A Call to the Colours

GENEALOGIST'S REFERENCE SHELF

A Call to the Colours

Tracing Your Canadian Military Ancestors

KENNETH G. COX

DUNDURN
TORONTO

Editor: Ruth Chernia
Copy Editor: Cheryl Hawley
Design: Jesse Hooper
Printer: Webcom

Library and Archives Canada Cataloguing in Publication

Cox, Kenneth G.
    A call to the colours : tracing your Canadian military ancestors / Kenneth G. Cox.

(Genealogist's reference shelf)
Co-published by: Ontario Genealogical Society.
Includes bibliographical references and index.
Issued also in an electronic format.
ISBN 978-1-55488-864-1

1. Soldiers--Canada--Genealogy--Handbooks, manuals, etc.   2. Canada--Genealogy--Handbooks, manuals, etc.   3. Archival resources--Canada.   I. Ontario Genealogical Society   II. Title.   III. Series: Genealogist's reference shelf

CS83.C69 2011   929'.371   C2011-900943-9

1   2   3   4   5   15   14   13   12   11

We acknowledge the support of the **Canada Council for the Arts** and the **Ontario Arts Council** for our publishing program. We also acknowledge the financial support of the **Government of Canada** through the **Canada Book Fund** and **Livres Canada Books**, and the **Government of Ontario** through the **Ontario Book Publishers Tax Credit** program, and the **Ontario Media Development Corporation**.

Care has been taken to trace the ownership of copyright material used in this book. The author and the publisher welcome any information enabling them to rectify any references or credits in subsequent editions.

J. Kirk Howard, President

Printed and bound in Canada.
www.dundurn.com

Ontario Genealogical Society
Suite 102, 40 Orchard View Boulevard
Toronto, Ontario, Canada M4R 1B9
tel. (416) 489-0734   fax. (416) 489-9803
provoffice@ogs.on.ca   www.ogs.on.ca

Dundurn Press	Gazelle Book Services Limited	Dundurn Press
3 Church Street, Suite 500	White Cross Mills	2250 Military Road
Toronto, Ontario, Canada	High Town, Lancaster, England	Tonawanda, NY
M5E 1M2	LA1 4XS	U.S.A. 14150

CONTENTS

INTRODUCTION

Prior to the rebellions of 1837, Anna Jameson toured Upper Canada and recorded her impressions in a book entitled *Winter Studies and Summer Rambles*. Her text offers Canadian historians an interesting glimpse into the early development of the Province of Ontario. For anyone interested in military history, she recorded the following review of an early militia muster in the community of Erindale, just west of Toronto. It speaks volumes about the state of our country's early military preparedness.

> On a rising ground above the river which ran gurgling and sparkling through the green ravine beneath, the motley troops, about three or four hundred men, were marshalled — no, not marshalled, but scattered in a far more picturesque fashion hither and thither. A few men, well mounted, and dressed as lancers, in uniforms which were, however, anything but uniform, flourished backward on the green sward, to the manifest peril of the spectators; themselves and their horses, equally wild, disorderly, spirited,

undisciplined: but was perfection compared to the infantry. Here there was no uniformity attempted of dress, of appearance, of movement; a few had coats, others jackets; a greater number had neither coats nor jackets, but appeared in their shirt sleeves, white or checked, or clean or dirty, in edifying variety! Some wore hats others caps, others their own shaggy heads of hair. Some had firelocks, some had old swords suspended in belts, or stuck in their waistbands; but the greater number shouldered sticks or umbrellas.

Mrs. M. told us that on a former parade day she heard the word of command given thus — "Gentlemen with the umbrellas take ground to the right! Gentlemen with the walking sticks take ground to the left!" Now they ran after each other elbowed and kicked each other, straddled, stooped, chattered; and if the commanding officer turned his back for a moment, very cooly sat down on the bank to rest. Not to laugh was impossible, and defied all power of face.[1]

From the earliest days of this country, our ancestors were required to perform some form of military service, often as militia. At least once a year, or as commanded by the military authorities, all able-bodied men between the ages of sixteen and sixty were required by law to muster for military training. Indeed, a myth developed that, during the various conflicts it endured, this country was saved by the local militia. It is hard to believe, after reading Anna Jameson's account, that the men who mustered in Erindale in 1837 were capable of stopping

Militia drilling, Elora, Ontario. Archives Ontario, C 286-1-0-6-31.

a determined enemy or eventually serving, as many of their descendents did, in major world conflicts. Or that many of these men had ancestors who had served during the War of 1812 or even farther back in time during the American Revolution. But they did.

By 1856 the British government had decided that it was about time for their North American colonies to take more responsibility for their own defence. Many of the British regiments that had been stationed in the colonies had been withdrawn during the Crimean War, and British taxpayers were already overburdened. So a more professional militia was recommended for Canada. Uniforms, arms, equipment, and professional training were provided by England and our militia took on a more professional look. Militia regiments like the Queen's Own Rifles and the 48th

Highlanders are good examples of the result of this change in policy. It soon became fashionable for young gentlemen with money to join one of the more prestigious militia regiments. By 1870–71 the remaining British regiments were withdrawn and Canada found itself responsible for its own defence. However, when necessary, Britain did send regiments back to Canada during periods of international or internal tension, such as during the Red River and North West Rebellions.

Canada's involvement in the Boer War heralded our first real military involvement beyond our own borders. Of course, by the end of the First World War Canadian soldiers proved that they were ready to be called upon to serve with distinction anywhere the country needed them. Unfortunately, this call would come again a mere two decades after the end of the "war to end all wars."

• • •

The discovery that an ancestor served during one of the major conflicts in our history is exciting. To find a family name on a Loyalist muster roll, a Canada General Service Medal with an ancestor's name engraved on it, a set of First World War attestation papers, or a box of Second World War medals says that one of our ancestors faced challenging events beyond the scope of everyday living.

It could have been that an ancestor served with a British regiment and chose to remain in Canada following his discharge or had seen service with one of the Provincial Corps established during the American Revolution and later applied for a land grant in Canada. You may discover that an ancestor served with a Canadian regiment during the First or Second World Wars, or with the 1st Polish Armoured Division attached to the Canadian Army in Northwest Europe. Polish Canadians who may have fought alongside our troops can access their records

Introduction

at The General Sikorski Institute and Museum, 20 Princess Gate, London, SW7, *www.pism.co.uk/archive/archive-documents.html*.

During times of peace or even insurrection, your ancestors may have served in the sedentary, active, or incorporated militia as part-time soldiers. You might even discover that a distant ancestor decided to join one of the early Fencible Regiments and saw more extensive action. It's exciting to discover an ancestor had seen action in one of the major battles of the War of 1812, fought the Fenians at Ridgeway in 1866, served on the Nile in 1884, or went west to fight the Métis during the Red River Rebellion in 1870 and again in 1885 during the North West Rebellions. There is a very strong likelihood that someone in your family served during the South African Boer War (1899–1902), First World War (1914–18), or Second World War (1939–45). Your female ancestors may have served as a nursing sister or with the Royal Flying Corps as a driver in the Second World War or even in the army, navy, or air force during the Second World War. Remember, some of our ancestors also served on sea and in the air throughout many of the conflicts mentioned in this resource guide. You will want to understand the events in which your distant relatives lived their lives and served their country.

The purpose of this educational resource guide is to offer archival, library, and computer resources that will provide the family historian with the tools to commence your own search for your ancestor's personal military history and surround his or her name with the appropriate context. I hope to provide you with the shovel to let you do the digging!

• • •

The limited scope of this guide precludes any in-depth history of battles and wars. That is left to the professional military historian.

The study of our military history, excluding wars and battles, can be compared to studying a new and unfamiliar culture with its own customs, laws, and mores. I have, however, attempted to provide a basic knowledge of military structure at one particular point in history.

Each military event also includes an introduction to a research subject as a focus for discovering the records. I trust this makes the guide more personal and relevant.

I have focused only on the periods of our history when we were involved in active military events. A brief outline of these events introduce each chapter. Each chapter ends with resources and a bibliography that researchers can use to acquire more knowledge about the events.

I have also included additional information that I hope will be of some use to those family historians who have discovered old photographs, documents, uniforms, and other "militaria" owned by their ancestors. An old uniform; rank, skill at arms, or trade badges; hat badges or collar dogs; pieces of webbing; and especially old medals all tell us something about the times in which our ancestors served. Medals, in particular, are the one item that our ancestors tended to keep and, for this reason, I have included pictures of the type of medal you might expect to find in a family collection.

Finding a family name on a monument, muster roll, medal, land grant application, or any other resource is not the end of the search. You need to prove that person is your relative by consulting other sources. This guide deals only with military records and assumes that you will also include in your final product references to vital statistics, census returns, land records, and church registers.

You will soon discover that researching military records requires that you learn about a whole new "culture" with its own language, structure, and customs. For instance, the title *A Call to the Colours* refers to the flags that every regiment holds in esteem: the king's or queen's colours and regimental colours. In early periods, both flags were carried into battle as a rallying point for the men of the regiment. In later wars they were given into the care of the regimental garrison church for safekeeping until hostilities ended. Our early militia's colours were often made by some of the women in the community. During the War of 1812, for instance, these ladies joined what was referred to as a "Loyal and Patriotic Society," made clothes for the troops, conducted fundraising activities, and, in the case of the 3rd Regiment of York Militia, sewed its colours. Every regiment in Canada has a set of colours (also referred to as standards), often bearing the names of past battle honours. These flags are well worth viewing, especially if your ancestor served with one of these regiments during a past war.

Many of the regiments your ancestors might have known still exist, either on their own or through amalgamation with another unit. Most have headquarters in various cities throughout the country and websites highlighting the history of the regiment. These regimental websites can offer a wealth of information and sometimes provide resource material to help with your search.

• • •

Searching for your military ancestors and placing them in historical context can be a rewarding experience. Good luck and I hope that this resource guide helps you start the search for your military ancestors.

PREFACE

How to Make the Best Use of This Guide

Your family history comes alive, then you add details about events that had an impact on your ancestors' lives — the battles, equipment used, medals earned, or interesting family stories — all create historical context. Otherwise, the history is merely a collection of names and a list of vital statistics: birth, marriage, death.

Throughout this book, many websites or textbooks have been referred to as potential sources of information. Only include any web address as a source after you have verified the material. There are six basic online resources:

- national archival web pages
- provincial archival web pages
- city, historical society, and museum websites
- free information sources prepared by either organizations or individuals
- gateway websites allowing access to a variety of specific pages
- pay-per-view websites

BOOLEAN SEARCH

Remember, once you identify the regiment/squadron/ship in which your ancestor served, you can do a boolean search to discover more specific details. Many search engines, such as Google or Yahoo, automatically implement a boolean search. When searching a site with an "advanced" function, use this excellent tool.

- Use **AND** to find both words. This will only open pages that have both words: "Italy" **AND** "star."
- Use **OR** to find all instances of either one word or another. This will find all pages that mention either word or both.
- Use **NEAR** to find words close to each other. This will provide pages that have both words and return pages ranked in order of proximity. So the first pages will have the words closer together than items lower on the list.
- Use **AND NOT** to exclude certain text from the search.
- Use * to look for words that start the same. Thus capture * will find capturing, captured, etc.
- Use ** to search for all forms of a word.
- Put quotation marks ("Canadians in Italy") around phrases you want the search engine to take literally.

LIBRARY AND ARCHIVES CANADA

When you discover an RG (record group) that might contain important information about your topic, open this page. Then select "Show Arrangement Structure." In RG 24-D-1, for instance, when you check the "show arrangement structure" icon, list of HMCS ships and related archival resources appears. Click on the small + icon beside the name of the ship to display the information that the archives holds related to that vessel. The specific RG that holds the information is listed beside each archival resource. This should help you narrow your search considerably. However, LAC is currently revising its search tools. Be aware that you may be directed to another area of LAC or to ArchiviaNet to continue your research.

Through both its archival and library records and books, and the Canadian Genealogy Centre portal, LAC should be your first stop. LAC is constantly posting new sources of data. For instance, early in December 2010 it launched a new online database, "Medals, Honours and Awards." "Through this online database, researchers can access more than 113,000 references to medal registers, citation cards and records of various military awards. In addition to archival references, this research tool includes digitized images of some medal registers. The database is available at: *www.collectionscanada. gc.ca/databases/medals/index-e.html.*"[1]

You should also become familiar with Amicus and ArchiviaNet through the Collections Canada site. These research tools can help you access the archival collections throughout Canada. LAC also offers an interlibrary loan service.

When you visit LAC in person, the following record groups contain military records:

- RG 8 — British Military and Naval Records
- RG 9 — Militia and Defence
- RG 15 — Department of the Interior (western land grants related to Red River, North-West Rebellions, and Boer War)

- RG 24 — National Defence Records
- RG 28 — Munitions and Supply
- RG 38 —Veterans' Affairs
- RG 44 — National War Service records
- RG 49 — Defence Production during the war
- RG 57 — Emergency Measures Organization
- RG 61 — Allied War Supplies Corporation
- RG 83 — Defence Construction Limited
- RG 117 — Office of the Custodian of Enemy Property
- RG 150 — Ministry of the Overseas Military Forces of Canada (First World War records)

Library and Archives Canada has prepared finding aids for most of their RGs and anyone doing research should automatically consult these when requesting information. Should you experience any difficulty identifying the appropriate RG, consult one of the on-site archivists. They should refer you to two resource guides:

- *A Guide to Sources Relating to the Canadian Militia* — finding aid RG 9-58 lists resources for infantry, cavalry, and armoured units.
- *A Guide to Sources Relating to the Canadian Militia* — finding aid RG 9-59 deals with the artillery.

OTHER RESOURCES

At Veterans' Affairs, *www.vac-acc.gc.ca*, you can learn about service medals and use a search engine that will allow you to visit the Book of Remembrance.

If you suspect an ancestor died in the war, visit the Commonwealth War Graves site at *www.cwg.org*. This site will provide you with date of death, service regiment, location of interment, and, perhaps, the address of next of kin.

Your provincial archives will have copies of many of the records available at the Canadian archives as well as records unique to your province.

Your local library and provincial genealogy society will also have their own records as well as some of the more popular LAC ones. For example, the Ontario Genealogical Society website is *www.ogs.on.ca* and the Toronto Reference Library web page is *www.torontopubliclibrary.ca*. Similar services are available throughout the country.

Canadian university libraries also hold material related to your military ancestors. Many of them contain valuable collections of scarce manuscripts or copies of LAC material. For instance, Brock University in St. Catharines, Ontario, has a complete set of the Upper Canada Land Books with an index, *www.brockloyalisthistorycollection.ca/collection.html*.

Before making a personal visit to any of the repositories, be sure to phone or email for hours and restrictions. When visiting an archives, expect that you will not be allowed to take in any writing implements beyond a pencil.

Portals, such as Cyndi's List, *www.cyndislist.com*, or pay-per-view sites like Ancestry.com and Findmypast.com allow access to a wide variety of resources. Don't forget to access the Church of Jesus Christ of Latter-Day Saints (Mormons, LDS) site at *www.familysearch.com* or visit one of their Family History Centres. Both Ancestry.com and Findmypast.com are free to view at the LDS Family History sites. Ancestry.com is also free to use at most public libraries.[2]

When you find yourself seeking reference material specifically related to the regiment or battle in which your ancestors served and fought, there are several book sites to search:

Grenadier Militaria, *www.grenadiermilitaria.com.*

Naval and Military Press, *www.naval-military-press.com.*

Pen and Sword Books, *www.pen-and-sword.co.uk.*

WHAT CAN MEDALS AND OTHER ARTIFACTS TEACH YOU?

Military medals issued before the Second World War were engraved around the rim with the name of the soldier, his or her rank, regimental number, and battalion or regiment. They were also issued with a ribbon that was unique to that medal. Sometimes in an old black-and-white photograph that patterned ribbon is enough to allow you to identify the military event in which an ancestor may have served.

Similarly, the "crown" you will find on cap badges will help you identify relevant time periods. During Queen Victoria's reign, cap badge design included what is commonly referred to as a "Queen's Crown" over the regimental number. This design changed when Edward VII and later George the V & VI assumed the throne, replaced by a "King's Crown," and then changed back to a "Queen's Crown" for Elizabeth II. British medals were issued with clasps or bars denoting the military event in which the participant saw service.

As you continue researching an ancestor's military history, expect to develop an awareness of the changes to the uniforms worn by your ancestor over the decades as well as the development of various patterns of "webbing" (military harness designed to support necessary equipment) and the type of weapons you might discover a family member carrying in some old photograph. This knowledge also helps you place an ancestor into context.

The infantry webbing worn by your ancestor will certainly help identify a time period in an old photograph. Often you will see a photograph of a soldier wearing Slade-Wallace harness, Oliver Pattern harness, 1908 or 1936 Pattern webbing, or, if your ancestor was an officer, wearing what was referred to as Sam Browne harness. Each piece of equipment carried by a military ancestor during certain time periods represents a change in the military culture. Refer to the glossary for an explanation of khaki, webbing, collar dogs, flashes, service and battle dress, puttees, and other uniquely military terms that will help you complete your search for your ancestor's military history.

Always make sure your sources are trustworthy (especially online). And remember, just because you cannot find a record does not mean that it does not exist; it could be that an ancestor's name was not recorded on the muster rolls or that the name was spelled differently than you expect it to be. You will quickly learn to distinguish between primary and secondary sources and some of the inherent weaknesses in the documents you may have to use as references. For example, when I searched the published rolls for the North West Canada Medal, they simply showed that a family member qualified for the medal and clasp (M. & C.) with nothing else of significance in the transcription. However, when I checked the original rolls I discovered that the transcriber had omitted a small, handwritten note. The note, which stated simply "12/05/85 wounded," added a significant footnote to my family narrative. It meant this individual had fought in the Battle of Batoche (8–12 May 1885) and consequently would have been entitled to the Batoche clasp with the medal because he had served under fire.

All researchers should note that many early military medals were awarded well after the event. The British Military General Service Medal for the War of 1812 was commissioned in 1847 and debate about the "bars" to be awarded continued into 1856. The North West Canada General Service Medal issued for the North-West Rebellions in 1885 was last awarded in 1945 to the men of the transport corps. Your ancestor had to apply for these medals, so if he or she did not there's a good chance he was either too busy to bother or had already died.

There are military terms and abbreviations that you will need to become familiar with in order to decipher any documents that you discover. The same applies to any photographs that show division, rank, skill at arms, trade, wound, battalion cap badges, or dog tags. A working knowledge of all of these will help you add to your narrative and enhance your research.

• • •

The websites in this book are correct as of the end of 2010. If you cannot find a site, do a Google search for the original URL or try to delete some of the letters after the first slash.

Remember that online resources are usually transcribed by volunteers and are therefore subject to mistakes. They also seem to have a "shelf life" and authors who include them in research texts often run the risk of having the site disappear before the printing of the text, including this one.

CHAPTER ONE

The War of 1812: Were My Ancestors Involved?

Have you ever wondered if you had any ancestors who served with the British forces during the Napoleonic period or were part of the militia that helped defend Canada during the War of 1812? If your family history has its roots in England, Scotland, Ireland, or French or British North America, there is a good chance that somewhere in your genealogy one of your relatives served in the British Army or Navy. After all, from the beginning of the Seven Years' War in 1756 through the American Revolution, which ended in 1783, to the battle of New Orleans in January 1815, North America was at war.

On 18 June 1812, the war in Europe came to North America. England and France had been locked in war since the end of the eighteenth century. In order to hamper the French war effort, British naval vessels had blockaded French ports hoping to deny Napoleon needed war materials. Indeed, Britain's control of the seas, blockade of French ports, and the stopping and searching of American naval vessels (that were trying to supply France) seemed to be just the excuse the young United States needed to threaten war.

Expansion of the United States across all of North America, including Canada, became what was to be considered their "manifest destiny." What better time to declare war and invade Canada? There were only approximately 1,600 British troops in North America and very little likelihood of any more being sent from England. As the American statesman Thomas Jefferson said, "[T]he acquisition of Canada … as far as the neighborhood of Quebec will be a mere matter of marching."[1] There were probably many individuals in British North America and England who agreed with him. The only thing in Britain's favour was the fact that the British regulars stationed in Canada were better trained than their American counterparts and England hoped it could depend on two other factors: the Loyalists and the Natives.

To begin your search for possible 1812 ancestors, you should gain some knowledge of Loyalist records. Approximately 50,000 people left the United States either during or shortly following the American Revolution. Their arrival in Canada had a huge impact on our history. The provinces of Nova Scotia, New Brunswick, and what later became Upper Canada were shaped by their arrival. The Loyalists and their children were entitled to free land. In the years following 1791 a large number of Americans also came north for free land with the only proviso that they swear loyalty to the British Crown. These people were later referred to as the "late Loyalists" and, to some in the colony, their loyalty was always suspect.

To provide land for the Loyalists, the British government surveyed large tracts of land in New Brunswick, Nova Scotia, and Upper Canada into the grid pattern we see today in the province of Ontario: concessions, lots, lines. The Loyalist muster rolls, land grant applications, and other related documents are valuable tools for a family historian. They contain a wealth of information on each of the individuals who applied for free government land.

The Provincial Corps (Loyalists) established by the British during the American Rebellion were assigned to four military districts: Eastern District, Northern District, Central, and Southern Commands. The Eastern and Northern Military Districts were mostly in what was called the "Canadian Establishment." For instance, if your ancestors served in the following Loyalist Regiments: Loyal Nova Scotia Volunteers, Royal Fencible Americans, Callbeck's St. John Island Volunteers, or Pringle's Foot — Royal Newfoundland, they were in the Eastern District. The Royal Highland Emigrants (84th Foot), King's Royal Regiment of New York (Yorkers), Butler's Rangers, King's Rangers (Rogers), Mohawk Corps of Rangers, Queen's Loyal Rangers (Jessup's Corps), and the Loyal Rangers (Jessup's Canadian Rangers) were in the Northern Command.

There were well over thirty Loyalist Corps/Provincial Regiments raised during the American Revolution. The following list will give you some idea of the Provincial Corps records you can search for at LAC

> Armed Batteau-men
> Armed Boatmen
> Arnold's American Legion
> Black Pioneers
> British Legion
> Buck's County Light Dragoons
> Callbeck's Company
> Carolina King's Rangers
> De Diemar's Hussars
> De Lancey's Brigade
> Emmerick's Chasseurs
> Ferguson's Corps
> Georgia Light Dragoons
> Gov'r Wentworth's Volunteers
> Hierlihy's Corps

Independent Troop of Cavalry
King's American Dragoons
King's American Regiment
King's Orange Rangers
King's Royal Reg't of New York
Loyal American Rangers
Loyal American Regiment
Loyal Foresters
Loyal New Englanders
Loyal Nova Scotia Volunteers
Maryland Loyalists
Nassau Blues
New Jersey Volunteers
New York Volunteers
North Carolina Dragoons
North Carolina Highlanders
North Carolina Volunteers
Pennsylvania Loyalists
Philadelphia Light Dragoons
Prince of Wales American Regiment
Provincial Light Infantry
Queen's Rangers
Roger's King's Rangers
Roman Catholic Volunteers
Royal American Reformers
Royal Fencible Americans
Royal Garrison Battalion
Royal Guides and Pioneers
Royal North Carolina Regiment
South Carolina Dragoons
South Carolina Rangers
South Carolina Royalists

Volunteers of New England
Volunteers of Ireland
West Florida Foresters
West Jersey Volunteers
Royal Highland Emigrants[2]

When the revolution started, many of the men who volun-teered for service were used as a local police force but, by 1776, the army in New York had received 5,000 green uniforms to be distributed to Loyalist regiments. The early uniforms were "faced" in white, green, or blue. This means that your ancestor's coat would have been green with white, green, or blue lapels. Later thousands of yards of red cloth were provided by the British authorities and some of the Provincial Corps began to look like regular establishment regiments. As the war progressed almost all Loyalist units began to take on the structure of regular British line regiments with a strict command structure, light and grenadier companies, their own regimental "colours," regimental bands, and cavalry units.

In 1779 the British authorities, in recognition of the importance of the Provincial Corps, created an "American Establishment"; renamed the Queen's Rangers to the 1st American Regiment; the Volunteers of Ireland became the 2nd American Regiment; and the New York Volunteers, the 3rd American Regiment. In 1781, the King's American Regiment became the 4th American Regiment and the British Legion, the 5th American Regiment. These designations were in recognition of each unit's proficiency. Your Loyalist ancestor may have also chosen to join a colonial militia unit used for scouting or other related activities.

There are a number of military resources available to consult. Your ancestor could have been part of a British regiment, referred to as Regulars; a member of a Loyalist/Provincial Corps, often referred to as Colonials; a member of the Loyalist Militia, who seem to have been predominantly established in the New York command; or a member of one of the corps that formed the American Establishment and thus more closely related to a British Line regiment or even a member of the Native Establishment based out of Fort Niagara. If your family has a German background then they could have seen service with one of the German/Hanoverian Regiments that operated in North America, often referred to as Hessians.

Some men served in more than one corps and, following the surrender of Cornwallis at Yorktown in 1781 and the beginning of peace negotiations in 1782, the muster rolls of the various provincial corps began to dwindle. Many of your ancestors who had served with a Loyalist corps either elected to try to return to their homes or chose to accept the British offer to relocate. Sometimes you may see the word "deserter" beside your ancestor's name but this may only mean that he elected to take a chance on either travelling north on his own or trying to re-establish himself in the new United States. Little effort seems to have been made by the British authorities to apprehend these men. You really have to appreciate what these men must have felt when they realized that they had lost everything they had struggled to build in the former Thirteen Colonies before the rebellion.[3]

If your ancestor chose to disband in New York, he could have gone to the West Indies, Quebec (then the name for what is now Quebec and Ontario), Nova Scotia, or Saint John, New Brunswick. It appears that the greatest number of disbanded Loyalists settling in one place were those who arrived in Saint John in 1783 under the command of Lieutenant Colonel Hewlett of De Lancey's Brigade. It is estimated that well over 3,000 men, women, and children settled there. This huge influx of settlers resulted in the creation in 1784 of the new colony of New Brunswick with Saint John as its administrative centre. By 1791, the colony of Upper Canada was created from the former colony of Quebec because of the volume of Loyalist settlers.

You can imagine the amount of record keeping that was done by the British authorities as they attempted to settle the displaced Loyalists and their families. You will discover muster rolls and pay lists, lists of individuals receiving rations, land grant records, claims for losses or requests for food rations and tools, petitions for increased acreage, inclusion of names on district records, petitions for title/deed for land, and, later, petitions from family members based on their Loyalist status. You will also discover gratuities granted by early colonial legislatures/Parliaments to ease the financial burden of Loyalist refugees. Many of these acts of Parliament were initiated years after the formation of the colony.

If you want to fully utilize the land-grant records, an excellent resource guide is *United Empire Loyalists: A Guide to Tracing Loyalist Ancestors in Upper Canada* by Brenda Dougall Merriman.

If you do discover an ancestor on a Loyalist muster roll you will want to check if he or she applied for a land grant. Start by checking the information found at, *www.collectionscanada.gc.ca/genealogy* and following the prompts for Loyalists/land.

So what happens if you do discover a name on a muster roll that you suspect may be an ancestor and someone who may have later served during the War of 1812? Many of the Loyalist regiments raised during the revolution came from specific areas in the thirteen colonies. For instance, the King's Royal Regiment of New York was originally composed of men from the Mohawk Valley in upper New York State. During the war, they were very active up and down the valley. The regiment was raised and led by Sir John Johnson whose family home was called Johnson Hall.

The Johnson home is maintained by the State of New York and is open to the public. At the end of the war the regiment settled along the St. Lawrence River near present-day Cornwall and Kingston, Ontario. Thus, if you discovered an ancestor who served with this regiment, search records in the former colony of New York's Mohawk Valley and also in the Cornwall and Kingston area of Upper Canada.

There are some excellent histories available on some of the Loyalist regiments. For example, in 1931 the Ontario Historical Society published a book by Ernest Cruikshank about the King's Royal Regiment, *The History and Master Roll of the King's Royal Regiment of New York, Revised Edition*, which was republished in 1984 with the addition of an index, appendices, and a master muster roll prepared by Gavin Watt. As a point of interest, this unit has been recreated by local military enthusiasts and has an excellent web site offering a great deal of information related to the original Provincial Regiment: *www.royalyorkers.ca*.

It has been suggested by some historians that by 1812 the population in Upper Canada was approximately 70,000+ individuals. Of these, 40 percent were Loyalists and their descendants, former members of British regulars who elected to remain in Canada following their term of service, or immigrants from England.

However, the remainder of the non-Native population was "late Loyalists" or, more specifically, Americans who had come north for free land.[4] So when war was declared, Upper Canada military authorities were a little concerned about the loyalty of these new settlers. For the American military authorities, it certainly made sense to plan any major invasion of the country through Upper Canada.

My own family research in this period began when I received an email from family in England with a copy of an oil painting attached, suggesting that the painting's subject was a member of my grandmother's Hinds family. Tradition stated that he had served with the British forces at the battle of Waterloo and before that at the battle of New Orleans. A second reason to research this period was the search for my wife's ancestor Jean Baptiste Turcott, whom it was believed had served during the War of 1812 and was granted land on Wolfe Island just south of Kingston, Ontario. Two quests necessitated two different approaches to researching War of 1812 records. The first individual would have served in a British regiment — in this case the artillery. I assumed the second was of French Canadian ancestry. Where did I begin?

First establish a historical reference point from which to begin your research. So ask yourself, is it possible that someone could have been involved in the British defeat at New Orleans and later fought at the Battle of Waterloo?

The Battle of Waterloo was fought July 1815 following Emperor Napoleon's return from his first exile, and the battle of New Orleans occurred January 1815. The incident in New Orleans was a bit of a blunder and certainly an embarrassment for the British. The War of 1812 had actually come to a close with the Treaty of Ghent in December 1814. Word didn't reach the British forces as they prepared to attack New Orleans and the battle ended in defeat. The Battle of New Orleans, although officially not part of the War of 1812, is still considered a major event in that conflict. To the Americans it was a positive event in a war that had not gone all that well for the United States Army.

Could this individual (Edward or William Hinds) have fought in both battles? The answer is, possibly, "yes." According to family sources the individual in the picture had served in the Royal Horse Artillery, achieved officer rank, and later died in India. That he may have started in the ranks and become an officer is possible. Rank in **corps units** (artillery, engineers) was often achieved through ability and not always, as in **line regiments**, through purchase.

If he died in India, he could have achieved officer status while serving with the East India Company's European Regiments. The company recruited extensively among disbanded soldiers shortly following the war with France.

The second research request offered an interesting all-Canadian element to my research. I would need to access a different set of records to prove a War of 1812 connection. The British Army during this period was divided into line regiments, cavalry regiments, and support corps. Line regiments could be referred to as a regiment of foot (infantry) with grenadier and light companies. Cavalry could be designated as heavy or light while corps units were artillery and engineers. Over the course of history, the artillery could be designated as garrison, horse, or field units. Thus, if your ancestor was in the Royal Horse Artillery you would know that he was part of a gun crew who serviced a field gun (artillery pieces are referred to as guns), drawn by horses. In this period of history the men who "drove" the horses were referred to as members of the Corps of Drivers while those who serviced the gun were recorded as Gunners. Near the end of the war with France, the Corps of Drivers was abolished as a separate unit and amalgamated with gunners as one unit of artillery.

My first suggestion to anyone searching for military ancestors is to start with the medal rolls. Many of the prominent British awards have been indexed and transcribed. This is certainly the case with both the Military General Service and Waterloo Medal Rolls. So what did a preliminary search show? The Waterloo Medal rolls did record a William Hinds, who had served in the Royal Horse Artillery and was entitled to the Waterloo medal with two bars: Badajoz and Vittoria. A search of the British Military General Service Medal rolls showed that he was also entitled to this medal for service with Ross's Battery of artillery, serving first as a driver and later as a gunner.

The Waterloo Medal was engraved with the recipient's name and was the first medal issued with a ribbon to general enlisted men. The Military General Service Medal presented for service between 1793 and 1814, was issued with several bars/clasps. Private collection.

Canadians who fought during the War of 1812 were also entitled to the Military General Service Medal. A search of the rolls for this medal did indicate that a Turcott was awarded the medal for service with the Canadian Voltigeurs at the battle of Chateauguay. Further research showed that the Voltigeurs had fought with the 104th Regiment from New Brunswick at the attack on Sackets Harbor. Both the Voltigeurs and New Brunswick Fencibles (104th Regiment) had a Turcott listed in their ranks, although the name on the 104 Muster roll was spelled differently. I already knew the 104th New Brunswick Regiment had recruited extensively in the Province of Quebec before the war. Perhaps they had recruited another Turcott? By consulting a road map, I could see that Sackets Harbor in the United States and Kingston, Ontario, are just across the river from each other. It was possible that Jean Baptiste Turcott had chosen to remain in the Kingston area and settle on Wolfe Island at the end of the war, perhaps applying for a land grant. That he was a member of the militia is indisputable.

The early militia was divided into sedentary units, which were basically farmers or tradesmen who were expected to serve when called upon and then return to their former occupation after hostilities had ended, and fencible units, which were better trained and expected to serve anywhere within their respective colony but not beyond its borders. Many of these better-trained fencible units applied for and were granted line regiment status. Thus, the Royal Newfoundland Regiment served in Upper Canada, as did the former New Brunswick Fencibles when they were granted status as the 104th Regiment of New Brunswick. The 104th regiment won considerable recognition by marching over land from New Brunswick to Upper Canada during the winter without losing a man.

So with this basic information in hand how can I prove if there was a Hinds or even a member of the Cox side of the family at the battle of New Orleans, and also a Turcott connection to the war: the former from either Derbyshire or Warwickshire in England and the latter from Lower Canada in British North America? My grandmother's family were Hinds — my grandfather's family Cox — both came from England's Midlands Region.

You could start your research by spending a few minutes reviewing War of 1812 background information. For instance, *www.warof1812.ca/voltigeurs.htm*, has some excellent descriptions of the Canadian fencible/militia regiments that were involved in the war. Wikipedia, *en.wikipedia.org/wiki/Canadian_units_of_the_War_of_1812*, has information on various British regiments that could provide some historical background to your research. However, the first place to start your search for primary and secondary resources is our own archives. When you visit LAC, the information related to 1812 military records is mostly found in Record Group 9. Nominal rolls are in RG 9, series IB7, vols. 1–39 while discharge certificates and land grant applications are in RG 9, series IB4, vols. 18–24. If a militiaman applied for a pension, for whatever reason, these will be found in RG 9, series IB4, vols. 1–17; or RG 9, series IC5, vols. 1, 3–4 and 8–27. You can also order some of this material through interlibrary loan.

In general, War of 1812 records contain two basic types of information: nominal returns for each unit and monthly pay lists, sometimes with lists related to prisoners of war. Nominal rolls will provide you with the name, rank, and remarks about service. These remarks can tell you about an ancestor's date of enlistment, period of service, if he was killed in battle or died during service, if he deserted the army or was taken prisoner. Muster rolls or monthly pay lists will provide you with name, rank, and period of service for which he received pay. Be aware that the majority of records are organized according to county so if you know in which county your ancestor lived it might make your search a little easier.[5]

In 1875, Parliament offered a gratuity to anyone who had fought in the war. A list of names, age, residence, and corps or division in which they served was printed in 1876 with comment on whether or not the individual qualified for the gratuity. This list provides a reference number for each application and can prove useful when verifying an ancestor's involvement in the war.

When doing any military research, remember to seek out private collections or visit your local regimental museums and/or archives. For instance, at the Royal Canadian Military Institute, *www.rcmi.org*, you can find some rare publications that might help in your search. However, while the RCMI is under construction the library is closed. As with any resource, contact the organization by email or phone before you visit.

WAR OF 1812 BATTLES

1812

- 8 June — War proclaimed by U.S. President James Madison.
- 11 July–11 August — U.S. General Hull invades Upper Canada with a large force; retreats in panic.
- 17 July — Capture of Fort Mackinac (on an island in Lake Michigan, near Sault Ste. Marie, Ontario).
- 16 August — Major-General Brock captures Detroit with only 1,300 regulars, militiamen, and Natives.
- 12 October — Battle of Queenston Heights, death of Brock, defeat of U.S. forces under General Van Rensselaer.

- 19–20 October — Action at Lacolle (9 kilometres from the border with New York State).

1813

- 22 January — Battle of Frenchtown (or River Raisin), major victory for British and Native allies, U.S. battle cry becomes "Remember the Raisin."
- 27 April — Capture, pillaging of York, Upper Canada, by U.S. forces, attacked again 31 July.
- 1 May — Battle of Fort Meigs (Ohio).
- 25–27 May — Assault on Fort George (near Newark, now Niagara-on-the-Lake).
- 29 May — Assault at Sackets Harbor (New York State).
- 6 June — Battle of Stoney Creek.
- 24 June — Battle of Beaver Dams.
- 10 September — Battle of Lake Erie, defeat of British fleet under Captain Barclay, British forces forced to retreat from western province.
- 5 October — U.S. victory at Moraviantown in battle of the Thames, great Native leader Tecumseh dies.
- 26 October — Battle of Châteauguay, Lower Canada.
- 11 November — Battle of Chrysler's Farm, major victory for the British.
- 10 December — Burning of Newark, Upper Canada, by the retreating U.S. forces.
- 12 December — British capture of Fort Niagara, guerrilla warfare commences on Niagara frontier.

- 29–30 December — burning of Lewiston, Tuscarora, Fort Schlosser, Black Rock, and Buffalo, New York, by British forces in retaliation for U.S. burning of York and Newark.

1814

- 30 March — Action at Lacolle.
- 5 May — Amphibious assault on Oswego, New York.
- May — Abdication of Napoleon — war ends in Europe.
- 3 July — Capture of Fort Erie.
- 5 July — Battle of Chippawa.
- 13–15 September — Bombardment by British of Fort McHenry, writing of "Star Spangled Banner."
- July–August — Twelve thousand British veterans arrive in Canada because of the end of war with France. Assault on Plattsburg, New York, poorly planned and leads to British withdrawal, over 1,000 British troops desert.
- July–August — Washington captured and burned.
- 24 December — Treaty of Ghent ends the war, all captured territory returned to previous owner.

1815

- 1 January — Battle of New Orleans ends in defeat for the British forces.

Of course, this is only a partial list of the many battles and small actions fought during the course of this war. I have purposely not included all naval engagements fought between Great Britain and the United States on the Great Lakes and the oceans of the world because that is beyond the scope of this guide.

It will take some research before you can place an ancestor in a specific regiment and ultimately at a specific battle. However, once you have accomplished this it is time to become a historian and commence fitting historical details into your own family narrative. Spend time researching some of the information available on the life of a soldier or militiaman of the period. Uniforms, weapons, equipment, and military tactics all help you understand your ancestor's military world. Stories about the life of a militiaman or British regular abound. The quantity/quality of food issued, the length of service, the harsh discipline, the horrible wounds sustained in battle, the nature of guerilla warfare all add interest to your narrative.

For instance, if your ancestor fought in this war, he carried a weapon referred to by the ordinary soldier as a "Brown Bess." The official name for this weapon was the East India Pattern Long Land Musket and it was a muzzle-loading gun. A good, well-trained soldier could load and fire this weapon three to four times in a minute. It should never be referred to as a rifle because it had a smooth bore in the barrel. "Rifling" the barrel was a later invention designed to add accuracy to the shot.

You may also discover that one of your ancestors served with the American forces during the war as a "licensed freebooter." These were men, many of whom were former "late Loyalists" (families who came up to Canada seeking free land in the years following the American Revolution before the War of 1812), who made the decision to join a band of American-sponsored marauders to terrorize their former neighbours. Men like Abner Chapin, William Markle, and Andrew Westbrook led bands of guerrillas who burned mills, destroyed crops, drove off cattle, and burned the homes of anyone who was a government official or served in the Upper Canada militia. Interestingly, they could often rely upon former neighbours to provide them with information about British troop movements.

As a matter of fact, following the capture of York and the burning of Newark, the whole Niagara frontier settled into a conflict between neighbours. British forces rampaged up and down the American side of the river burning Buffalo, Tuscarora, and Little Rock. In response to the threat from American raiders, the British eventually detached Lieutenant James FitzGibbon from his regular duties and assigned him a group of Mounted Regulars. His job was to intercept communications between American forces and seek out and destroy American freebooters. The American forces called his men the "Green Tigers" because of the green facings on their uniforms. It was FitzGibbon who, with help from his Native allies, was able to take the information provided by Laura Secord and prepare an ambush of a far superior American force at the Battle of Beaver Dams.

Following the war, the civil authorities in Canada initiated court proceedings against former settlers accused of high treason. Angela Files and Tess Rowe compiled a list of these.[6] At *Ancestry. com* you can access the nominal roll of the men who belonged to the Canadian Corps of Volunteers who fought with the American forces during the war.

Your ancestor may have served with the British Army as a regular and chose to remain in (or return to) Canada following his term of service. Archives Canada has acquired a significant number of microfilm reels concerning the British Army (1713–1940) all of which can be borrowed on interlibrary loan. At present there are 844 microfilm reels. However, the following are British Army regiments that would be of interest to anyone doing family history research related to the War of 1812:

a. Infantry of the Line
    1st Regiment of Foot
    6th Regiment of Foot
    8th Regiment of Foot
    9th Regiment of Foot
    13th Regiment of Foot
    37th Regiment of Foot
    41st Regiment of Foot
    42nd Regiment of Foot
    49th Regiment of Foot
    52nd Regiment of Foot
    57th Regiment of Foot
    60th Regiment of Foot
    77th Regiment of Foot
    81st Regiment of Foot
    82nd Regiment of Foot
    89th Regiment of Foot
    99th Regiment of Foot
    100th Regiment of Foot
    103rd Regiment of Foot
    104th Regiment of Foot
    De Watteville's Regiment
    7th West India Regiment

b. Fencible Regiments
    Canadian Fencible Regiment
    Glengarry Light Infantry Fencible Regiment
    New Brunswick Fencible Regiment
    Newfoundland Fencible Regiment

c. Royal Marines

d. Canadian Militia Units
    Canadian Voltigeurs
    Incorporated Militia Battalion of Upper Canada

e. Native Warriors
    Caughnawaga
    Huron
    Micmac
    Oneida
    Ottawa
    Tuscara

You can find many of the nominal rolls/muster, pay rolls for these units in the LAC manuscript groups. Records for Native Warriors are mostly non-existent. You may, however, discover a Military General Service Medal with the name of a Native Warrior engraved around the rim. These are very scarce.

Those who wish to learn more about the British regiments and Canadian militia should consult Michael Gregory's book, *Compendium of Canadian Regiments* (Ottawa: Lorimer Printers Ltd., 2005).

What Has My Own Research Proven?

Is there any truth to the Hind's story that an ancestor served at the battle of Waterloo and earlier at New Orleans? And did a member of the Turcott family also serve during the War of 1812 and eventually settle on Wolfe Island near Kingston, Ontario?

William Hinds is listed as receiving the Waterloo Medal and Military General Service Medal with two clasps. A search of the Military General Service Medal rolls shows the same individual entitled to this medal as a gunner in Ross's E Troop Royal Horse Artillery. So this individual must have transferred from the Corps of Drivers to become a gunner in a Troop of Artillery. Ross's troop, Royal Horse Artillery (R.H.A.) served in the Peninsula and Southern France, (1809–14), from Busaco to Orthes with the Light Division, and at Helder in 1799 and at Waterloo in 1815. A check of the Battery Records of the Royal Artillery, 1716–1859, definitely shows three batteries in service at New Orleans: Carmichael's Corps, Michell's Corps, and Munro's Corps, but not Ross's Corps. Also, no mention was made of any Royal Artillery officer by this name on any medal rolls. My next step was to search for a will left by William Hinds and any online records of the British East India Company's European Regiments organized for service in India following the war with Napoleon. I also discovered an Edward Cox, ensign 6th Foot, 17th September 1805, Captain 6th Foot, 18 May 1809, who served in North America, November 1814–February 1815 at Fort Erie and died 27 August 1825 in Bombay, India! Perhaps the Hinds portrait was incorrectly identified. Maybe it was sent by a relative on the Cox side of my family? The 6th Regiment of Foot was a Warwickshire unit and the Coxes are all from the Birmingham region. This could take my research in a new direction. Now I have to research early parish records in Warwickshire/Derbyshire England and check the Indian army records at the National Archives in England.

The Turcott story is a little more interesting. I already knew a Turcott had fought at the battle of Châteauguay and so was entitled to the Military General Service Medal with Châteauguay clasp. Originally this medal was to be issued to senior officers only. However, after some protest, Lord Elgin, the governor general of Canada, was informed on 2 August 1847 that the Military General Service Medal was to be awarded to Canadian militia and Indian warriors as well. There were only three clasps awarded for this medal: Fort Detroit (16 August 1812), Châteauguay (26 October 1813), and Chrysler's Farm (11 November 1813). At the urging of the Parliament of Canada a request was made for further clasps: Queenston Heights, Lundy's Lane, Ogdenburg, Lacolle, and Plattsburg. These requests were refused by the authorities in England because it would be too difficult to identify the appropriate recipients. By 1853 the whole matter of additional clasps seems to have been dropped, probably because of the situation developing in the Crimea and the fact that the British Parliament did not want to incur any more expense.[7]

Remember, all British medals were engraved around the edge with the name of the recipient and the regiment in which they served. This practice only stopped with the issue of Second World War medals. Thus, if you discover a British military medal with a "bar" or "clasp" it is relatively easy to trace the individual and acquire knowledge of the military action for which they were awarded the medal.

In 1875 the Parliament of Canada did decide to reward the remaining veterans of the war with a gratuity. Anyone wishing to claim the gratuity had to submit an application proving he had served in the militia during the war. The list of claimants was published in 1876 showing name, age, place of residence, and name of division or corps in which he served. This is an interesting source of information for anyone doing genealogical research because not only does it give some important statistics but also provides two important file numbers: the government file and the case file.

In this record I found the name Jean Baptiste Turcott, age seventy-eight, living on Wolfe Island, Frontenac County, private in the Boucherville Division. I had already traced the family back to this Jean Baptiste, establishing connections through the 1851 census and earlier church records. Because he had provided, on his gratuity request, the name of the division in which he served, I now had a location in Lower Canada (Quebec) in which to conduct further searches. Boucherville, Quebec, is on the south shore of the St. Lawrence River, just south of the city of Montreal. It was originally settled in 1660 and is just north of Châteauguay.

A later search of the nominal/subject index to British and Naval Records did provide information that Turcott, Jean Bte., did apply in 1841 for one-hundred acres of land for service during the war.[8] A search of Lower Canada land petitions showed that a Jean Baptiste Turcott had also applied earlier, in 1838.[9] My future searches will attempt to connect the Turcotts who served with the 104th New Brunswick Regiment and the Canadian Volitgeurs. Interestingly, the 1838 land grant application added another piece to the puzzle when it stated that Turcott was living in Sainte-Marie, Beauce, and had been a corporal in the 4th Battalion during the war. His 1838 application had been published in the *Quebec Gazette.*

Jean Baptiste Turcott's 1841 application was a group application made on his behalf by an independent applicant. I'll have to get a translation because it will be interesting to discover if he had requested a further land grant because he had fought with the government forces during the rebellions of 1837.

LAC PRE-1812 RECORDS

- RG 1, L3, Upper Canada land petitions, 1788–1848.
- RG 1, L1, Upper Canada land and state books, 1787–1841.
- RG 5, correspondence of the civil and provincial secretaries.
- RG 8, finding aid 1800, British records, muster rolls of Loyalist Provincial Corps, volumes 1851 to 1908, microfilm C-3873 to C-3874, C-4216–4217 to C-4224.
- Black Loyalist muster rolls can be found at *epe.lac-bac.gc.ca/100/200/301/ic/can_digital_collections/blackloyalist/index.html.*
- WO 17/24, if your ancestor served in a British or German regiment.
- War Office (WO) 28, volumes 2–10, microfilm reels, B-2862-2867, finding aid 87, British records of many of the Northern Dept. Loyalist units.

- Manuscript Group (MG) 13 and WO 36, the American Rebellion Entry Books (1775–83). These records contain information on the history of the revolution, British Army returns, France and Spain — armed forces, Order Books — Britain plus Prisoners of War and Prisons.
- MG 21 contains five volumes of reference material containing northern command muster rolls, lists of provisions to refugees, and service lists for the Provincial Marines. These are the records most used by researchers, finding aids 599 and 90, indexes on microfilm C-1476.
- MG 23, B1, microfilm M-341 to M-370, the records of Sir Guy Carleton, who was responsible for the evacuation from New York, references to soldiers, ships, refugees, and Loyalists.

WAR OF 1812

This is only a small part of the resources you can use to research your 1812 ancestors.

- MG 13, WO 10, Reel C-12568 contains muster books and pay lists for the Royal Artillery serving in Canada.
- MG 13, WO 12, 1759–1839. British Regiments of the Line who served at Louisburg and Quebec, 1759–67; Fencible Regiments, 1791–98 and 1812–16; Canadian Volunteers 1838–39. On microfilm reel C-9202 you will find the 1795–1816 reference material. The microfilmed

originals are on microfilm reels B-110 to B-118 and B-3196.

- MG 13, WO 17 — 1758–1865 — vols. 1489–1569, "Canada," 1758–1865, vols., 1570–80, "British, Provincial, and German Troops serving in Canada," 1776–86, microfilm B-1585 and B-1587 to B-1590, vols. 2241–2293, "Newfoundland," B-1591 and B-1606 to B-1613. These records show the distribution of British forces in North America, records effective strength of all ranks in each regiment with the names of all commissioned officers present and absent. The returns also provide information on the dates of any officers dying since the last return, the rank and file fit for duty, and the number of men discharges for any reason since the last return.

- RG 10, microfilm, C-11120, claims for pensions by veterans, contains a list of Natives who served during the War of 1812.

LAC LAND GRANT RECORDS

- RG 1 - 9, Crown land admin., Subject files. This file contains correspondence regarding requests for land grants for militia service.

- RG 1 - 54, Petitions relating to land received by the Crown Land Department. Here you will find petitions from veterans of the war that may provide some details about military service.

- RG 1 - 100, Patent Plans. The material found in this file may be useful in locating the land granted to your 1812 ancestor.
- RG 1 - 52, Registers of Militia Grants. Gives reference to acreage granted to men of the militia, provincial dragoons, or provincial marine. Name, rank, and unit are provided.

NOVA SCOTIA ARCHIVES

Military Land Grant Map. Nova Scotia Archives, Map Collection, V7/239-1785 Pictou.

- RG 1, Great Britain — Army — Volume 376, 1784, Muster Rolls of Loyalists and military settlers at Annapolis, Digby, and adjacent places in that county, also on the island of St. John (Prince Edward Island) and other settlements on Gulf Shore of Nova Scotia, 28 May to 28 September 1784 (transcribed in 1880 from the muster rolls in possession of J.W. Lawrence of Saint John, NB, formerly among the papers of the late Honourable Ward Chipman, chief justice of New Brunswick). These records contain names with class, numbers in family, and remarks as to where they settled, as well as names of the disbanded corps to which many of them had belonged.
- MG 12 — Headquarters office papers, vol., nos.0-236, 1783–1907, record of regiments and corps that have served in the Nova Scotian Command since October 1783 when the troops arrived from New York after the American Revolutionary War.

If you visit the Nova Scotia Archives in person, these are two useful finding aids:

Marion Gilroy, comp., Halifax, 1937, *Loyalists and Land Settlement in Nova Scotia*, is a transcribed list of Loyalist land grants providing name, date, situation, acres, and origin or rank for the nine counties of Nova Scotia. Included are grants, warrants, and escheats. Often the name of the loyalist corps, rank, and status are provided on each individual.

Jean Peterson, assisted by Lynn Murphy and Heather MacDonald, *A Detailed List of Archival Resources Available to Researchers*, Public Archives of Nova Scotia. Page 85 lists books

related to the military in Nova Scotia and available at the archives.
Page 239, Chapter 15, Military — offers general correspondence,
regiments and "soldiers," which includes uniforms etc., providing
reference numbers for research purposes.

NOVA SCOTIA WEBSITES

The following websites list either original or transcribed nominal
rolls of members of the Provincial Corps who settled in one of
the eastern provinces.

- The Genealogical Association of Nova Scotia
  www.chebucto.ns.ca/Recreation/GANS.
- At Genealogy Links *www.genealogylinks.net/
  canada/nova_scotia/nova_scotia_military.htm*,
  Loyalist records and lists of British regiments
  stationed in Nova Scotia.
- The Nova Scotia Genealogical Network
  Association. Go to *nsgna.ednet.ns.ca*, and check
  Military.
- The Nova Scotia Museum has a surname search
  function for Black Loyalists at *museum.gov.ns.ca/
  blackloyalists/names/default.htm*.
- At Mary's Genealogy Treasures (Nova Scotia)
  www3.telus.net/public/mtoll, check Military.
- On Roots Web *freepages.military.rootsweb.ancestry.
  com/~bonsteinandgilpin/gatnc.htm*, you can trace
  your Hessian ancestors.

NEW BRUNSWICK

At the New Brunswick Archives, *www.archives.gnb.ca*, you can access all the records of the 1839 Act, "An Act for the Relief of Old Soldiers of the Revolutionary War," granting financial assistance to soldiers or their widows who had fallen on hard times and were applying for government assistance. The petitions and the schedules of payment are available. The petition often includes the number of years the applicant has lived in the colony, his or her economic condition, information about military service, and in the case of widows when and where the couple was married. The payment schedules contain lists of names and in some cases information about the recipient. All the records have been digitized and are available online. At the archives website, check Search then Other to access the records. If you view these records online, check the Help option, especially the "Guidelines for Performing an Effective Search." If you visit the archives in person, look at the following record sources:

- Record Source (RS) 566 — Provincial Secretary: Old Soldiers and Widower Pension Admin. Records.
- RS 146/148/153/154/157 — County records: Albert, Charlotte, Northumberland, Queens, Sunbury for record of payments.
- RS 9 — Executive Council Meeting Files, contain lists of soldiers and widows, and sometimes include information about individual soldiers.
- RS 24 — Sessional Records of the Legislative Assembly.
- MG 24 8-1, Ref. # 6886-0-2-E, a transcript of a "List of Veterans of 1812–1815" of Upper Canada to whom medals have been granted.

- Similar but not identical to records found 8, vol. 1202, reels C-3519.

Websites

University of New Brunswick Library, *www.lib.unb.ca*, allows you to browse the collection of military/loyalist records.

Ancestry.com, *search.ancestry.ca/search/*. Available on this site are a list of volunteers who served with Major Willcocks and a nominal roll of the men belonging to the Corps of Canadian Volunteers in the service of the United States during the war. There are also Loyalist muster rolls online.

Canadian Military Heritage Project, *www.rootsweb.ancestry.com/~canmil*.

Cyndi's List, *www.cyndislist.com/milcan.htm*, select Military Resources Worldwide then Canadian.

Early Canadiana Online Project, *www.canadiana.org/ECO*. At this site you can access the books listing the militiamen of the 1812 war wounded or killed in action and entitled to a government pension/gratuity.

Families in British India Society, *www.fibis.org*, if you suspect your ancestors may have served in India during the Raj.

Family Search, *www.familysearch.org*, this site will give you access to the records of the Church of Jesus Christ of Latter-day Saints (Mormons). The Library Search tab will provide you with a list of the records held at Salt Lake City. Once you know the microfilm number, the film can be borrowed on inter-centre loan. You do not have to be a member of the church to use the research facilities.

Friends of Fort York, *www.fortyork.ca*, check the links to re-enactor groups. Many of these groups have done extensive research related to the personnel who served during the war.

General Society of the War of 1812, *www.societyofthewarof1812. org/links.html*, this is an American site but does provide some good links to Canadian information.

Google Books, *www.googlebooks.com*. Here I found *A Narrative of the Affair at Queenston Heights: in the War of 1812* with a review, published 1836, Van Renssaelaer, John Armstrong. Van Renssaelaer was the American commander at the battle of Queenston Heights who was removed from command following the American defeat. He spent years trying to clear his name.

Imperial War Museum, U.K. *www.iwm.org.uk*.

Library and Archives Canada, *www.collectionscanada.ca/archivianet*, access the list of research tools, then general inventory, for government of Canada files, land grants, and other archival resources across Canada.

McGill Library, *digital.library.mcgill.ca/CountyAtlas*. The university has scanned county atlases and provided an index so you can search for ancestors who may have owned land in Canada. The site is titled; "In Search of Your Past: The Canadian County Atlas Digital Project." Here, I found the Turcott farm in an 1878 atlas of Frontenac County.

National Archives U.K., *www.nationalarchives.gov.uk*.

Olive Tree Genealogy, *www.olivetreegenealogy.com/mil/1812*, focus on Canadian genealogy, then military.

Rootsweb Freepages hosted by Ancestry, *freepages.genealogy. rootsweb.ancestry.com/~crossroads/regiments/regiments-guards. html*, will provide you with information about the British Regiments in Canada.

Ancestry.com has posted U.K. military campaign medals and awards roll, 1793–1949, on their website. Check the right-hand side to browse the collection at *search.ancestry.co.uk/ search/category.aspx?cat=131*.

Books

Loyalists

Cook, S.H. and G.R. Hodges. *The Black Loyalists Directory:African Americans in Exile After the American Revolution.* New York and London: Garland Publishing, 1996.

Cruikshank, E. *The King's Royal Regiment of New York.* With index, appendices, and a master muster roll provided by Gavin Watt. Toronto: Ontario Historical Society, 1931, reprinted 1984.

Dubeau, S. *New Brunswick Loyalists, A Bicentennial Tribute.* Agincourt, ON: Generation Press, 1983.

Fryer, Mary Beacock. *Rolls of the Provincial (Loyalist) Corps, Canadian Command, American Revolution Period.* Toronto: Dundurn Press, 1981.

Gregory, M. *Compendium of Canadian Regiments.* Ottawa: Lomor Printers Ltd., 2005.

Hughes, G.W. *A Marchpast of the Corps and Regiments of the Canadian Army Past and Present* (three Volumes). Calgary: [s.n.], 1993.

Katcher, P. *Armies of the American Wars 1753–1815.* New York: Hastings House, 1975.

Raymond, W. O. *Loyalist Arms, 1775–1783: A Short History of the British American Regiments with the Rolls of Officers.* Milton: Global Heritage Press, 2001.

Rees, R. *Land of the Loyalists, Their Struggle to Shape the Maritimes.* Halifax, NS: Nimbus Publications Ltd., 2000.

Wilson, Barbara. *Military General Service Medal, 1793–1814, Egypt Medal, 1882–1889, North West Canada Medal, 1885 (Canadian Recipients).* London, U.K.: Spink & Son Ltd., 1975.

War of 1812

Cruikshank, E.A. *Record of the Services of Canadian Regiments in the War of 1812: The Militiamen of the Eastern District: Glengarry, Stormont and Dundas.* Canadian Military Institute, 1915, reprinted Toronto: Canadiana, 196?.

Gray, W.M. *Soldiers of the King: The Upper Canada Militia, 1812–1815: A Reference Guide.* Erin, ON: Boston Mills Press, 1995.

Lauber, W.R. *An Index of the Land Claim Certificates of Upper Canada Militiamen Who Served in the War of 1812.* Toronto: Ontario Genealogical Society, 1995.

MacLean & Rogers. *Militiamen of 1812–1815: Showing the Names, Ages and Residence of Militiamen of 1812–15 Who had Applied for the Government Gratuity of 1875.* Ottawa: Department of Militia and Defence, 1872.

Merriman, Brenda Dougall. *United Empire Loyalists: A Guide to Tracing Loyalist Ancestors in Upper Canada.* Milton, ON: Global Heritage Press, 2009.

Books Containing Lists of Names of Medal Recipients or Information About Military Service Medals

Berton, P. *Flames Across the Border, 1813–1814.* Toronto: Anchor Canada, 2001.

___. *The Invasion of Canada, 1812–1813.* Toronto: Anchor Canada, 2001.

Blatherwick, Francis, J. *Canadian Orders, Decoration & Medals, 4th Ed.* Toronto: Unitrade Press, 1994.

Duckers, P. *British Campaign Medals, 1815–1914.* Botley, Oxford: Shire Books, 2000.

Irving, L.A. *Officers of the British Forces in Canada during the War of 1812–1815*. Welland, ON: Welland Tribune Press, 1908, reprinted 1992.

Mullen, A.L.T. *The Military General Service Medal Roll, 1793–1812*. London: London Stamp Exchange, 1990.

N.A. *The Waterloo Medal Roll: Compiled from the Muster Rolls*. Dallington, East Sussex: Naval and Military Press, 1992.

Vigors, D., and MacFarlane, A.M. *The Three Great Retrospective Medals, 1793–1840 Awarded to Artillerymen*. Salisbury, U.K.: Vigors & MacFarland, 1986.

RCMI Library

Arkwith, W.N. *List of Officers of the Royal Regiment of Artillery, 1716–1899*, 4th Edition. London, U.K.: William Clowes & Sons, 1900.

Government of Canada. *Statement the Names, Age and Residence of Militiamen of 1812–15, Who Have Applied to Participate in the Gratuity Voted by Parliament in 1875, With the Name of the Corps or Division and Rank in Which They Served*. Ottawa: Maclean, Rogers & Co., 1876.

Laws, M.E.S. *Battery Records of the Royal Artillery, 1776–1859*, Woolwich, U.K.: Royal Artillery Publication, 1952. In this book I discovered which batteries of artillery were in action at the battle of New Orleans.

Sutherland, S. *His Majesty's Gentlemen: A Directory of Regular British Army Officers of the War of 1812*. Toronto: Iser Publications, 2000.

CHAPTER TWO

The Rebellions of 1837–38: I Think My Ancestors Were Rebels!

Many historians will tell you that American history is one of revolution while Canada's is one of evolution. In many cases this is true, but not in 1837. If you ask Canadians about this period in our history most will shrug and give you a blank look. This shouldn't be the case! From the end of the War of 1812, in 1814, to the creation of the Union Government in 1841, this country was in social upheaval. Indeed, the system of government we have today, created 1 July 1867 and referred to as Confederation, is a direct result of this period of rebellion.

Jean Baptiste Turcott applied for a land grant twice. His 1838 application was made to John George Lambton, Earl of Durham (Lord Durham), governor general of Canada, and was discovered at LAC. The finding aid stated, "Turcott, Jean Bte — St. Marie, Beauce, corpl. 4th Btn. Que. 21/1/41 script for 100 acres of land, list 4, Que. Gazette, 21-1-1841." I assumed the entry was for service during the War of 1812 but was intrigued by the application to Lord Durham.

John George Lambton was appointed governor of Canada following the rebellions that had broken out in Upper and Lower Canada in 1837. In England he had been referred to as "Radical

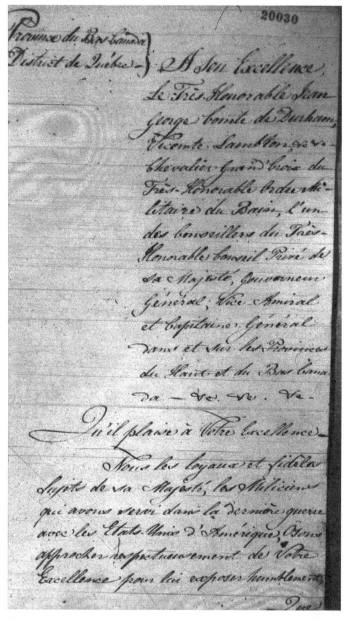

Land grant application submitted on behalf of Jean Baptiste Turcott.
LAC 20030, also available in list 4, Que. Gazette, 21-1-1841.

Jack" because of his liberal views on social reform. He was sent to the colonies in 1838 to report on the reasons for rebellion. His *Report on the Affairs in British North America,* commonly called The Durham Report, changed the face of government in Canada, eventually led to the establishment of Bytown (Ottawa) as the capital of a united colony, and ultimately the Confederation of the colonies with the British North America Act in 1867.

There was a chance that my wife's ancestor, Jean Baptiste Turcott might have served in one of the loyal militia units that had fought the rebels in Lower Canada. After all, his 1838 application stated that he had served as a corporal with the 4th Battalion and lived in Ste.-Marie, Beauce, while his 1878 application for the gratuity granted by Canada's Parliament stated that he had served in the Boucherville division during the War of 1812.

What happened in the twenty years following the War of 1812? These are some of the topics you should research to gain some knowledge of the Rebellions: life in Canada in the 1830s, causes of the rebellions, the lists of those captured and tried for treason (over 1,000 individuals), what militia or regular British regiments served during the period, and how to discover if one of your ancestors was transported to Australia.

Because this chapter focuses on military ancestors and, in this case, rebels (Upper Canada) and patriots (Lower Canada) as well, I leave it to you to discover any vital statistics on your ancestors. Although this period is before formal censuses, there are some church records and militia lists. The earliest censuses of 1842, 1848, and 1852 list heads of families only and are incomplete for many areas. Quebec records are more complete.

First, what background information can you learn about your 1830s British North American relatives? I would recommend you start your research by reading *Roughing It in the Bush* by Susanna Moodie, *A Veteran of 1812* by Mary FitzGibbon, and *Winter Studies and Summer Rambles* by Anna Jameson. These first-hand accounts will give you a sense of what your 1830 ancestors faced when they left England to start a new life in the colonies.

The FitzGibbon book, in particular, gives insight into the rebellions in Upper Canada. There we find an outline of the order of battle for the loyal forces. FitzGibbon recorded this "Rough Sketch of Distribution for the Attack on the Morning of December 7 1837." It can be of use if you discover an ancestors was one of the "Men of Scarboro, in the woods with Colonel McLean (Allen)."

Colonel Macnab.

Lieutenant Nash ... ... 1st Company ... ... .Advance Guard.

Lieutenant Coppinage ... 2nd Company ... ... Advance Guard.

Lieutenant Garrett ... ... .3rd Company ... ... .Advance Guard.

Major Draper.

Henry Sherwood.

Two Guns.

Captain Wm. Jarvis ... ... 1st Company ... ...Battalion.

Captain Campbell ... ...2nd Company.

Captain Nation ... ...3rd Company.

Captain Taylor ... ... 4th Company.

Captain Jno. Powell ... ... .5th Company.

Henry Sherwood ... ... .6th Company.

Henry Draper ... ...7th Company.

Donald Bethune ... ... 8th Company.

Colonel Samuel McLean ... ... *Lieutenant Cox to aid.

Lieut.-Colonel George Duggan.

Major Jno. Gamble.

Judge Macaulay.

Colonel McLean.

Colonel Jones ... ... For the Left Battalion.

Colonel Jno. Macaulay.

Captain Macaulay.

Captain Durnford.

Artillery.

Captain Mathias.

Captain Carfrae.

Captain Leckie.

Dragoons.

Three Companies in Front.

One Gun, Major Carfrae.

Four Companies:

The men of Gore, under Colonel Macnab.

One Gun.

Four Companies:

Right Flank under Colonel Jarvis.

One Company, Men of Scarboro, in the woods with Colonel McLean (Allen).

Left Flank under Colonel McLean (Archibald).

Two Companies under Colonel Jones.[1]

Susanna Moodie's husband, J. Dunbar Moodie, was a former army officer who had been placed on half pay following the war with France. He elected to apply for a land grant in Upper Canada and eventually settled near present-day Peterborough, Ontario. During the Rebellions he was recalled to duty at present-day Cobourg, Ontario, leaving his wife and children on their bush farm trying to survive the winter. These books may help you to understand why your ancestors either remained loyal or chose to fight with the rebels. Susanna wrote the following concerning the causes of the rebellion:

> Favouritism was, of course, the order of the day;
> and the governor, for the time being, filled up all

offices according to his will and pleasure, without many objections being made by the people as to the qualifications of the favourite parties, provided the selections for office were made from the powerful party. Large grants of land were given to favoured individuals in the colony, or to immigrants who came with recommendations from the home government. In such a state of matters the people certainly possessed the external form of a free government, but as an opposition party gradually acquired an ascendancy in the Lower House of Parliament, they were unable to carry the measures adopted by their majority into operation, in consequence of the systematic opposition of the legislative and executive councils, which were generally formed exclusively from the old conservative party. Whenever the conservatives obtained the majority in the House of Assembly, the reformers, in retaliation, as systematically opposed every measure. Thus a constant bickering was kept up between the parties in Parliament; while the people, amidst these contentions, lost sight of the true interests of the country, and improvements of all kinds came nearly to a stand-still.[2]

SO, WHAT ELSE SHOULD I KNOW ABOUT THIS PERIOD?

Any time a rebellion occurs, there are usually some major grievances that have gone unresolved over a period of time. Eventually the grievances become so overwhelming that normally law-abiding citizens feel they have no choice but to take up arms and bring about change, often through force. If the rebellion is successful, a new order arises that, one would hope, rectifies the injustices that brought about the violence.

In Upper and Lower Canada, even though the rebels were defeated and those captured tried for treason, change resulted because England was shocked by what had occurred. A young Queen Victoria and the British Parliament wanted to make sure they weren't facing a repeat of the American Revolution.

The library is full of Canadian history books that will give you detailed accounts of the grievances that led up to the rebellions: the clergy and crown reserves, colonial government, the Family Compact/Château Clique, funding for the "Established Church," poor roads, lack of publicly funded education, and various other grievances. You can also find biographical sketches of key political figures such as William Lyon Mackenzie and Louis-Joseph Papineau.

If you think one of your ancestors might have played a leadership role in the rebellions, spend a few minutes researching some of these following key players. In Upper Canada: Robert Baldwin, John Beverley Robinson, Sir Francis Bond Head, Dr. Charles Duncombe, James FitzGibbon, Robert Gourley, Samuel Lount, Peter Matthews, Alan McNabb, Dr. Wolfred Nelson, Dr. Edmund Bailey O'Callaghan, John Rolf, Egerton Ryerson, Thomas Storrow Brown, Reverend John Strachan, and Anthony Van Egmond. In Lower Canada: Jean-Olivier Chénier, Lord Colborne, Dr. Cyrille Côté, Amury Girod, Louis LaFontaine, Robert Nelson, André Ouimet.

The one grievance common to Upper and Lower Canada was the colonial government. Each colony had a lieutenant governor who was appointed in England. The Houses of Assembly in each of Nova Scotia, New Brunswick, Lower, and Upper Canada had two levels: the Legislative Council, appointed for life, and the Legislative Assembly, which was elected by the colonists. The governor also had the right to appoint an executive council as his advisors. The crux of the problem was the issue of elected-versus-appointed representatives.

In addition, the people holding power in the colonies had a fear of American Republicanism. Remember that a large segment of the population in Upper Canada originally came from the United States in search of free land. Many brought their "republican" beliefs with them. Included in this mix were new immigrants from the British Isles who expected the same political freedoms they had enjoyed back in England.

Often, when the new governor arrived from England he selected individuals for his executive council whom he saw as the leading educated and loyal members of the colonial society he was going to govern. Soon these select few not only had direct access to the governor but also could recommend political appointments for individuals they saw as worthy, especially to the appointed legislative council. In Upper Canada this group became referred to in the local newspapers as the Family Compact and in Lower Canada, the Château Clique. Those terms were used because the more radical newspapers often made headlines by pointing out the family connections among government appointees. The lower house, or legislative assembly, was elected by the voters of the colony and, therefore, seemed more democratic.

It's not difficult for anyone to see that this system had built-in flaws that would ultimately lead to conflict. The extract from Susanna Moodie's book does an excellent job outlining the resulting frustration. The elected assembly saw many of the laws it wished to enact disallowed by the legislative council and governor. In turn the assembly refused to vote the monies the governor needed for his own initiatives. William Lyon Mackenzie in Upper Canada, Joseph Howe in Nova Scotia, and Louis-Joseph Papineau in Lower Canada presented lists of grievances directly to the Home Office in England with no satisfaction. The stage was set.

When you construct your family narrative, include some of the following key events from the Rebellions:

In Upper Canada:
- Mackenzie is defeated in the election of 1836, mostly because of the direct interference of Governor Bond Head during the campaigning.
- Vigilance Committees are formed following Mackenzie's call for armed resistance.
- The Committees start to collect fire arms and to drill.
- October 1837, Mackenzie receives word from Lower Canada that the Patriotes are ready to strike a blow for liberty.
- Date is set for rebellion, 7 December 1837, plan calls for 5,000 men to assemble at Montgomery's Tavern just north of Toronto.
- In November word is received that rebellion has broken out in Lower Canada.
- In spite of advice from James FitzGibbon, Governor Bond Head sends all available troops to Lower Canada.
- 4 December 1837 rebels start to assemble at Montgomery's Tavern.
- 5 December 1837 they begin to march on Toronto.

- About 300 men, loyal to the Family Compact, assemble in Toronto.
- Thirty government supporters, under the command of Sheriff Jarvis, stand guard at a barricade just north of the city.
- A brief skirmish results and the rebels retreat back to the tavern.
- The government forces, under the direction of James FitzGibbon, march north on Yonge street and defeat the rebels.
- Montgomery's Tavern is burned along with other buildings associated with known reformers.
- Mackenzie escapes to the United States, establishes a provisional government on Navy Island in the Niagara River from which he initiates raids on Upper Canada.
- The American steamer *Caroline*, used to supply the group, is burned by government supporters.
- 14 April 1838, prisoners from Dr. Duncombe's Rising, near Brantford, and the Short Hills engagement are sentenced to death.
- Several men, including Samuel Lount and Peter Matthews, are hanged for treason and almost one hundred are sent into exile.
- Mackenzie is finally arrested by U.S. authorities, spends a year in jail, eventually settles in New York City, and returns to Upper Canada in 1849 when a general amnesty is declared.

In Lower Canada:

- By 1837 there is deadlock in government — the assembly refuses to grant money to pay the salaries of the governor and councillors.
- The Ten Resolutions are passed by the British Parliament allowing the governor to pay out funds without the consent of the assembly.
- Patriotes (supporters of Papineau) start to collect arms and secretly drill.
- The rebels start to refer to themselves as the "Fils de la liberté" hold rallies and use slogans like "La nation Canadienne" and "Papineau et l'independence."
- November 1837, the rebellion begins with a clash between the Doric Club, which supports the government, and the Patriotes who support reform.
- Papineau leaves Montreal, Patriotes start to assemble in the Richelieu Valley region, and the government decides to send troops to take prisoners and disperse any armed Patriote groups.
- 22 November 1837, a force of British Troops march toward the village of Saint- Denis, a five-hour battle is fought with a large body of Patriotes who put up such a strong resistance that the troops retreat.
- 24 November 1837, a second clash occurs at the village of Saint-Charles, Papineau flees to the U.S., and the rebels are defeated.
- December 1837, the battle at Saint–Eustache, just north and west of Montreal, results in 120 Patriotes being taken prisoner and many more killed and wounded.

- Trials begin and eventually over one thousand prisoners are tried for treason.
- Papineau eventually leaves the United States, lives in France, and returns to Canada in 1845.

The rebellions in Upper and Lower Canada did not end with the defeat of the rebels. For the following few years Hunters' Lodges, mostly situated in the U.S., organized and planned raids on Upper Canada. The lodges seemed to be mostly located in New York State and indeed a meeting did occur in Lockport, New York, in March 1838 attended by William Lyon Mackenzie. These lodges were responsible for the burning of the steamer *Sir Robert Peel* and various raids across the border at Niagara. In November 1838, a major engagement was fought at Prescott, Ontario, which is commonly referred to as the Battle of the Windmill. What is left of the windmill is still on the site and Fort Wellington is open to the public.

As an interesting aside, you may want to spend some time researching William Johnson, the Thousand Island Pirate. It is claimed Johnson was responsible for the burning of the *Peel* and generally harassing boat traffic on the St. Lawrence River. That he was a member of a hunters' lodge is not totally verified; that he was a pirate whom authorities would have like to apprehend is not in doubt. I don't believe he was ever captured, nor was his base in the Thousand Islands discovered. Johnson is one of the many interesting characters who appear in Canadian history from time to time and about whom very few Canadians know.

So, what about your military ancestors who served during the rebellions? The governor of Upper Canada, Sir Francis Bond Head, upon a request from the authorities in Lower Canada, sent almost all the regular British troops then stationed in the colony to Quebec. Thus, by January 1838 the defence of the colony of

Upper Canada depended on local militia units raised specifically for the duration of hostilities. Several hundred volunteers flooded into the city of Toronto in response to the December threats and it is estimated that by February there were almost two thousand militiamen available for service. They were formed into units with names like the Toronto City Guards, Queen's Lancers, and Royal Volunteers. To counter the hunters' lodge threat several 600-man battalions were incorporated and specifically equipped by the government for full-time service. By the end of 1838 these battalions were reorganized into thirty companies and sixteen battalions.[3]

Your ancestors would have been organized into incorporated, provisional, or sedentary militia units. The incorporated militia served for eighteen months, full-time. The provisional battalions volunteered for six months. The sedentary units and Aboriginal peoples were called out when it was felt necessary. England responded by dispatching over five thousand regulars to Upper and Lower Canada. The Great Lakes were protected by several specifically designed steamers, manned by members of the Provincial Marine.

LAC's MG 13, WO 13, holds the nominal rolls of the "Coloured" companies raised by the British to help track down rebels. The authorities knew that they could depend on Upper and Lower Canada's black citizens to support the government because slavery had been abolished in Upper Canada in the 1790s and in the British Empire in 1834. The British were counting on the black settlers (mostly Loyalists and escaped and freed slaves) and Native population of British North America to want no part of American republicanism. Four battalions were formed.

The Durham Report resulted in the 1841 Act of Union uniting Upper and Lower Canada and changing their names to Canada East (Quebec) and Canada West (Ontario). The geographic origin of public records for these two regions from 1841 until 1867 were referred to as CE (Canada East) and CW (Canada West). Likewise the government offices for the Parliament of the United Canadas alternated between Kingston, Canada West, and Montreal, Canada East.

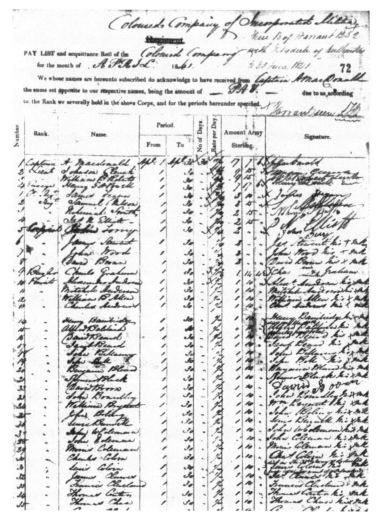

Muster Roll of Coloured Troops. LAC, MG13, muster rolls of militia, 1837–1850, B series.

In 1849 the Government of the United Canadas passed into law the Rebellions Losses Bill compensating former Reformers/Patriotes for damages committed by government troops during the Rebellions. The result was riots in Montreal and the burning of the Parliament buildings in that city. In 1854, Queen Victoria decided to resolve the issue of the capital of Canada by selecting Bytown, later Ottawa, as the seat of government.

The Act of Union was designed not only to unite the provinces of Upper and Lower Canada with an equal number of seats assigned to each in the new Parliament, but also to assimilate the French Canadians and encourage them to give up their language and customs. By the early 1860s, the Parliament of the United Canadas was again in deadlock. Eventually the British North America Act would create the Confederation of Ontario, Quebec, New Brunswick, and Nova Scotia on 1 July 1867.

WHAT HAPPENED TO THE HUNDREDS OF INDIVIDUALS WHO WERE TRIED AND SENTENCED FOR TREASON?

If one of your ancestors was a Reformer in Upper Canada or a Patriote in Lower Canada he might have been sent to Botany Bay in Australia onboard a convict ship. The only way you will know is by checking some of the lists of individuals tried by court martial found in archival documents or online.

You can find a list of the 1,048 individuals tried for treason and acquitted or either executed or transported to Australia in *The Patriots and the People*. There I found Louis Turcott — acquitted — in the list of names.[5] The actual document published by the Colonial Office in 1840 provides a complete return of the persons imprisoned in Lower Canada. A great deal of information about the individuals is provided, including whether or not their sentence was executed or commuted. The report, entitled "Return to an Address of the Honourable the House of Commons" and dated 27 February 1839, is available at the Toronto Reference Library.

> On Olive Tree Genealogy you can find a list of men sentenced to death as a result of Dr. Duncombe's rising near Brantford: Horatio Hill, Stephen Smith, Charles Walworth, Ephraim Cook, John Tufford, and Nathan Town, as well as the names of those charged in the Short Hills Insurrection: Samuel Chandler (banished), James Morreau (executed), William Reynold, Garret Van Camp, August Linus, Wilson Miller, George Cooley, Norman Mallory, Loren Hedge, George Buck, James Genmill, Murdoch McFadden, Freeman Brady, Robert Kelly, Ebenezer Rice, David Taylor, Abraham Clarke, John T. McNulty, John Grant, Street Chase, James Waggoner, Edward Seymour, Alexander McLeod, Benjamin Wait (banished).[4]

In Upper Canada, only two individuals were hanged for their part in the rebellions: Samuel Lount and Peter Matthews. Many of those condemned to death had their sentences commuted because of general indignation amongst the people of the colonies. For instance, Joseph Sheard, architect and later mayor of Toronto, blatantly refused to build the gallows for Lount and Matthews's execution, stating, "Lount and Matthews have done nothing that I might not have done myself, and I'll never help to build a gallows to hang them."[6]

WHY MIGHT MY ANCESTORS HAVE BEEN SENT TO AUSTRALIA?

It was Captain James Cook's report that convinced the British Admiralty of the suitability of Botany Bay as a prison for convicts. Previously, Britain had been in the habit of sending undesirables convicted of a wide variety of crimes to the Thirteen Colonies. However, the end of the American Revolution and the creation of the United States put an end to the availability of this region. The first fleet of prisoners arrived at Sydney Cove on 26 January 1788, and the final group arrived in 1868. Some 150 persons convicted of treason were sent to Australia on two ships, the *Canton* and the *Marquis of Hastings.*[7]

Your ancestors who lived during this period saw some interesting changes as the colony of British North America slowly assumed more responsibility for government and military defence. By the 1850s England was beginning to distance herself from Canada, allowing the colonies to rely more on their own militia for defence. After the Aroostook War in the mid 1850s, over the boundary between New Brunswick and the State of Maine, the whole structure of our military changed. In 1855 the government enacted the Militia Act, which established an Active Militia (permanent) of 5,000 officers and men, and a Sedentary Militia (only called out in times of need to supplement the active militia) of 100,000 officers and men. The Militia Act saw the growth of many new units, each assigned a battalion number and title. These changes occurred just in time to face the challenges of the upcoming decades.[8]

Jean Baptiste Turcott must have received his land grant as his name doesn't appear on any of the lists of individuals tried for treason; he clearly states in his application that he served in the 4th Battalion as a corporal. A relative, Louis Turcott, must have been accused of treason by someone or was seen in the company of suspected Patriotes but was acquitted by the court in Montreal. Shortly after the events in Lower Canada, Jean Baptiste must have moved to Wolfe Island, Frontenac County, Canada West. There he and one of his sons, Joseph, refer to themselves as sailors when registering children on the local Catholic parish registers. They can both be found in archival documents working for the government, transporting immigrants to the quarantine station on Grosse Isle. Perhaps that is where Joseph, my wife's great-grandfather, met his future wife, Mary O'Herne.

RESOURCES FOR THE REBELLIONS OF 1837–1838

LAC

These records will provide you with the nominal rolls, pay lists, etc. of the British units stationed in North America as well as the Canadian militia units.

- RG 9, series IB5, vols. 5–10, reels T3488 and T3489 contain militia records, 1824–47.
- RG 9, series IB7, vol. 8, 1837/38, hold registers of officers of the militia units involved in 1837/38.
- RG 9, series IA5, vol. 20, ref. R1023-13-7-E, available on microfilm, contains a list of militia officers dismissed for disloyalty.
- RG 9, series IA5, 1808–1846, provides a register of officers, Lower Canada, reels: T6943 and T6944 (1831–46), T6945 — officers dismissed (1837/38).
- RG 5 – B36 & B37, trials (37/38) and court martial (1838/39) in the London District.

- RG 5 – B38, results of Court of Queen's Bench in England, releasing 10 of 23 men slated for transportation to Australia.
- RG 5 – B39, review of conduct of Colonel J. Prince at the Battle of the Windmill.
- RG 5 – B41, an outline of the court martial at Kingston's Fort Henry.
- RG 5 – B44, covers claims for losses incurred during the rebellions.
- WO 13, NA, MG 13, vols. 3673–3717, reels B2916–B2917, B2976–B2977, B2995, B3159 to B 3196 will provide you with muster rolls etc., of British units stationed in North America during the rebellions.
- MG 24 – B2 Ref. #R12320-0-5-F contain the family papers of Louis-Joseph Papineau.
- MG 24 – A25 Ref. # R2451-0-5-E allows access to the family papers of Sir Francis Bond Head.
- MG 13, WO 67 hold the depot description books 1803–92, reels B-3661 to B-3663 — finding aid 90.
- MG 24 – G35 Ref. #R6679-0-8-E, are the Upper Canada Militia Unit Account Books.
- MG 24 – G40-0-2-E, Ref. #R6683-0-2-E contain the Volunteer Militia Force of Canada West fonds.
- MG 13, WO 13, hold the Muster Rolls, Canadian Militia 1837–50, reels: B2916-2917, B2976-2977, B2995, B3159-B3196, listed alphabetically according to unit.
- WO13, MG13, offers a list of officers and men killed and wounded during the 1837–38 rebellions.

WEBSITES

Australia, *www.naa.gov.au*.

Canadian Institute for Historical Microreproduction, *www2. canadiana.ca/en/home*, now part of the early Canada Online Project, always check this site for early documents.

City of Montreal, *ville.montreal.qc.ca/archives*.

City of Toronto Archives, *www.toronto.ca/archives*.

Eastern Townships Heritage WebMagazine, *www.townshipsheritage. com*.

Independence of Québec, English language page *www.english. republiquelibre.org/1837-38-patriot-war.html*, an excellent list of the events in Lower Canada.

Internet Archive, *www.archive.org/stream/cihm_00186/cihm_00186_ djvu.txt*, where you can read Reverend John Douglas Bothwick, *A History of the Montreal Prison from A.D. 1784 to A.D. 1886*. It contains a complete record of the Troubles of 1837/1838, Burning of Parliament Buildings in 1849, the St. Albans Raiders 1864, the Two Fenian Raids of 1866 and 1870. You will also find a list of the over one thousand individuals tried for treason as well as the verdict of acquittal, transportation, or execution.

Library and Archives Canada, "From Colony to Country, Rebellions of 1837 and 1838: A Reader's Guide to Canadian Military History," collectionscanada.gc.ca/military/025002-3000-e.html.

Library and Archives of Quebec, *www.banq.qc.ca*.

Military Heritage, *www.militaryheritage.com/pastprojects.htm*, you can see excellent images of the type of uniform worn by British units in this period.

National Archives U.K., *www.archives.gov.uk*.

Olive Tree Genealogy, *www.olivetreegenealogy.com/mil/can/1837*, click on Rebellion 1837, Patriot War.

Olive Tree Genealogy, *www.olivetreegenealogy.com/mil/can/1837/ data_duncombe.shtml*, for those sentenced to death after the Dr. Duncombe Rising.

Province of Ontario Archives, *www.archives.gov.on.ca.*

To the Outskirts of Habitable Creation, *www.1837rebellion.net/ linksto1837rebel.html*, a gateway to a variety of websites.

BOOKS

Life in 1830s Upper Canada

These nineteenth century books are available in many editions. These are the ones I used in preparing this book.

FitzGibbon, Mary Agnes. *A Veteran of 1812.* Toronto: William Briggs Pub., 1894, reprinted by Coles Publishing, 1979.

Jameson, Anna. *Winter Studies and Summer Rambles.* Reprint. Toronto: McClelland & Stewart, 1990.

Moodie, Susanna. *Roughing It in the Bush.* Ottawa: Carleton University Press, 1995, originally published in 1852.

The Rebellions

Bercusion, G. *Dictionary of Canadian Military History.* Toronto: Oxford University Press, 1992.

Brooke, A., and D. Brandon. *Bound for Botany Bay, British Convict Voyages to Australia.* London, U.K.: The National Archives, U.K., 1993.

Cahill, J. *Forgotten Patriots: Canadian Rebels on Australia's Convict Shores.* Toronto: Robin Brass Studio, 1998.

Colborne, Sir John. *Report of the State Trials before a General Court Martial Held at Montreal (1838–1839)*, Vol. II. Montreal: Armour and Ramsay, 1839.

Duclos, DeCelles, A. *The "Patriotes of 37": A Chronicle of the Lower Canada Rebellion and Theller, E.A., Canada in 1837–38: Showing, By Historical Facts the Causes of the Late Attempted Revolution and its Failures.* Washington: Library of Congress, 1841.

Graves, D.E. *Guns Across the River: the Battle of the Windmill, 1838.* Toronto: Friends of Windmill Point Publishers, 2001.

Greer, A. *The Patriotes and the People: The Rebellion of 1837 in Rural Lower Canada.* Toronto: University of Toronto Press, 1993.

Kilbourn, W. *The Firebrand: William Lyon Mackenzie and the Rebellion in Upper Canada.* Toronto: Dundurn Press, 2008.

Marteinson, J. *We Stand on Guard: An Illustrated History of the Canadian Army.* Montreal: Ovale Press, 1992.

Read, C., and R.J. Stagg. *The Rebellion in Upper Canada.* Ottawa: Carlton University Press, 2000.

CHAPTER THREE

1866 to 1898: My Ancestors May Have Defended Canada or Served in the Sudan

What an interesting period this is in Canadian history. At the end of the American Civil War (1865), we were not yet an independent country. Yet events on the world stage and developments within North America were soon to test the resolve of Canadian statesmen, result in the creation of the Dominion of Canada, and challenge the new country's right to govern. The conflicts that form the basis of this chapter tested the resolve of our ancestors and helped to further forge our military heritage.

My interest in this period started with an old photograph and an interesting story. The old photo shows two soldiers, one sitting the other standing. One of the soldiers seemed to be an officer while the other wears corporal stripes on the arm of his tunic. One of the men was supposedly James Forbes Foley, the first husband of my wife's grandmother. The photograph showed James in a uniform commonly worn by the local militia in the mid-nineteenth century. The uniform and cap badge gave me a point of reference for my research. The uniforms were certainly of the period: Wolseley pith helmets, 1871 (or earlier), valise pattern equipment, and what appeared to be scarlet tunics with appropriate piping on the sleeves.

William and James Foley. Private collection.

All this information was helpful in placing the individuals in a particular time period. British uniforms had gone through significant changes since the War of 1812 and Rebellions of 1837. The Crimean War (1853–56) and the need to wear appropriate service clothing in the far-flung areas of the British Empire had necessitated changes in weaponry, clothing, and equipment. Indeed, military uniforms went through the same fashion changes as civilian clothing.

Another interesting family story took place during the Fenian Raid on 2 June 1866, in the Niagara Peninsula near Ridgeway (now part of Fort Erie), Canada West. The Teal family lived on a farm close to Lime Ridge, where the battle took place. Family history relates that the husband heard from neighbours that the Fenians where raiding farms in the area looking for food or anything else they could plunder. He had his wife take their children and hide in the woods while he placed an old pot on his head, took his rifle, and defended his farm. Being such an accurate shot, he discouraged the raiders from entering his house. The farmhouse still stands and still displays the results of this action — some bullet holes from the event. The story did not mention whether Teal was a member of the local militia. The Teals were the ancestors of another family relative and not directly related to me. They had photos of the farmhouse and had even visited the site

WHERE SHOULD YOU BEGIN RESEARCHING THIS ERA?

Certainly either of these men, if they served with either the regular army or local militia, would have been entitled to the Canada General Service Medal with bar(s). The medal was approved by Parliament in 1899 and only issued to men who applied for it. There were approximately 16,668 Canada General Service Medals issued, over 15,000 to Canadians. There were three bars/clasps awarded: Fenian Raid 1866, Fenian Raid 1870, and Red River 1870. Over 500 Red River clasps were issued.[1] The British garrisons left Canada in 1870 so you should start with Canadian records. Unfortunately, there are no service files! The men who served during the Fenian period were paid and then released from service.

What's available in the archives or online which may be of use to family historians seeking information about ancestors in service during the 1860s and 1870s? One early source is *Troublous Times in Canada* by John MacDonald detailing the rise of the Fenian movement and the subsequent invasions of Canada. It is an excellent resource because it details all the militia units that were called up to serve during this crisis.

But first you need some working knowledge of this period. The Fenian movement in the United States was connected to the rise of the Irish Republican Army in Ireland and the fight for independence from British rule in that country. Many Irishmen had served during the American Civil War and, upon the end of that conflict, were available and well-trained, ready to take up the Fenian Brotherhood's goal of invading Canada and using the occupation as a point for negotiating the independence of Ireland. The Fenian threat was very real. Thousands of Irishmen in the United States volunteered to serve and large stores of weapons and equipment were available for purchase by the Brotherhood. They even believed they had the tacit approval of the United States government. Britain had quietly supported the Southern cause during the Civil War and had even turned a blind eye to the activities of Southern spies operating out of British North America. A number of locations in Canada were designated

Canada General Service Medal with Fenian Raid Clasp, issued for service during the Fenian Raids. Private collection.

as invasion routes: the Niagara region near Buffalo, New York; Cornwall, Canada West, across from Malone, New York; and the Vermont border south of Montreal, Quebec.

On 1 and 2 June 1866 the invasion began near Ridgeway, Ontario. The Queen's Own Rifles, the York Rifle Company, the Thirteenth Battalion, and the Caledonia Rifle Company were directly involved in the fighting at Lime Ridge. Even though the Fenians were victorious, their commanders decided to retreat back across the American border. Throughout the remainder of the year, the Fenian threat continued until the U.S. government finally decided to enforce the Neutrality Act, arrest the leaders of the Brotherhood, and confiscate any weapons. Large numbers of Canadians had served in their local militia units and were called out on a number of occasions to defend the border.

Early photograph showing militia "forming square." It was a similar movement that hampered the militia at the Battle of Ridgeway when they suspected the Fenians of having cavalry. Toronto Reference Library photographic collection.

When the Fenian threat finally ended a court martial was held in Hamilton, Canada West, in July 1866, into the conduct of the Canadian militia commander, Lieutenant-Colonel Booker, at the battle of Ridgeway. Family historians who discover an ancestor served with the militia during this period will find the following excerpt provides an interesting insight into militia training.

> ... this court are further of the opinion that the entire force under command of Lieut.Colonel Booker, from the formation of the expedition to the time it came out of action, was under disadvantage with which Her Majesty's regular forces have seldom or ever, it is submitted, had to contend — in the want, of cavalry, artillery, commissariat arrangements, or even the requisite means of carrying with them cooked provisions, or supplying themselves with water in the country through which they were about to move ...
>
> Further, that more than half of the two battalions forming the largest proportion of the whole force which left Port Colborne for Stevensville on the morning of the 2nd of June, was composed of youths not exceeding, and in many instances not having reached twenty years of age; that a large proportion of the force had been for a very short time accustomed to bear arms; that a somewhat less proportion had not even been exercised with blank cartridge, and that practice with ball cartridge was by very many of the rank and file of that force to be entered upon for the first time in their lives that day.[2]

So, was James Foley entitled to the Canada General Service
Medal and did the Teal family actually serve with the militia or
defend the family farm against Fenian marauders? My search
of the records for claims against damages turned up three Teal
family members making claims. Two claimed they were veterans
and one stated that he was living in Chicago at the time of his
application. The Chicago application was not surprising as a unit
of approximately thirty men did form an American detachment
and come north to fight against the Fenians. They arrived too
late to see any action but were treated to some adulation by the
citizens of Toronto. That local citizens who were not part of the
active militia became involved in the fighting cannot be denied.
The fighting that took place at Eccles Hill on 24 May, just south
of Montreal, Canada East, is a prime example of this type of
involvement. The local farmers, knowing the Fenians were preparing to enter the province and realizing the militia were not
ready to advance, took it upon themselves to purchase weapons
and occupy the heights known as Eccles Hill. There they delayed
the Fenian advance until the militia moved into position.

Research at the Archives of Ontario indicated that James
Foley was born in Dundas, Ontario, on 11 November 1868, and
thus was too young to have served. His father, however, may have
been Thomas Foley, born in Newfoundland. When I checked the
names of the men who served during the Red River expedition
I found a Thomas Foley, born in Newfoundland. Perhaps the
family picture was of James's father. The 1871 and 1881 censuses
indicate that James lived with his family on a farm in Waterloo
County. The census states that James's father was William Foley,
born in Ireland, and not Thomas. That a Foley served on the Red
River expedition is still rather interesting and something I must
still check. The family recently discovered a picture of William
Foley shown in the uniform of an officer in the 10th Royal

Grenadiers, allowing for more detailed research into a specific and significant regiment.

THE RED RIVER EXPEDITION — 1870

Three years after Confederation the Canadian government purchased all the former Hudson's Bay Company territory. This was a huge acquisition and resulted in settlers from Ontario going west in search of land, the appointing of a lieutenant-governor for the Territory and the establishment of Canadian sovereignty. Unfortunately no one thought to consult the Natives and Métis people already living in what was to become the Province of Manitoba. When news of the sale reached them, the Métis appointed Louis Riel as their leader and established their own provisional government. Things came to a head after negotiations failed and the provisional government tried and executed Thomas Scott and denied entry to the territory of the new lieutenant governor. Originally from Ireland and a member of the Orange Order, Scott had come west from Ontario. The Government of Canada commissioned British Colonel Garnet Wolseley to lead a military force west to settle the situation. By Order-in-Council, 16 April 1870, the government authorized a military contingent to serve in the new province of Manitoba. This adventure became known as the Red River Expedition.

The force was to consist of two battalions of riflemen. One unit was designated the First (Ontario) Battalion and the other the Second (Quebec) Battalion. These battalions were to be composed of volunteers from the active militia, drawn from the seven military districts of Ontario and Quebec. They were to serve for one year or longer if required. The force eventually numbered 1,200 men, including 350 officers. Accompanying the force were the 60th Royal Rifles, detachments of Royal Artillery and Engineers, as well as a contingent of Canadian Voyageurs.[3]

After an arduous trip, the force reached Manitoba only to discover that Riel and some of his followers had escaped to the United States. Wolseley left a detachment of troops and returned to Ottawa. In 1873 the Canadian government established the North-West Mounted Police to act in civilian matters and confirm Canadian sovereignty of the newly acquired land. The history of the force and a search of their records are beyond the focus of this text but something that family historians should not ignore if they suspect an ancestor may have served with the unit in either western Canada or later with the police in South Africa.

My search for James Forbes Foley did not end with the Red River Expedition files. Perhaps he had served with General Middleton during the North-West Rebellion or even went with General Garnet Wolseley when he travelled down the Nile River in Egypt to save General Gordon.

THE NILE EXPEDITION, 1884–85

The action on the Nile in Egypt is an interesting event in our country's young history. In reality, it is the first time that Canadians were asked to participate in a foreign war and were recognized as citizens of a new country — albeit, under British control and without direct support from the Canadian government. In Sudan, British General Gordon faced an uprising led by the Muslim prophet, the Mahdi, Muhammad Ahmad bin Abd Allah. Eventually Gordon found himself under siege in the city of Khartoum and Britain was forced to organize a relief column. Garnet Wolseley, the same man who had led the

Red River Expedition, was assigned the task of saving Gordon by leading an expedition down the Nile River from Egypt.

Men of the Voyageur contingent photographed outside Parliament before departure for the Nile. LAC C-002877.

Wolseley realized that the only way he was going to save the British garrison at Khartoum was by moving his men and supplies through the many rapids on the river, a job for which Voyageurs were well-suited. In August 1884 an advertisement was placed in Canadian newspapers for a "few good boatmen."[4] Frederick Dennison eventually recruited 377 men, seven officers, and eight "wheelmen," mostly from Ottawa and Manitoba, a few from Peterborough, Ontario, and Trois-Rivières, Quebec, and 56 Natives from Caughnawaga.[5]

The group left Montreal on 16 September 1884 and arrived in Egypt on 7 October. The men signed on for a six-month engagement terminating 13 March 1885. Later an appeal was made for volunteers to extend the term of enlistment and eighty-three boatmen and six officers remained for the final push to Khartoum. On 10 February 1885 news reached the relief column that General Gordon had been killed in Khartoum. Sixteen members of the Voyageur Contingent died on the expedition: two fell from a train, six drowned, and eight died of disease. The men received two medals: the Egyptian Medal with either "The Nile" clasp or, if they were at the battle of Kirbekan, a "Kirbekan" clasp. Eventually the men were also entitled to the Khedive's Star. On 24 February, the river column stopped near the village of Abu Hamed and were informed that Khartoum had fallen and General Gordon had been killed. This was as close

The Nile Medal and Khedive Star issued to men who served with the Nile Voyageurs. Private collection.

to Khartoum as the Canadian Voyageur Contingent got before being ordered to return to Egypt and eventually Canada.[6]

THE NORTH-WEST REBELLION, 1885

Although by 1871 the last of the British regiments had departed Canada and left the defence of the country to the new Confederation, our government was loath to accept this responsibility and originally only reluctantly assumed the military role. Only two small batteries of artillery were created to take over the abandoned fortifications at Kingston, Ontario, and Halifax, Nova Scotia.

It also became common practice to only assemble the militia once every two years for a summer camp. The transport corps, medical corps, and any means of feeding men during a campaign were totally ignored.

This was the basic situation when Louis Riel decided to return to Saskatchewan on 5 June 1884. It didn't take long for Riel to submit a list of grievances to the Canadian government on behalf of the Métis and Natives. By 19 March 1885, he had proclaimed a new provisional government at Batoche and declared Gabriel Dumont as his adjutant general. Events quickly unfolded: at Duck Lake, on 26 March, a detachment of Mounted Police were defeated and on 1 April, nine whites and Métis were murdered by Chief Big Bear's Cree Indians at Frog Lake.

The government again found itself seeking a commanding officer who had the experience to lead a force to the Saskatchewan Territory and called upon the volunteer militia to muster for the duration of hostilities. Eventually, Major General Frederick Middleton was appointed commander of the force, and by 22 April almost three thousand volunteers joined the North West Field Force.

Timeline

A detailed description of the engagements fought during the rebellion is readily available in many books and is beyond the scope of this text. However, if you discover ancestors who served during this period, you need to be aware of some specific dates.

25 April — General Middleton clashes at Fish Creek with Métis under the command of Gabriel Dumont.

3 May —At the Battle of Cut Knife Hill, Colorado, Otter is defeated by Indian Chief Poundmaker's warriors.

9–12 May — Middleton's forces reach Batoche and a four-day battle is fought, resulting in a successful assault on the Métis settlement.

15 May — Riel surrenders, followed on May 25 by Chief Poundmaker.

27 May — General Strange fights Big Bear's Native warriors at Frenchman's Butte.

2 July — Chief Big Bear surrenders.

16 November —Louis Riel is hanged for treason.

As important as these events are, you should not ignore some of the harrowing narratives available concerning the journey that the Field Force had to make from eastern Canada to the

Saskatchewan Territories. The Canadian Pacific Railroad was still under construction and large open stretches existed in the line. The men were forced to march through wet, snow-covered forests and bogs, and often travel on open carriages when the railroad was available. The journey was a particular nightmare for the artillery.

The following military units served during the Batoche campaign with General Middleton:

- 10 Royal Grenadiers, Toronto
- Midland Battalion, Belleville, Lindsey, Port Hope, Kingston
- 90 Battalion of Rifles, Winnipeg
- Regiment of Canadian Artillery, Quebec
- Winnipeg Field Battery, Winnipeg
- Assorted local mounted units

The Battleford column with Lieutenant-Colonel Otter:

- Regiment of Canadian Artillery, Kingston
- North-West Mounted Police, Regina
- Queen's Own Rifles, Toronto
- Infantry School Corps, Toronto
- Governor General's Foot Guard, Ottawa
- Battleford Rifles, Battleford

The Alberta Field Force with Colonel Strange:

- Steele's Scouts (including N.W.M.P.), Regina
- 65th Mounted Rifles, Montreal
- Winnipeg Light Infantry, Winnipeg

Other units involved used to garrison specific locations along the route of the march:

- Cavalry School Corps, Quebec
- York and Simcoe Rangers, formerly 12th and 35th Battalions
- 7th Fusiliers, London
- 9th Voltigeurs, Quebec
- Montreal Garrison Artillery, Montreal
- Winnipeg troop of Cavalry/Infantry, Winnipeg
- Rocky Mountain Rangers, Southern Alberta
- Yorkton Militia, Yorkton
- Halifax Provisional Battalion, Halifax[7]

Perhaps James Forbes Foley served in one of the militia units that went west to fight Riel. You can tell by the number of men who served and the events that occurred that this was a major historical occurrence for a young country and resulted in a large amount of research material. You should start by checking the Department of Militia and Defence annual report for the year ending 31 December 1885. There you'll find information related to all aspects of the rebellion: nominal rolls, lists of killed and wounded, pensions applied for/granted, and so on. The Dominion government issued Certificates of Service to all men who served with the North-West Field Force. The certificates are arranged by unit and at present there is no index of names. The certificates indicate the person's name, unit and, in some cases, details about date and place of service. You will have to visit the archives and request, RG 9, II-B-1, vols. 77 to 79 to access these certificates.[8]

I know that James Forbes Foley was born on a farm near Hamilton in 1868 and later moved to Toronto, so there was a good chance that he enlisted in one of the Toronto units and went west in 1885. If he did then he would certainly have been entitled to the North-West Canada Medal and should be mentioned on the medal rolls. There were two clasps awarded for this medal: "Saskatchewan" for the men who served at Fish Creek, Cut Knife Hill, Frenchman's Butte, and Batoche; and a "Batoche" clasp for those men who served under fire at Batoche or on board the steamer *Northcote.* A search of the medal rolls shows a James Foley, corporal, serving with the 10th Royal Grenadiers, wounded at Batoche, 12 May 1885, and entitled to the medal with clasp. The 10th Grenadiers served with Middleton at Batoche and a check of the nominal rolls of the regiment gave me more details about James Foley.[9] That he was wounded means I need to check the records to see if he applied for a pension or a land grant. Interestingly, the picture we had of William Foley, James's father, showed him as an officer in the 10th Grenadiers. Discussions with family members confirmed that they had heard of the family owning land in the Thunder Bay region of Ontario.

THE YUKON FIELD FORCE: 1895–1904

No Foley or any other of my ancestors served with the Yukon Field Force. However, many were assigned the arduous duty of helping the North-West Mounted Police defend the Dawson goldfields against potential lawlessness. What was this small force all about and where can you search for the records of the men and women who served in its ranks?

Learn about the gold rush in the Klondike, starting with the discovery of gold by George Carmack, Skookum Jim, and Tagish Charlie on the Kondike River in 1896. It will also be necessary for you to research the life of men like James M. Walsh, the first Territorial commissioner, and Sergeant Sam Steele of the NWMP.

The national police force we know today has gone through some name changes since its inception in 1874. At first it was called the North-West Mounted Police then the Royal was added and, finally, when they became a national force the name was changed to the Royal Canadian Mounted Police. When you start your research into this historical period don't forget to include some of the poems written by Robert Service. His "Cremation of Sam McGee" and *Songs of a Sourdough* are certainly worth reading.

Following the discovery of gold in the Klondike in 1896 there was a stampede that forced Canada to pass the Yukon Act in 1898, establishing the region as a separate territory with its capital at Dawson City. For Canada this was the easy part! The real problem was the establishment of sovereignty and then law and order. Miners streamed into the area from the American cities of Skagway and Dyea, climbed the Chilkoot or White Horse passes into Canadian territory, or built barges and sailed down Lake Lindeman or Lake Bennett to the Yukon River and on to Dawson. Soon a form of miner's justice developed in the gold fields; decisions were made by a "committee of the whole" without recourse to the laws established by Ottawa. Into this scenario stepped the North-West Mounted Police led by Sam Steele.

The police established control points on the passes, barring entry to anyone without the required supplies and enforcing law and order. This was in contrast to what was happening on the American side at Skagway and Dyea. Read about Soapy Smith to understand the difference between the two regions.

In *Klondike*, Pierre Berton describes the Field Force:

> And in the midst of all this hurly-burly, the most
> outlandish sight of all: two hundred and three
> uniformed soldiers in scarlet jackets and white

helmets marching as best they could in close order, with the help of Hudson's Bay packers and mules, trudging in step through mud holes and over rocks and stumps, performing barrack-square evolutions, spearing fish with their bayonets, and dragging their Maxim guns along with them. This was the Yukon Field Force, made up of officers and men from the Royal Canadian Rifles, the Royal Canadian Dragoons and the Royal Canadian Artillery, and sent north to reinforce the Mounted Police by a government which feared that the influx of foreigners might cause an insurrection that could wrench the North from Canada.[10]

Berton failed to mention that this small detachment was supplemented by five female nurses whose job it was to tend not only to the soldiers but also the inhabitants of Dawson City. In reality, there were probably more police officers serving in the Yukon than regular military personnel.

FENIAN RAID

LAC Records

Nominal lists of those who served during the Fenian Raids and the Red River Rebellion of 1870.

- RG 9, series IIA4, vol.16, those who received a pension for injuries suffered while on active duty.

- RG 9, series IC5, vols. 30–32, those making claims for injuries etc., following the raids. Here I discovered the Teal family.
- RG 9, series IIA4, vols. 39–150, those granted the 1912 bounty for all surviving Fenian veterans.
- RG 9, series IIA5, the medal rolls, where you can request a search for a medal recipient.

Websites

Canadian Military Heritage, *www.rootsweb.ancestry.com*.

Olive Tree Genealogy, *www.olivetreegenealogy.com*, focus on Canadian genealogy/military/Red River for Dr. Shore's excellent resource listing the individuals who served at the Red River.

Rootsweb, *freepages.genealogy.rootsweb.ancestry.com/~crossroads/regiments*, for a list of British Regiments that served in Canada before 1870.

Veterans' Affairs, *www.vac-acc.gc.ca*, where you can view the Book of Remembrance and learn about the Canada General Service Medal.

RED RIVER

LAC

- RG 9, series IIB2 and 4 for a register of service officers — also on reel T6955.
- RG 9, series IIF7, vols. 1–4, the nominal rolls and pay lists for members of the expeditionary force.

- RG 9, series IIB2, vols. 34–35, correspondence related to the organization of the force and some hospital returns.
- RG 9, series IIB2, vol. 33, information about court martials.

British Military Records at LAC

- MG 13, WO 32, Registered Papers, General Series, 1848–1913, subjects include: defence of Canada; raising of Canadian Troops for Imperial Service; military lands; the Red River and Nile Expeditions; designation and accoutrements of Canadian Militia Units; relationship of Canadian Militia Units to the British Army; Royal Military College, reels B-1820, B-2991 and B-3080 to B-3093, finding aid #575, No.MSS0090 and MSS0575-1.
- MG 13, WO 67, Depot Description Books, 1803–92, reels B-3661 to B3663, finding aid #90, "nominal and descriptive rolls of non-commissioned officers and enlisted soldiers in regimental depots." They record physical descriptions, giving age, place of birth, trades, promotions, etc.
- MG 13, WO 73, Monthly Returns, Distribution of the Army, 1861–1906, 24 microfilm reels, available on reels B-1750 to B1770. "Showing the monthly distribution of the British Army by division and station." Finding aid #90, No. MSS0090-1.

Books

Brown, G.A. *Canada General Service Roll, 1866–1870*. [n.p., Canada]: Battleline Books, 1983.

Neale, Graham H. and Irwin, Ross W. *The Medal Roll of the Red River Campaign of 1870 in Canada*. Toronto: Charlton Press, 1982.

NILE EXPEDITION

LAC

- RG 7, Government House records. Here you'll find the original documents related to the Nile Expedition including the nominal roll.
- MG 13-WO 100, Campaign Medals, 1884–89, "names of officers and men entitled to campaign medals and clasps between 1793-1912." Copied extracts of the medical staff, nursing sisters and Canadian Voyageur Contingent who participated in the Egypt and Sudan campaigns of 1884–85, microfilm B-1820, transcripts available on reel C-12585.

Websites

Toronto Star, pagesofthepast.ca, check this pay-per-view site, which may be available free from your local library, for period articles.

University of Calgary Libraries and Cultural Resources Centre, *lcr.ucalgary.ca*, offers scanned books online. Many are scarce and most contain nominal rolls for the regiment. This is a useful site because most of the books also cover the Boer War and First World War, as well as the North-West Rebellions.

University of Manitoba, *umanitoba.ca/libraries/archives*, the university archives holds records about the Nile Voyageurs available online.

Books

Benn, C. *Mohawks on the Nile, Natives Among the Canadian Voyaguers in Egypt, 1884–1885*. Toronto: Dundurn Press, 2009. Lists the Natives who served along with biographical sketches of many of the men.

Blatherwick, Francis, J. *Canadian Orders, Decorations, Medals, 4 ed.* Toronto: Unitrade Press, 1994. For a description of the Egyptian Medal.

MacLaren, Roy. *Canadians on the Nile, 1882–1898: Being the Adventures of the Voyageurs on the Khartoum Relief Expedition and Other Exploits.* Vancouver: University of British Columbia Press, 1987.

Stacey, C.P. *Records of the Nile Voyageurs, 1884–1885: The Canadian Voyageur Contingent in the Gordon Relief Expedition.* Toronto: Champlain Society, 1959. This book also contains the nominal roll for the expedition.

NORTH-WEST REBELLION, 1885

LAC

- RG 9, series IIF7, vols. 4–9 reel C4494, nominal rolls and pay lists for all the units that served.

- RG 9, series IIA4, vol. 17, pension claims by those who were injured while on active duty.
- RG 9, series IIA5, vol.11, reel C1863, medal rolls for all those who served with the government forces. Recorded here are names, unit and marital status.
- RG 15, series DII9, vols. 1629–1644, lists of those who served and were issued land grants in western Canada.

Websites

Cyndi's List, *www.cyndislist.com/milres.htm*, select Military Resources worldwide, then Canada.

Olive Tree Genealogy, *www.olivetreegenealogy.com/mil/can/nw*, for a historical overview, books online, battles, biographies, databases, and regimental histories.

University of Saskatchewan, *library2.usask.ca/northwest/index/subject/150.html*.

Books

Morton, Desmond. *The Last War Drum: The North West Campaign of 1885.* Toronto: Hakkert Press, 1972.

Morton, Desmond. *Telegrams of the North West Campaign 1885.* Toronto: Champlain Society, 1972.

Stonechild, Blair. *Loyal Till Death: Indians and the North West Rebellion.* Calgary: Fifth House, 1997.

Wallace, Jim. *A Trying Time: The North-West Mounted Police in the 1885 Rebellion.* Winnipeg: Bunker to Bunker Books, 1998.

An interesting history, as the men of the NWMP had to petition the government for their medals. It was only issued to the members of the force who could prove they came "under fire."

Wilson, Barbara. *Military General Service Medal, 1793–1814 (Canadian Recipients): Egypt Medal, 1882–1889 (Canadian Recipients), North West Canada, 1885: Index to the Medal Rolls.* London, U.K.: Spink Publishers, 1975.

THE YUKON FIELD FORCE

LAC

Check the nominal rolls for the two permanent militia units that served in the Yukon as well as the Artillery Corps.

- RG 18-A-1, volume 214, subject file R196-26-3-E.
- RG 9-II-A-1, numbered files, R180-41-8-E.
- RG 15-D-V-1, 1896-1901 file, for information about Fort Constantine, Fort Cudahy, land applications, and so on.
- RG 13-A-2, 1896/01, 1896/06.

Websites

Yukon Genealogy, *www.yukongenealogy.com/content/dawson.htm.*

Books

Berton, Pierre. *Klondike: The Last Great Gold Rush, 1896–1899.* Toronto: McClelland & Stewart Ltd., 1972.

Greenhouse, Brereton. *The Story of the Yukon Field Force.* Toronto: Dundurn Press, 1987.

CHAPTER FOUR

The Boer War: I Think My Ancestors Served in South Africa

The Boer War (1899–1902), also known as the Anglo-Boer War or the South African War, marked the first time Canada become involved in a foreign war as an independent nation. In many ways this war established a unique Canadian identity in terms of the military discipline, strategy, and individualism that would manifest itself in future conflicts. My interest in this period started with a flag and a photo.

In an antique store I discovered a small Red Ensign flag printed with the word Paardeburg and ten names that looked like they had been added in pen and ink. The flag had been printed on cotton, was about the size of a sheet of paper, and listed ten names with a statement to the effect that the individuals had died during the South African War. Fakes and forgeries of militaria abound. I felt this flag was no exception and, besides, the price was prohibitive. What intrigued me though were the names on the flag and the possibility that they just might have served in the Boer War. I copied some of the names and decided to do some research.

The second incentive was a picture of William Martin, my wife's great-grandfather on her grandmother's side of the family.

Family photograph of William Martin, shown wearing his Distinguished Conduct and Long Service and Good Conduct Medals.

The picture was engraved with the name of a photographer's studio in Vancouver, British Columbia. The image showed William Martin wearing three medals that appeared to be a coronation medal and two others that were not common campaign issue. My search for the Martin family resulted in a review of the causes, campaigns, equipment, and medals issued for service in this war.

Where to Start?

The South African war, also referred to as the Anglo-Boer War or Boer War, was the first time that Canadians fought overseas in their own units. This involvement resulted in the creation of forms and files for over seven thousand individuals and, ultimately, disability requests and land grant applications. The records are quite extensive. The war was fought between Britain and the Boer farmers in South Africa and was really imperialistic in nature. The Boers, Dutch farmers living in the Orange Free State and Transvaal regions of South Africa, referred to themselves as Afrikaners. They controlled territory that Britain was interested in annexing to their own South African colony.

Gold and diamonds had been discovered in Boer territory, resulting in a large influx of miners, most of them English-speaking. The Boers were worried that these *Uitlanders* (strangers) would eventually control the territories and had refused them the right to vote. Under the pretext of protecting the rights of British subjects living in the Boer republics, and still smarting from an earlier defeat in 1881 at the hands of the same Boers, England declared war on 11 October 1899.

This was a time in our history when any schoolchild could point to a map of the world and claim that the "sun never set on the British Empire." British subjects around the world were proud of this fact and saw nothing wrong in this type of expansionism. This was the first major conflict Britain was involved in since the Crimean War of 1854 and it was unprepared for the type of campaign the Boers were able to conduct.

Typical Boer War Commandos armed with German-made Mauser Rifles. They knew the territory well and were accurate shots and excellent horsemen. The Boers were more than a match for the early British troops. LAC R9271-5-2-E, #128778.

Supplied with bolt-action Mauser rifles from Germany, mounted on tough ponies and organized into commandoes, the Boers staged a hit-and-run campaign that soon resulted in major British defeats and ultimately the sieges of the British garrisons at Mafeking, Kimberley, and Ladysmith. Further major British defeats at Stormberg, Magersfontein, and Colenso, from 10 to 15 December 1899, became known as the "black" week for Britain's army.

The British were finally able to defeat the Boers with help from their colonies, the introduction of systematic control points throughout the country, and the establishment of concentration camps. By limiting the movement of the Boer Army, burning their farms, and concentrating their women and children in camps, the British forced the Boers to surrender. The whole issue of concentration camps and the subsequent death of thousands of women and children from disease and malnutrition is certainly a stain on the history of England. When the war finally ended in 1902, the cost to England was over £200 million. It cost the lives of over 21,000 British soldiers: 8,000 died in action and 14,000 of disease. An estimate of Boer losses is 6,000 killed in action with more than 26,000 women and children dying in concentration camps.[1]

Non-commissioned officers of the 3rd Regiment Canadian Mounted Rifles, Halifax. The men are wearing typical Canadian uniforms. Notman Photographic collection, NSARM, 1983-310, #9771.

Canada's role in all this started with a request from England, in October 1899, for a contingent of troops. Mr. Chamberlain, British colonial secretary, had received an offer of support from Canada's Major-General Hutton, the officer commanding the militia, to provide troops if necessary. A reply sent by Mr. Chamberlain on 3 October 1899 stated the conditions of service:

> Firstly, units should consist of about 125 men; secondly, may be infantry, mounted infantry, or cavalry; in view of numbers already available, infantry most, cavalry least, serviceable; thirdly, all should be armed with .303 rifles or carbines, which can be supplied by Imperial Government if necessary; fourthly, all must provide own equipment, and mounted troops own horses; fifthly, not more than one captain and three subalterns each unit. Whole force may be commanded by officer not higher than major … Troops to be disembarked at port of landing South Africa fully equipped at cost of Colonial Government or volunteers. From date of disembarkation Imperial Government will provide pay at Imperial rates, supplies and ammunition, and will defray expenses of transport back to Canada, and pay wound pensions and compassionate allowances at Imperial rates. Troops to embark not later than 31st October, proceeding to Cape Town for orders.[2]

The original offer had been made without the consent of Parliament and this created a small problem for Prime Minister Wilfred Laurier (1896–1911). There was no interest in Quebec for any involvement in an imperial war that many in that province felt was unjust. The reaction in English-speaking Canada was completely opposite.

Eventually Ottawa agreed to send four units of 250 men each to South Africa by 30 October. The Canadian government would organize, equip, and transport the volunteers but once in South Africa they would be totally financed by Britain. Lieutenant-Colonel William Otter was given command and on the promised date 1,061 volunteers boarded the steamer S.S. *Sardinian* and sailed to war. This first contingent was mustered from the twelve existing Canadian military districts, with the force divided into eight companies — A to H. If your ancestor was part of this group, you can find pictures of the *Sardinian* online.

- A Company was raised at Victoria and Vancouver, British Columbia, and Winnipeg, Manitoba.
- B Company in London, Ontario.
- C Company at Toronto, Ontario.
- D Company at Ottawa and Kingston, Ontario.
- E Company at Montreal, Quebec.
- F Company in Quebec City, Quebec.
- G Company at St. John, New Brunswick, and Charlottetown, Prince Edward Island.
- H Company at Halifax, Nova Scotia.

The men who joined signed Attestation Papers and swore an oath designed for the occasion:

> I swear that I will well and truly serve our Sovereign Lady the Queen in the Canadian Volunteers for active service, until lawfully discharged and that I will resist Her Majesty's enemies, and cause Her

Majesty's peace to be kept on land and at sea, and
that I will in all matters appertaining to my service faithfully discharge my duty, according to law,
So help me God.

I hearby declare that I am willing to serve
wherever Her Majesty the Queen may direct in
the Canadian Volunteers for active service under
the provisions of the Militia Act of Canada, so
far at it applies, under the Queen's regulations
and orders for the army and the Army Act for a
term of six months, or one year if required, or
until sooner lawfully discharged or dismissed, at
the rate of pay fixed for the Permanent Corps
of Canada, until landed in South Africa, and
after disembarkation to serve in Her Majesty's
regular forces, at the rates of pay fixed by the
Royal Warrant for the pay of the British Army,
and I have accordingly taken the above Oath of
Allegiance.[3]

Later, the government agreed to send two more battalions
of mounted rifles and three field artillery batteries, totalling
1,320 men. A 3rd battalion of the Royal Canadian Regiment
replaced the British troops at Halifax and Esquimalt. At his own
expense, Lord Strathcona, Donald Smith, raised a mounted unit
from cowboys and the North-West Mounted Police officers,
placed it under the command of Sam Steele, and sent it to South
Africa. Ultimately, twelve squadrons of South African Police, four
regiments of mounted rifles, and a field hospital were all sent
at Britain's expense. Of the 8,300 Canadians who enlisted only
3,499 served at Canada's expense. Two hundred-and-forty-two
Canadians died in the war.

The war also produced a number of Canadian Victoria Cross recipients. Sergeant Arthur Herbert Richardson of Lord Strathcona's Horse won the medal for action at Wolver Spruit on 15 July1900, when he gallantly saved the life of Corporal McArthur whose horse had been shot by Boer marksmen.

Besides the many books published at the time, there are also a substantial number of newer military history texts related to the politics of the Boer War. Consult the catalogue at your local library.

Canadians fought in most of the major engagements of the war but were specifically present in the following battles. If you discover an ancestor had served during this period and was entitled to a Queen or King's South African Medal, you would definitely want to add some information about the following battles to your family history. The Canadian War Museum webpage can also provide more specific details about each of these battles *www.warmuseum.ca/cwm/exhibitions/boer/boerwarbattles_e.shtml.*

- Paardeburg, 18–27 February 1900
- Israel's Poort, 25 April 1900
- Zand River, 10 May 1900
- Relief of Mafeking, 17 May 1900
- Doornkop, 28–29 May 1900
- Taber's Put, 30 May 1900
- Honing Spruit, 22 June 1900
- Lelienfontein, 7 November 1900
- Hart's River (Boschbult), 31 March 1900

For Britain this war was unique. The Boer's basic fighting unit was the commando. Every Boer between the ages of sixteen and sixty was expected to belong to a "commandoe" based on the area in which they lived. A commando could be anywhere from 300 to

1,000 men depending on the turnout to the call to assemble. The men were expected to muster with a horse, ammunition, weapon, and suitable clothing. The units were highly manoeuvrable and mobile, and also very successful against British infantry. Much of the fighting took place on land that was relatively treeless with rolling hills and open plains (veldt). The area was also interspersed with rocky outcrops called *kopje* that were excellent for taking cover. The Boers had also been trained in the use of artillery and the Mauser rifle during the decades before the First World War, when Britain and Germany were competing for new colonies and challenging each other in an arms race.

Early in the war, British tactics were still based upon the use of infantry. However, when you pit slow-moving infantry against mobile cavalry, and fight over ground that is relatively open, the results are predictable. Because of their knowledge of the territory, the Boers inflicted significant defeats upon the British Army. Readers will remember that Britain's first request for colonial troops specifically requested infantry over cavalry units. Realizing their mistakes, the British commanders requested more mounted units equipped with rifles and, when necessary, troops able to live off the land. They expected these units to ride into battle, dismount, and take cover. The British wanted the Canadian mounted units to be prepared to fight in the Boer style. Thus, Canada's second contingent was organized around the following qualifications,

> The mounted men must ride well and shoot well, must be thoroughly self-reliant, know how to take cover, follow a trail, find their way without a map, must have the wariness and persistence of old hunters, and be clear grit to the backbone. In a word, they must have, in a high degree, the

typical qualities of pioneers in a new country. A
few hundreds of such men could scout for any
army corps and give the Boers lessons in their
own style of fighting.[4]

These men were to be referred to as Mounted Rifles but
later the name was changed to the 1st and 2nd Battalions, Royal
Canadian Dragoons. Three batteries of artillery were also sent
and designated as C, D, and E. Family historians who wish to
narrow their search should note that the government decided
to assign specific areas for recruitment of each battalion. If you
know where your ancestor lived during this period of history and
suspect they served during the Boer War, then this information
could help narrow your search.

1st Battalion A Squadron: Toronto, St. Catharines,
Peterborough, Ottawa, London, and Kingston, Ontario;
and Montreal, Quebec.

1st Battalion B Squadron: Winnipeg, Portage la Prairie,
Virden, Brandon, Yorkton, Manitoba, and the North-
West. Montreal, Quebec, and Cookshire, Quebec; and
Sussex and Saint John, New Brunswick, were included,
as was Canning, Nova Scotia.

2nd Battalion: was to be drawn from the ranks of the
North-West Mounted Police.

The same applied for the artillery.

C Battery: Kingston, Gananoque, Hamilton, St.
Catharines, Toronto, Ontario; and Winnipeg, Manitoba.

D Battery: Guelph, Ottawa, London, and Port Hope, Ontario.

E Battery: Quebec, Montreal, and Granby, Quebec; Woodstock and Newcastle, New Brunswick; and Sydney, Nova Scotia.[5]

On 11 January 1900, Lord Strathcona offered to raise, equip, and pay at his own expense 500 "rough riders" until they arrived at Cape Town, after which the British government would assume responsibility for the unit. Lord Strathcona's Horse became a Special Service Corps of Mounted Rifles and was enrolled between Winnipeg, Manitoba, and Victoria, British Columbia. The S.S. *Monterey* was chartered to carry the unit and they sailed on 16 March 1900.

The Canadian units adapted quickly to fighting in South Africa and soon had a reputation for hard riding, bravery, using the land to advantage, unconformity when it came to military dress, foraging (military term for looting), and dependability. There are some interesting accounts of Canadians written by observers from other countries commenting on their "resourcefulness" and preference for "profane" language. E.W.B. Morrison describes the "Canadian" method of fighting the Boers:

> "Making good" a kopje is done in this way: One horseman, called a pointer, advances straight toward the rocky crest of a kopje; a quarter of a mile behind him two more advance, and about the same distance in rear the rest of the troop in line, with wide intervals. When the pointer gets within a couple of hundred yards from the kopje if they shoot him you know the Boers are there.

Of course, they don't always hit him; but the chances are that way. It requires a lot of nerve and courage on the part of the pointer, but it is a great improvement on the late lamented British method of advancing infantry brigades in quarter column or artillery brigade divisions in line — and discovering the Boers were there. Or even the British mounted infantry method — all bunched up. It takes a high order of courage in the individual men of the force to do it properly; but the relatively small proportion of Canadian troops in this army of a quarter of a million men did not win their reputation as fighters for nothing.[6]

WHERE CAN I FIND MY ANCESTOR'S RECORDS?

According to LAC, 7,368 men and twelve nursing sisters served in this conflict and so there is a substantial amount of material available. The basic RGs you will search are:

RG 9 – Militia and Defence

RG 24 – National Defence

RG 38 – Veterans' affairs. Veterans' Affairs includes the South African War service files and any land grant applications.

You'll discover that almost 75 percent of South African service records have survived and often contain a soldier's attestation papers, service card, medical report, service in South Africa and military medal record. If you check RG 38, volumes 1–116 and 412–418, you'll note that these records have been microfilmed and are available on interlibrary loan. In RG 9 you will also have access to nominal rolls for all units, pay lists, and hospital lists. Don't forget to include in your research the Book of Remembrance for the South African War found at *www.vac-acc.gc.ca*.

WHAT MEDALS WOULD MY ANCESTOR HAVE EARNED?

If you discover a medal that you think was issued to a Canadian and you were wondering if the bars/clasps were correct, you can again check the medal registers in RG 9 IIA5. In general, the Queen's South African medal was issued to those who served from 11 October 1901 to 31 May 1902. There were over eighty engagements fought during this war but the British government decided to award only twenty-six bars. Canadians were most likely to be granted one of the following: Transvaal, Natal, Cape Colony, Orange Free State, Dreifontein, Johannesburg, or Belfast.

Queen Victoria died in 1901 and her son Edward assumed the throne as Edward VII. Another medal, referred to as the King's South African Medal, was issued to those who served from January to June 1902 during his reign. The King's Medal had two bars: South Africa 1901, and South Africa 1902, and was always issued with the Queen's medal. In most photographs of Boer War veterans you will see them wearing the two medals.

Always check the rim of the medals; they are inscribed with the name of the recipient, regimental number, rank, and unit. These inscriptions are an excellent means of tracing the veteran and also proving that the bars/clasps are legitimate. You should also become familiar with the colour pattern of the ribbons. No two British campaign or bravery/service medals have the same ribbon colour or pattern. When searching for personnel files or medal registers keep in mind that the following units served during the war:

- 2nd Battalion, Royal Canadian Regiment (RCR) — they were the first unit sent.
- The Royal Canadian Dragoons (RCD) — second detachment raised.
- 1st Battalion, Canadian Mounted Rifles (CMR) — men of the NWMP and cowboys.
- Brigade, Royal Canadian Field Artillery (RCA) — a brigade had three batteries. Each battery had three sections. Each section had two 12-pounder breech-loading guns.
- Lord Strathcona's Horse (LSH) — unit privately raised by Lord Strathcona (Donald Smith) and led by Superintendent Sam Steele, three squadrons of 162 men from Manitoba, North-West Territories, and British Columbia with fifty-three officers.
- 2nd Regiment, Canadian Mounted Rifles.
- 10 Canadian Field Hospital — personnel include nursing sisters.
- The Canadian Scouts
- South African Constabulary (SAC) — fifty-seven Canadians died in action while serving with this unit.
- 3rd, 4th, 5th, and 6th Regiments, Canadian Mounted Rifles — arrived in South Africa after the war had ended.

- 3rd. (Special Services) Battalion (Royal Regiment of Infantry) — relieved British troops at Halifax and Esquimalt.

A group of Canadian enlisted men and an officer somewhere in South Africa — a good example of their uniforms. With permission of the Canadian Military Institute, Toronto.

I HAVE AN OLD PHOTOGRAPH.
IS IT FROM THIS PERIOD?

This war also produced interesting changes in basic infantry uniforms, equipment, and weapons. Gone were the red woollen battledress jackets of earlier wars, replaced with khaki-coloured cotton uniforms more suitable for camouflage and the climate. Pith helmets, Stetsons, and a wedge-shaped field-service cap became the common headgear and Canadian units wore their own unique cap badge: a large maple leaf with the word Canada scrolled across the bottom. White Slade-Wallace harness had been replaced by Oliver gear: a combination of leather and woven web material. Officers wore leather Sam Browne belts from which their pistol, ammunition pouch, and sword were suspended.

If you discover what you assume to be equipment from this war it is likely to be a cap badge, leather belt with a "snake" clasp, or a leather ammunition bandolier. The pith helmets issued have mostly disappeared into military collections or museums, or not withstood the ravages of time. The Stetsons most Canadians wore, which look like the Scout hats worn by previous generations of boys, often did not survive either.

As an interesting aside the scouting movement originated with this war. Lord Baden-Powell, who fought in the war, was responsible for creating the boy scouts. He applied the tracking, camping, and basic field strategies he learned to his scouting philosophy.

The average Canadian soldier who served in South Africa received either the 40 cents per diem paid to privates in the permanent force or the 50 cents per diem paid to the active militia while in camp. However, once the troops were in South Africa, Britain assumed responsibility for paying them and the amount was almost one-half the Canadian level of pay. The Canadian government decided to make up the pay for the term of a volunteer's enlistment, guaranteeing the difference in pay and offering it to the dependents of a soldier or handing it to the volunteer upon his or her return to Canada. Interestingly, this allocation to dependents amounted to 50 cents for a wife and 5 cents for children of a sergeant per diem, and 35 cents and 25 cents for corporals and privates. In one account, a member of Lord Strathcona's Horse stated that he was receiving 25 cents per day but had the amount doubled by Lord Strathcona to 50 cents. It certainly doesn't seem like a significant amount of money to earn for suffering through the hardships of campaigning and the very realistic possibility of being shot at by some Boer marksman.[7]

What did I discover about the flag and the picture that had triggered my interest in this period of our military history? The flag may very well have been a fake. I could find no names on the list of Canadian causalities at Paardeburg that matched the names on the flag. Of course, this doesn't mean that these men didn't serve and pay the ultimate sacrifice. They could have very well been British soldiers whose relatives had moved to Canada and who, in remembrance, had written the names on a Canadian flag. I will have to check the British records at *www.nationalarchives.gov. uk* or to see if their Anglo-Boer War records were available online, or even pay a researcher in England to check the records.

The picture proved a little more interesting. Members of the Martin family still live in British Columbia, which explains the Vancouver address on the picture. The medals William Martin was wearing are the Coronation Medal (right breast) either for Edward VII or George V and the Distinguished Conduct Medal and Long Service, Good Conduct Medal. The Distinguished Conduct Medal is issued for bravery in the field and is a gallantry award while the Long Service, Good Conduct Medal is granted for twenty-five years service in the military without major infraction. Or, as old soldiers will tell you, without being caught for anything! Just looking at the picture told me this much about William Martin.

After I searched the 1901 Scottish census records I was able to add a little detail to the family history. I discovered the Martin family living in Ayrshire, Scotland; William's occupation was listed as soldier. In 1915, his daughter Ruby Martin married William Thomson Murchie, 2nd Lieutenant in the Royal Scots Fusiliers. On their marriage registration, William Murchie's occupation is listed as photographer. This could explain the connection with a photographic studio in Vancouver. Perhaps William moved his family to Canada and continued in this profession. When I continued my research into the Martin family, I discovered that William Martin had married in Ireland and been born in Balteagh, Armagh, Northern Ireland.

Checking the British military records, I discovered that the 1st Royal Inniskilling Fusiliers recruited in Armagh. An online search generated the website for the present-day regiment and an email request resulted in a reply that a William Martin had been a sergeant-major with the Fusiliers and had been awarded a Distinguished Conduct Medal, April 1901, for service in South Africa, a Long Service and Good Conduct Medal for his service from 1894 to 1902, and was entitled to both the Queen's and King's South African Medals with bars. The Queen's South African Medal included clasps for Belfast, Cape Colony, Tugela Heights, Relief of Ladysmith, and Orange Free State.

The non-commissioned rank of sergeant-major is quite significant and certainly of some prestige. A person who holds this position commands respect from not only the men of the regiment but also the officers and would certainly be someone who had served for a long time. Because William was not a Canadian citizen when he served, my military research ended with the information I had discovered. Any family member wanting to access his military records would probably have to hire a researcher in England.

It is interesting that he was not wearing his South African medals in the photograph. Perhaps he was prouder of the two medals he is displaying or maybe he had misplaced his Queen's and King's medals. We'll never really know. However, a subsequent contact with a family member did produce a family photograph of William Martin wearing his Mess Dress (formal attire) with the rank badges of a sergeant-major.

WHEN I FIND MY ANCESTOR'S RECORDS, WHAT CAN I EXPECT TO DISCOVER?

If you do discover an ancestor who served with the Canadian forces you can expect to find four basic records in the file. The first would be his attestation paper, which will give you a basic description of the height, weight, and age of your ancestor. It will also provide you with place of birth, which can be useful when searching census records. The attestation papers are accompanied by a recruit declaration giving a medical description of the volunteer as well as location of recruitment. The third would be the roll of individuals entitled to a South African Medal while a fourth would be a land grant application if your ancestor made application for the gratuity.

If your ancestor served in the British forces perhaps before arriving in Canada, there are a few resources you will want to consult. As expected, start your search at the National Archives in England. Use their online subject guide at *www.nationalarchives.gov.uk/records/looking-for-subject/boerwar.htm* to discover what Anglo-Boer War service records are available. British Army records before 1913 will provide you with the age, place of birth, age upon enlistment, length and location of service, character report, details of appearance, trade or occupation, and reason for discharge. The pay-for-view site, *www.findmypast.co.uk* has recently digitized these records. If your British ancestor wasn't in a regular British regiment and served as a volunteer in the Imperial Yeomanry, you can discover an account of this unit with details of the men who served at *www.britishmedals.us/kevin/iyhistory.html*. If you just want to discover what British units served in South Africa then visit *www.angloboerwar.com/imperial-units*.

Should your ancestor have served with a Canadian unit, you might want to consult the regimental museum as well as any regimental histories. Once you know where the regiment served and what clasps your ancestor was entitled to, it becomes a matter of historical research to surround his name with the appropriate details of service. Remember to do an online search of your ancestor's name. You may be surprised to discover someone else researching the same individual or even some related historical material.

You may also find in your Boer War ancestors file a "special services forces" form that will also provide you with place of birth, father's name, and confirmation of clasps awarded for service in South Africa. If your ancestor was wounded during his service expect to find a medical report. It will provide you with the nature of the wound, the battle in which the wound was received, and the date of return to Canada.

The end of the Boer War saw some changes occur to the basic structure of the Canadian Military. In 1904 a new Militia Act was legislated by the Canadian Parliament. From then on the commanding general of militia had to be a Canadian officer. A Militia Council was established and new powers and responsibilities were given to the minister of militia and defence. The council was to be composed of the minister as chair, the deputy minister, the chief of general staff, the adjutant general and quartermaster general, with the director of artillery and judge advocate general as associate members. Later other branches of the service were added to the council. The Act also provided for the establishment of the Army Service Corps, Corps of Engineers, Ordnance Corps, Corps of Guides, Corps of Signals, Army Medical Corps, Pay Corps, and Chaplain Service. Administrative staff was also employed to help prepare the country for a more permanent military force. One of the initiatives undertaken by the Militia Council was the outfitting of the Canadian military by Canadian contractors. Eventually, this led to some unwise choices in the quality of Canadian web gear and the insistence that the Canadian soldiers be issued with the Ross rifle during the First World War.[8]

BOER WAR RESOURCES

LAC

- RG 9 IIA3, vol. 28-30, nominal rolls of units.
- RG 9 IIA3, vol. 32-34, reports and diaries.
- RG 9 IIA5, vol. 13-15, reel C-1863, Register of Canadian Recipients of the Queen's South African Medal.
- RG 9 IIB1, vol. 220, AG Docket #93706, South Africa, Return of Troops.
- RG 9 IIB1, vol. 222, AG Docket #94930, South African Constabulary.
- RG 9 IIB1, vol. 234, AG Docket 1277/01, Casualty lists (fatalities), arranged by unit. Includes SAC and CDN Scouts, Memorial Cape Town Cathedral.
- RG 9 IIB1, vol. 263, AG Docket 1840/02, war diary 10, Canadian Field Hospital.
- RG 9 IIB1, vol. 235, AG Docket 1379/01, list of Canadian Scouts returning to Canada.
- RG 9 IIB1, vol. 252, AG Docket 5574/01, names of those who remained after contingents returned. Includes reason for remaining.
- RG 9 IIF7, vol.10-11, nominal rolls and pay lists, South African Contingents, 1899–1902.

- RG 24, vol. 6562, nominal rolls, Department of National Defence fonds.
- RG 24, acc. 584, vol. 408, file 63-1-33, number of officers, non-commissioned officers and men who served in the South African War.
- RG 24, vol. 6309, file HQ-63-16-4, nursing sisters in Boer War, 1909.
- RG 24, vol. 369, file HQ54-2-7, list of engagements in South African War of 1899–1902 for which clasps were awarded, 1910.
- RG 38, A1a, vols. 1-116, reel T-2060 to T-2090, personnel service files, 1899–1902, includes applications for land grants by veterans.
- RG 38, IB, vols. 117-136, land grants, South African War, applications by individual veterans under the Volunteer Bounty Act.
- RG 38 A2a, vols. 412-418, personnel files, 1899–1902, files relating to veterans of the South African War.

Websites

Anglo-Boer War website, *www.angloboerwar.com*.

Australian site, *www.au.af.mil/au/aul/bibs/boer/boerwr.htm*, offers an excellent list of websites and resources related to the Anglo-Boer war.

Canadian Military Heritage Project, *www.rootsweb.ancestry. com/~canmil*.

Canadian War Museum, *www.warmuseum.ca/cwm/exhibitions/boer/ boerwarbattles_e.shtml*, for a list of units, battles, personalities, awards, uniforms, equipment, weapons, maps, etc.

Cyndi's List, *www.cyndislist.com*, click on Military, Canada.

Errol Luys' website, *www.erroluys.com/BoerWarChildsStory.htm*, has an account of a concentration camp inmate.

Genealogy World, *www.genealogyworld.net/boer/tracing.html*, for British Boer War ancestors.

Olive Tree Genealogy, *www.olivetreegenealogy.com/mil*, for information related to the war.

Soldiers of the South African War, 1899–1902, *www.collectionscanada. gc.ca/databases/south-african-war/index-e.html*.

The National Archives, U.K., *www.nationalarchives.gov.uk/ documentsonline*, is always adding new material that can be digitally transferred for a small fee.

The *Toronto Star* newspaper site, *www.pagesofthepast.com*, for articles related to the war. Other newspapers may also have been digitized and can be searched online.

The war museum of the Boer Republic in S.A. has some interesting photos, *www.anglo-boer.co.za*.

Veterans' Affairs, *www.vac-acc.gc.ca*, for the Book of Remembrance

Books

Many of the books in this list contain nominal rolls, details of events, and often information about causalities.

Department of Militia and Defence. *The 2nd Regiment Canadian Mounted Rifles and 10 Field Hospital in South Africa*. Ottawa: King's Printers, 1902.

Hart-McHaig, W. *From Quebec to Pretoria, with the Royal Canadian Regiment*. Toronto: William Briggs Pub., 1902; provides a list of casualties at Paardeberg, 18 February 1900, and a list of non-commissioned officers and men who died of disease.

Marquis, T.G. *Canada's Sons on Kopje and Veldt.* Toronto: Canada's Son's Publishing Co., 1902; provides a list of officers and men plus a roll of honour of the 1st and 2nd contingent, the Royal Canadian Artillery and Strathcona's Horse. You can find this book online at the University of Calgary.

McCormick, A.S. *The Royal Canadians in South Africa.* Akron, OH: n.p., 1960.

Millish, Ann E. *Our Boys Under Fire: or New Brunswick and Prince Edward Island Volunteers in South Africa.* Fredericton, NB: Examiner Office, 1900.

Morrison E.W.B. *With the Guns, D. Battery, Royal Canadian Artillery.* Winnipeg: Hignell Printing Limited, 1901 (available in reprint from Eugene G. Ursual, Ottawa, ON).

Morton, Desmond. *Canada at Paardeberg.* Ottawa: Balmuir Books, 1986.

Penlington, Norman. *Ontario's Contribution to the South African War.* Toronto: Ontario Historical Society, vol. 42, 1950.

Roncetti, Gary. *The Canadians: Those Who Served in South Africa, 1899–1902.* Toronto: E. Denby & Assoc., 1979; names, units, campaigns and casualties of the Canadian Contingent as well as the nominal rolls of the Canadians who served in the South African Constabulary.

Ursual, E. *Canadians in Khaki: South Africa, 1899–1900, Official Correspondence, Nominal Roll, Casualties, etc.* Winnipeg: Hignell Printing Co., 1994.

CHAPTER FIVE

The Great War:
I Believe My Ancestors Fought with the CEF

If we look closely enough reminders of the First World War surround us everywhere in this country. It is there in the names of
some schools, it is remembered when we pass monuments to the
dead, it is on plaques in public buildings, and it is present every
year on November 11th when we attend memorial services or
stop for a moment's silence. It is there when we pass a legion
hall in some small town and see a trench mortar or machine gun
cemented to a base and pointing off into the distance.

For me, it was obvious every day during the years I worked in
a school that had two brass plaques mounted just inside the front
door, dedicated to two young men who had died in the First
World War. The plaques had previously been in an old school
building that, I guessed, the two men had attended before the war.
When that building was replaced in the early 1960s workmen
had relocated the plaques and there they remained, unnoticed. I
believe both young men had belonged to the Canadian Machine
Gun Corps.

Almost 620,000 Canadian men and women out of a population of only eight million served. It is estimated that of this eight
million, 1.5 million were eligible for military service: quite an

accomplishment. Few people in our country know that 66,655 Canadians were killed and 172,950 were wounded. Fewer still know that 19,666 of our soldiers have no known grave.[1] Their names are commemorated on the National War Memorial in Ottawa, on the Commonwealth Memorial at the Menin Gate in Ypres, Belgium, and on the Vimy Ridge Memorial in France. As a matter of fact, the "Last Post" is still sounded every night at the Menin Gate in honour of those whose names are engraved on that memorial.

My great-uncle, Rupert Hinds, my neighbour's great-uncle, William Stanley, and my wife's grandfather, George Turcott, were among the Canadians who served and returned alive. These men and the nation in which they lived mobilized in September 1914, and eventually faced the horrors of trench warfare along a front that stretched for 966 kilometres through Belgium and France to the border of Switzerland. There are many accounts of the horror of trench warfare but a good description is provided by historian Desmond Morton:

> Between the lines lay "no man's land" pock-
> marked by shell holes, strewn with barbed wire,
> abandoned equipment, and fragments of human-
> ity. Snipers watched for the unwary. Machine-
> guns swept the landscape with random bullets.
> Heavy artillery, in growing numbers, searched out
> opposing guns or casually blasted trenches and
> dug-outs. Soldiers lived like moles, underground
> and in darkness. At night, they set out on weary,
> dangerous patrols or struggled to repair trenches
> and barbed wire. Working parties plodded up and
> down communication trenches, dragging food,
> water and ammunition to the front. An hour
> before dawn and dusk, every man stood guard,

for those were the likely times for an enemy attack. In daylight, a few men might sleep.[2]

Rupert Hinds, shown wearing the later pattern Canadian uniform, and the Canadian Machinegun Corps cap badge and collar dogs. Rupert's Casualty Form/Active Service Form shows that he arrived in France with the 74th Battalion and was later transferred to the 54th Battalion. Family photo.

This war was precipitated by the assassination of Archduke Franz Ferdinand of Austria-Hungary and the subsequent alignment of Germany, Austria-Hungary, and Turkey against England, Russia, France, and Italy. War was declared in August 1914 and it was automatically assumed that England's former colonies, then called Dominions, and all members of the British Commonwealth would automatically join Britain in that war.

The war has been documented in well over a thousand books. The causes, the battles, and the generals have been analyzed in depth. Veterans have written accounts of their experiences in the trenches and historians have debated the nature of the war ad nauseam. You can visit any local library to acquire background knowledge to help you understand the culture of war in that era.

WHERE DO I BEGIN MY SEARCH?

My own research started with my great-uncle Rupert Hinds. I remember visiting his family as a very young child and seeing Uncle Rup relaxing on his bed with his artificial leg standing beside the nightstand. This fascinated my brother and me and we couldn't help asking him how he had lost his real leg. His reply was to point to a military medal he had framed on the wall and tell us that he got "that" for his leg during the war. When pressed further, his answer was, "I did something stupid. An officer was trapped on the barbed wire and I went out to save him. He made it back to the trench just before me and as I was sliding over the edge an artillery shell took off my leg." For this act of bravery Rupert Hinds was awarded a Distinguished Conduct Medal.

Recently my neighbour showed me a picture of his great-uncle Billy. William Stanley was the name of the officer in the picture. He was a lieutenant and had won the Military Cross during the war. Included with the picture was a letter written by William.

The Distinguished Conduct Medal issued to men for outstanding bravery in the field. An officer had to witness the act of bravery and submit a request for the medal on behalf of the soldier. Rupert Hinds won the award for bravery at Bourlon Woods during the last days of the war. Private collection.

Wednesday, Sept. 12th France

Hello Bert.

Just a line to let you know that I came through the last two battles o.k. and at present am feeling fine and dandy.

It has been raining for the last four days and the trenches we are in are awfully muddy. We are in a dug-out but it has about a foot of water in it now and we had to build ourselves a place in the trench.

I am bombing officer and works officer for our Battalion and like the job very much. We have a headquarters mess consisting of the Col., the 2nd in command, adjutant, battalion officers and the specialist officers and of course get the best of everything. We have four cases of scotch whisky coming in tonight so expect to get wet inside as well as out.

I am the next officer in our Battalion to go on leave and my first stop is London. If I can get passed there, I may go on to Ireland but at present London looks awfully good to me.

I just finished censoring some letters and one lad said to his girl the only excitement we were having just now is wondering where the ground sheet is going to leak next as that is all the men have for cover from the rain. One lad spoke of our trip down south after a hard tour in the line in front of Opis. We had to march all night for six nights marching as high as 30 miles in one night from 9 p.m. to 9 a.m. and he remarked that he saw an article in the papers saying how romantic it was on these night marches. He says he would have used a different adjective if he had written it.

There is not much use of me telling you about the war that is the two big shows we have been in as the papers no doubt are full of news but after this last one they can call the war off any time and they will not make me mad.

The show down south was a surprise to the Huns and after we got through their trench system we had it fairly easy and captured all kinds of stuff including canteens with barrels of beer and wines etc.

My job for this show was liaison officer between the four Battalions in our Brigade and the four on the left and had Rumney with me and had to keep sending messages to different Colonels how the battle was going on their left or right as the case was.

This show up here in front of Arras was not a surprise to the Huns and they were just waiting for us and to give the devil their due they put up a damn good fight. They had all kinds of artillery and machineguns. I thought for awhile that they were throwing guns and all at us. We lost 17 officers but considered ourselves lucky as the 75th Battalion on our right lost 25. Even our Brigadier General was wounded. Arnold Nealon was with the 75 Bn. but was gassed in the show down south; I used to see a lot of him. He certainly thought a lot of you. He is a captain and is well liked by all the officers of their Battalion.

The Hun flying machines did great work in this last show. They would come down within 100 feet of us and fire at us with machine guns and drop bombs on us. I saw lots of planes on both sides fall from thousands of feet up. One

Lieutenant William Stanley with his "batman," Rumney, somewhere in France. Batmen helped officers with various duties. Rumney is mentioned in Lieutenant Stanley's letter. Family collection.

plane came down in flames right beside us. The two aviators fell out when the plane was about a thousand feet from the ground and you could see their bodies twirling in the air on the way down.

It looked like we would not be able to get through the famous Hindenburg line but the men certainly fought hard and that night when we dug in we were miles behind his famous line but were in a big Salient with artillery firing at us from both flanks as well as from in front of us and by the looks of his flares you would think that he was right behind us. I passed one boy limping out with a bad wound in his leg. He had 3 wound stripes up that is he had been wounded three other times before going into this battle. He was all smiles and I said hard luck old man and he says hard luck why I would not sell this one for a million dollars. About that time, I would have given all the money I owned to have one like his.

I passed an officer that I know real well. He was wounded and in a shell hole but I could not stop, his batman went to get a stretcher party but before he got back another shell came and killed the officer.

At the start of this show we were going forward and I had charge of head quarters of our Battalion and only had gone about a hundred yards when a shell dropped right on top of us and hit 5 batmen and both cooks on the officer's mess. I had only time to detail stretcher parties to get them out and had to move forward. The second in command was walking in rear of headquarters and just before I caught up to him a shell came and killed him, at least he was alive when we sent him out but died soon after.

We had 11,000 casualties in the show down south and up here we must have lost 15,000 making a total of about 26,000. That is a lot when you consider we only have 48 Battalions in the whole Canadian army. There is the artillery and engineers but on the outside we must have had about 75,000 men in action. So you can see a fellow kind of feels lucky at coming through both battles at least I do anyway.

Well Bert, will have to ring off as my hand is cramped with the cold. Give my love to the wife and family. Your loving brother.

Bill[3]

My third incentive was the story of George Turcott. Family members insisted that he never served during the 1914–18 war because they had never heard him talk about it. My research showed that George Turcott had two sets of attestation papers because he had deserted the army early in the war only to join up again at a later date. I was curious to know what had happened to him and if he had faced court martial charges.

Some Background

This war was a major event in our history. It touched the lives of almost every Canadian alive at the time. It was as challenging for Prime Minister Sir Robert Borden (1911–17) as the

Boer War had been for Sir Wilfred Laurier, probably more so as Borden had to deal with his minister of Militia and Defence, Sir Sam Hughes, as well as the challenges thrown up by the growing casualty figures. The resulting conscription debate polarized this country, setting English Canada against French Canada, and leaving a lasting legacy.

Any family historian conducting research into this period of their ancestor's lives should investigate at least three important individuals: Sir Sam Hughes, Sir Arthur Currie, and perhaps Sir Julian Byng. Having background information on these three should give you some interesting perspectives on the war.

Sir Sam Hughes was in charge of the initial stage of our war preparations, established the camp at Valcartier, Quebec, insisted our troops use the Ross rifle, demanded that Canadian troops be a separate army instead of being divided among British regiments, established the Battalion system in which Canadians served, and was finally relieved of his command by Sir Robert Borden in a controversial situation. At the end of the war, Garnet Hughes, Sam Hughes's son, charged Sir Arthur Currie with wasting Canadian lives during the last days of the war during the attack at Mons. The court case that ensued vindicated Currie but cost him his health

Sir Arthur Currie was a real estate developer who rose to command the Canadian Corps that captured Vimy Ridge, was successful at other fronts in the war when British and commonwealth troops failed, defined the use of the creeping artillery barrage, and believed firmly in making sure our troops understood completely what was going to happen in any given battle and what their objective was. He fully expected each man to assume command should his officer, sergeant, or corporal be killed or wounded, and complete the assignment.

Lord Byng was the British cavalry officer who was reluctantly assigned overall command of the Canadians when all other senior

British officers knew how independent Canadian soldiers were, often challenging what they thought were mindless British rules. He came to respect our soldiers for their fighting ability and they eventually referred to themselves as "Byng's Boys."

You should also learn about the Vimy Memorial and the architect who designed it — Walter Allward. It is truly an impressive monument and a fitting tribute to the Canadian Corps that captured the heights. Our corps and Arthur Currie were undoubtedly the best of any army that fought in the First World War.

As an aside, if you're really interested in this period spend some time reading about the peace negotiations that followed the end of the war. France, England, and the United States didn't want to give Canada the status of signing the Versailles Treaty as an equal partner. They were, however, going to give the right to Portugal, a country that had contributed fewer troops to the war than Canada had lost in killed and wounded. Had Prime Minister Robert L. Borden not insisted that the other countries recognize our contribution we would not have been given equal status as a nation. It was a very important step on our way to recognition as a partner on the world stage. There are even some interesting stories of Borden confronting the British Prime Minister Lloyd George in somewhat of a physical manner over the issue, although these stories, to my knowledge, have not been substantiated.

THE CANADIAN EXPEDITIONARY FORCE

Start your research in your local public library. It is important that you become aware of the nature of the Canadian Army, its organization, the equipment it used, the battles it fought, the medals that were earned, and the cap badges our ancestors wore with pride. The actual history of the causes of the war and the specifics about the battles, I leave for you to discover.

I strongly recommend that anyone interested in discovering the history of the battalion in which an ancestor served search ArchiviaNet for other resources. For instance, a search of the Royal Canadian Military Institute website, *www.rcmi.org*, would provide you access to their extensive library of military resource material, especially Battalion histories. However, a physical visit will not be possible for at least two years from mid-2010 because the building is being redeveloped.

WHAT CAN I LEARN FROM MY ANCESTOR'S SERVICE NUMBER?

When Sir Sam Hughes, minister of Militia and Defence, activated the Canadian Expeditionary Force in 1914, he ignored the existing structure of the Canadian Army and created a system of battalions based on geographical regions, with each region assigned a block of enlistment numbers. So, for example, the 154th Battalion mobilized in Cornwall, Ontario, included the counties of Stormont, Dundas, and Glengarry and was assigned serial numbers from 633001 to 636000. The 174th Battalion mobilized in Winnipeg enlisted men from Manitoba, North Saskatchewan, and Alberta and was assigned numbers 693001 to 696000. Eventually there were 260 battalions.[4] Your ancestor may have volunteered in a place other than where the family lived. Always check the attestation papers, especially the address of the next-of-kin. Support troops, engineers, transport, medical, artillery, and so on, referred to as corps (pronounced *core*), were also assigned blocks of enlistment numbers.

Military personnel could be transferred from one battalion to another, or even be trained in a new skill and assigned to a different branch of the corps, but would always maintain their service number. Your ancestor's documents will have the number of the battalion he or she initially joined listed as one of the finding aids. This battalion was not usually the one in which he or she served. Many of the 260 battalions played a reserve role, providing trained men for "overseas" units. In *The Madman and the Butcher*, Tim Cook mentions that "every battalion numbered from 90 to 258 was broken up" upon arrival in England and the men assigned to other active battalions. [5] The Canadian 5th Division, commanded by Garnet Hughes, was actually stationed in Britain and used for training purposes after which the men would be assigned to units serving on the Western Front.

If your ancestor was an officer, he would not have been issued a service number unless he had come up through the ranks. Officers' attestation papers provide just the commissioned rank they were granted upon enlistment plus personal information.

If your ancestor was a member of the permanent force before the war and elected to join a battalion for service overseas, he had to give up his years of seniority and rank. If he returned to the permanent force following the war, his First World War service files were transferred back to his pre-war regiment. These records were kept until the soldier reached the age of 90 and then destroyed. If you can't find a service record for an ancestor, he might have been in the permanent force and you may not be able to find anything about his war service.

I'VE DISCOVERED A CAP BADGE

Each battalion was expected to submit a design for a cap badge. Most were a large maple leaf with the number of the battalion imposed beneath a crown, with a motto on the bottom. Of course, there are many exceptions to this and so you should consult a good resource guide to Canadian cap badges when attempting to decipher an old photograph or identify a cap badge. Your First World War ancestor would also have worn a battalion insignia on the collar of his battledress tunic. Mostly these were a simple number over the letter *C*. The number would have been the battalion designation and was referred to as "collar dogs."

The battalion Rupert Hinds joined originally was a reserve battalion. When he reached England he was transferred to an active battalion. Later he joined a trench mortar unit and ended the war with the machine-gun corps. His photograph shows him wearing a machine-gun corps cap badge with collar dogs from that corps — crossed machine guns. Even with all these moves, he still maintained the same service number he was assigned when he joined the army.

Division, Corps, Battalion

The Canadian Corps in France contained four divisions and was commanded by a lieutenant-general. The Fifth Canadian Division was stationed in Britain and used for training purposes and to reinforce the other divisions because of high losses in killed and wounded.

The corps had four divisions, each commanded by a major-general — about 17,000 men each.

Each division had four brigades, each commanded by a colonel — about 4,000 men each.

Each brigade had four battalions commanded by a lieutenant-colonel — about 1,000 men each.

A battalion had four companies commanded by a major or captain — about 250 men each.

A company had four platoons commanded by a lieutenant or 2nd lieutenant — about 60 men each.

Each platoon was divided into Sections of six to ten men led by a sergeant or corporal.

Each section had two machine-gun units.

Each division would also include: a cyclist company, cavalry squadrons, brigades of artillery, an ammunition column, corps of engineers and signals, mobile ambulance workshop, sanitary section, medical unit, a labour battalion, service corps, and a veterinarian unit.

By the end of the war the Canadian Corps had evolved into the following organization containing over 102,000 personnel.

Corps Troops: Calvary, Artillery (Garrison, Field, and Horse), Engineers (Company, Searchlight, Tunnelling, Survey, and Tramway), Machine-gun Corps, Service Corp, Medical Corps (casualty clearing stations and field ambulance), Cyclist Battalion, and Signals Company. Each Division had a full complement of these specialists.

The Divisional Troops were organized thus:

1st Division

1st Infantry Brigade
1st (Western Ontario) Battalion
2nd (Eastern Ontario) Battalion
3rd (Toronto Regiment) Battalion
4th (Central Ontario) Battalion
2nd Infantry Brigade
5th (Western Cavalry) Battalion
7th (1st BC Regiment) Battalion
8th (90th Winnipeg Rifles) Battalion
10th (Canadians) Battalion
3rd Infantry Brigade
13th (Royal Highlanders of Canada) Battalion
14th (Royal Montreal Regiment) Battalion
15th (48th Highlanders of Canada) Battalion
16th (Canadian Scottish) Battalion

2nd Division

4th Infantry Brigade
18th (Western Ontario) Battalion
19th (Central Ontario) Battalion
20th (Central Ontario) Battalion
21st (Eastern Ontario) Battalion
5th Infantry Brigade
22nd (French Canadian) Battalion
24th (Victoria Rifles of Canada) Battalion
25th (Nova Scotia Rifles) Battalion
26th (New Brunswick) Battalion
6th Infantry Brigade
27th (Winnipeg) Battalion
28th (Northwest) Battalion
29th (Vancouver) Battalion
31st (Alberta) Battalion

3rd Division

7th Infantry Brigade
Royal Regiment of
Canada
Princess Patricia's
Canadian Light
Infantry
42nd (Royal Highlanders
of Canada) Battalion
29th (Edmonton
Regiment) Battalion
8th Infantry Brigade
1st Canadian Mounted
Rifles
2nd Canadian Mounted
Rifles
4th Canadian Mounted
Rifles
5th Canadian Mounted
Rifles
9th Infantry Brigade
43rd (Cameron
Highlanders of
Canada) Battalion
52nd (New Ontario)
Battalion
58th (Central Ontario)
Battalion
116th (Ontario County)
Battalion

4th Division

10th Infantry Brigade
44th (New Brunswick)
Battalion
46th (South
Saskatchewan)
Battalion
47th (Western Ontario)
Battalion
50th (Calgary) Battalion
11th Infantry Brigade
54th (Central Ontario)
Battalion
75th (Mississauga)
Battalion
87th (Canadian Grenadier
Guards) Battalion
102nd (Central Ontario)
Battalion
12th Infantry Brigade
38th (Ottawa) Battalion
72nd (Seaforth
Highlanders of
Canada) Battalion
78th (Winnipeg
Grenadiers) Battalion
85th (Nova Scotia
Highlanders)
Battalion

A researcher can well imagine that an organization that eventually encompassed 600,000 individuals created a massive amount of paperwork. When you start to access the forms, you should consult the excellent guide provided at LAC concerning military abbreviations. This can be especially helpful when trying to decipher medal cards.

Some Basic Terms

Rank: corporal (cpl.), sergeant (sgt.), lieutenant (lt.), captain (capt.), major (maj.), colonel (col.), general (gen.).

Some officers were attached to headquarters (H.Q.).

Corporals and sergeants are classified as non-commissioned officers (n.c.o.) and enlisted men can appear on forms as (enl.) or troops (trps.).

They were all members of the Canadian Expeditionary Force (C.E.F.) and also considered infantry (inf.).

If they served in France it would be considered overseas (o/s) and recorded so on military forms.

In all likelihood they received their training (trn.) in England and were sent as reinforcements (reinf.) to a unit in France.

Soldiers could be members of an artillery battery (art. bty.), cavalry (cav.), signals (sig.), be part of the Canadian Army Medical Corps (camc), part of the transport (trans.) corps, or even trained as machine gunners (m.g.). They may even have been assigned to mining duties as a tunneller (tun.).

If they were killed or wounded you could see them recorded as a casualty (cas.), killed in action (k.i.a), wounded in action (w.i.a), if the wound was caused by shrapnel from an artillery burst (s/w), or by bullet (b/w).

Army units: You would expect to see abbreviations for platoon (plat.), battalion (bn.), brigade (bde. or brig.), and company (coy.) or division (div.) used in reports and documents.

Every university in Canada had a Canadian Officer Training Corps (cotc) that provided officers for active service.

Of course, these are only a few of the hundreds of terms used by the military to create abbreviated records, many written by hand and later typed. You will also discover that the enlisted men developed their own language.

Hun or Boche were the common words used when referring to German troops.

A "coal box" was a term used to describe a German heavy-calibre artillery shell.

A "whizz bang" described the sound of other enemy shells.

A "minnenwerfer" was a trench mortar shell, fired by the enemy, which made little or no noise until it landed.

Pilots on patrol would record that they encountered "H.A." meaning Hun or hostile aircraft.

There were thousands of slang terms used to describe a multitude of trench experiences. There were songs and customs. David Love's *A Call to Arms* and other similar books contain invaluable appendices for those new to this type of research.

Most of us are interested in acquiring our ancestor's service files and surrounding the facts with the events of the conflict. This was, without a doubt, a world war. Canadians served in many theatres of the war, but mostly in France and Belgium. If you do a general search for First World War websites you will be overwhelmed by the quantity and quality of the material available to help you with your research. The same is true when you start to narrow your search using terms like Canadian Expeditionary Force, Soldiers of World War One, or even the name of one of the battles fought between 1914 and 1918. If you are tracing your English ancestors you should be aware that the German Luftwaffe bombed the building holding all the B.E.F. First World War records during the Second World War blitz bombing of London. Those that were saved are referred to as the "unburnt" records while what's left are called the "burnt" files.

If you are searching for an ancestor who has no known grave, it was recently reported that the Red Cross headquarters in Geneva, Switzerland, has opened its extensive files concerning the death, burial, hospitalization, and prisoners of war records, all of which had been carefully recorded in ledgers and on file cards during the war. Hopefully, in the years ahead, their resources will become available to family historians.

BATTLES IN WHICH THE C.E.F. FOUGHT AS A UNIT

- Battle of Ypres, 22–24 April 1915, 1st Can. Division — 6,035 casualties in forty-eight hours. More than 2,000 died of their wounds. It was here that John McCrae wrote "In Flanders Fields." Four Canadians won the Victoria Cross (V.C.): E.D. Bellew, F. Fisher, F.W. Fisher, and F.A. Seringer.

- Battle of Beaumont-Hamel, 1 July 1916, 1st Nfld. Regiment of the British 29th Division's 88th Brigade — 733 of 801 men are killed or wounded. This was the opening day of the Somme in which there were 57,470 casualties of which 19,240 were fatal. Keep in mind that Newfoundland fought as part of the British Army.

- Battle of the Somme, 1 July 1916, British forces had lost 57,500 killed or missing in one day. Canadians moved to the Somme in August and occupied a section of the line west of the village of Courcelette. By 15 September, they pushed on to Courcelette. By 11 November the fourth Canadian Division captured Regina Trench and a week later Desire Trench. The Somme cost us 24,029 killed or missing. The Canadian Corps then moved to Vimy.

- Battle of Vimy Ridge, 9 April 1917, four divisions of the Canadian Corps, commanded by Sir Julian Byng, with the 1st Division, commanded by Sir Arthur Currie, take Vimy Ridge after repeated attempts by British and Australian units had failed. On 12 April Canadians take Hill 145, the highest feature on the ridge as well as the

Pimple, another high feature. 10,600 Canadians are wounded, 3,598 are killed. V.C.s: W. Milne, E. Sifton, T. MacDowell, and J. Pattison.

- Battle of Passchendaele, (also called third battle of Ypres), 31 July to mid-November 1917. British, Australian, and New Zealand forces had suffered over 100,000 casualties before the Canadian Corps began their attack on 26 October 1917. The Corps lost 15,000 dead and wounded. V.C.s awarded to Canadians: C.F. Barron, T.W. Holmes, C.J. Kinross, H. McKenzie, G.H. Mullen, C.P.J. O'Kelly, G.R. Pearkes, J.P. Robertson, and R. Shankland.

- Battle of Amiens, 8–11 August 1918. Considered a "black day" for the German Army. Canadian Corps suffered 11,800 casualties, 4,000 on 8 August. Significant gains are achieved because of Currie's careful planning. A victory, some believe, equal to Vimy.

- Battle of Arras and Canal du Nord, known as the Hundred Days — August to November 1918 following the victory at Amiens. The capture of Arras results in 11,000 casualties. On 27 September the Canal du Nord is crossed and the strong points at Bourlon Wood and Cambrai are taken on 9 October. There are approximately 30,000 casualties but the end of the war is near. The Canadian Corps fights on the outskirts of Mons, 1–10 November.

You may also want to research the battle at Festubert in 1915, in which we suffered 2,468 casualties; Saint-Éloi, 3–16 April 1916, in which the 2nd Division lost 1,373 men; Mount Sorrel on 13 June 1916 with over 8,000 casualties; Hill 70 on 15 August 1916, in which we captured and held against twenty-one German counterattacks but suffered over 9,000 killed and wounded.[7]

The last Canadian soldier to die was Private George Price of the 28th Battalion, shot by a German sniper outside Mons just a few minutes before 11 a.m., 11 November 1918. Private Price's original grave marker can be found at the Canadian War Museum and is so placed that the sun strikes it on the morning of every Remembrance Day — 11 November.

Beyond the Infantry

You can read about those in the air and at sea in chapters eight and nine.

In August 1914, the Royal Flying Corps went to France with four squadrons, about forty-six planes, and almost 900 personnel. By 11 November 1918, the Royal Air Force had 188 squadrons and 22,000 aircraft; about 300,000 personnel had served in this service. Approximately 3,000 Canadians served with the Royal Navy and by the end of the war over 5,000 served in the Royal Canadian Navy. In 1914, the Canadian Navy had two ships, HMCS *Niobe* and HMCS *Rainbow*, and two submarines; by the end of the war the RCN numbered over 100 ships.

The Medals They Earned

There were two basic medals approved in 1919 for distribution to military personnel who qualified: The Victory Medal and the British War Medal. The Victory Medal was issued to those who served in a theatre of war between 5 August 1914 and 11

November 1918 or the mission to Russia 1919–20. There were 351,289 issued to members of the C.E.F. There were no bars or clasps issued for this medal but an Oak Leak was attached if a soldier was Mentioned in Dispatches. You will always find the Victory Medal issued with the British War Medal. The B.W.M. was issued for the same period of service as the V.M. with no bars or clasps. The British War Medal was issued to 427,993 Canadians. Both medals were engraved around the rim with the name, rank, serial number, and battalion of the recipient.

Some Canadians also qualified for the 1914 Star, called the Mons Star, or the 1914–1915 Star. The 1914 Star was issued to anyone who served in France or Belgium between 5 August and 22 November 1914. There was a bar issued for this medal: 5 August–22 November 1914 for those on duty during the period and under fire from enemy mobile artillery fire. Only 160 Canadians received this medal and all were with the 2nd Canadian Stationary Hospital attached to the British Expeditionary Force. The 1914–1915 Star was issued to personnel who served between 5 August 1914 and 31 December 1915. This medal was not issued to those who qualified for the 1914 Star. Canadians received 71,150 of these medals.

If your ancestor died in the war the next-of-kin would have received a Memorial Cross with the name of the recipient engraved on the back. Families of British and Commonwealth war dead were presented with a Memorial Plaque, which became known "a dead man's penny."

IDENTIFYING OLD PHOTOGRAPHS

You are more likely to discover old photographs from the First World War than an earlier event. Battalions were photographed as a group upon completion of training and individual soldiers had pictures taken of themselves, often with friends, to send back to loved ones. Official army photographic units were employed to record important events as they occurred and many of these photos are in our archives. Professional war artists recorded the contribution of the Canadian Corps and some of their work is displayed in the House of Commons chamber in Ottawa.

Many old photographs can be used to identify the battalion, rank, or division to which an ancestor belonged. Each Division in the Canadian Army had a unique rectangular patch that the men wore just below the shoulder. First Division had a basic red rectangular patch while 2nd wore blue, 3rd was grey blue, 4th was basic green, and 5th wore purple. Above each divisional patch was another piece of shaped fabric that indicated the battalion or if he was in engineers, machine gun corps, or a trench mortar battery.

Non-commissioned officers wore their rank badges halfway between the elbow and the shoulder. A basic sergeant wore three stripes; a corporal wore two. Lance corporals wore only one stripe. An N.C.O., above sergeant, would wear a small crown, crossed cannons, or engineer's insignia above the three stripes to denote if he was a sergeant-major or sergeant of artillery or engineers. Below the elbow were any trade badges or skill-at-arms badges earned by the enlisted man. These were worn halfway between the cuff of the jacket and the elbow. If a soldier wore crossed flags he was trained as a signaller, a stylized *L* meant he was a gun layer in an artillery battery, an S.B. badge would denote a stretcher bearer, and a small bugle meant bugler. If a man had been wounded he was entitled to wear a small wound stripe in the centre of the left sleeve just above the cuff.

In Lieutenant Stanley's letter he commented on seeing one of the troops with a serious leg wound who was already wearing three wound stripes. When Stanley says "bad luck old man" to the soldier, the fellow's reply is something to the effect that he wouldn't trade his wound for anything. The soldiers knew the only way out of the trenches was either to be killed or receive a wound that would send them to a hospital in England and perhaps even home. They believed that the lucky ones got a "blighty," which injured you enough to get you out of the hell of trench warfare but not kill you.

Ted Barris provides an excellent description of the kit your ancestor would have worn:

> As the battalions kitted up in Allied tunnels before the attack, every soldier's equipment weight began to increase. Each Canadian Corps infantryman's field service orders required him to wear his helmet and carry a box gas mask, an overcoat or leather jerkin, his Lee Enfield rifle with bayonet and 120 cartridges, a pick or shovel, four Mills bombs [hand grenades], two unfilled sandbags, a haversack on his back with two days' rations and an iron ration, two aeroplane flares, a Verey light, a candle, a box of matches, and his mess tin slung outside the haversack. The entire kit could add 50 or 60 pounds to his overall weight.[8]

Officers were not required to carry the same weight. Often, they would attack with a Webley pistol as their sole means of defence. To identify command they wore their rank either on their sleeves or on the shoulder flaps of their uniform. Second lieutenants (the most junior rank) wore one small star, called a pip, on their cuffs. Lieutenants wore two pips, captains wore three

First World War soldier in field kit with the officer who designed the "08" pattern webbing. This photograph provides the researcher with a good example of the uniform and kit of an enlisted man and officer. LAC, PA 000353.

pips, while a major wore one crown. A lieutenant-colonel had a crown above a pip and a colonel had a crown above two pips. Brigadiers had a plain cuff but wore a crossed sword and scabbard on their shoulder flaps while major-generals had a crossed sword and scabbard with a pip above it. Later in the war junior officers, who often lead attacks, did not display their rank insignia prominently for fear of attracting attention from enemy snipers.

WHAT HAVE I LEARNED ABOUT RUPERT HINDS, WILLIAM STANLEY, AND GEORGE TURCOTT?

When you apply for your ancestor's records you should also request a copy of the abbreviations you could expect to find on a set of First World War records. Usually they are included, but, if not, the following might help:

Adj.	Adjutant
Adm.	Admitted
Att'd.	Attached
Auth.	Authorized
AWL	Absent without leave
Bn.	Battalion
Bty.	Battery
CBD	Canadian Base Details
CCAC	Canadian Casualty Assembly Centre
CCD	Canadian Convalescent Depot
CCRC	Canadian Corps Reinforcement Camp
CCS	Canadian Clearing Station
CDD	Canadian Discharge Depot
CFA	Canadian Field Ambulance
CGH	Canadian General Hospital

CL	Casualty List
CMGC	Canadian Machine Gun Corps
C of I	Court of Inquiry
DCM	Distinguished Conduct Medal
Dis.	Discharged
DO	Daily Orders
D of W	Died of Wounds
Dvr	Driver
Emb	Embarked
GC	Good Conduct badge
GHQ	General Headquarters
Gnr	Gunner
GSW	Gunshot wound
GOC	General Officer Commanding
HMT	His Majesty's Troopship
Inv. "wd"	Invalided wounded
KIA	Killed in Action
LG	London Gazette
LMB	Light Mortar Battery
M&D	Medals & Decorations
MC	Military Cross
MD	Military District
MIA	Missing in Action
MID	Mentioned in Dispatches
Miss.	Missing
MM	Military Medal
NYD	Not Yet Determined
OMFC	Overseas Military Force, Canadian
O.S.	Overseas
P&S	Plaque and Scroll
Pres.	Presumed
Proc.	Proceeded

QRD	Pyrexia of unknown origin
RFB	Reported from Base
RTC	Returned to Corps
RTU	Returned to Unit
SEF	Siberian Expeditionary Force
SOS	Struck off Strength
Spr	Sapper
Staty	Stationary (hospital)
SW	Shrapnel Wound
TMB	Trench Mortar Battery
TOS	Taken off Strength
Tpr.	Trooper
Trans	Transferred
Unk	Unknown
w.(w)	wounded[9]

The first document you will probably find in your ancestor's file is his or her attestation papers. Attestation papers are available online at LAC. This two-sided document provides basic information about next of kin, address, physical appearance, and any declarations the volunteer was expected to sign. The document will also provide you with the service number and battalion assigned to your family member. Both of these are important because even though the enlisted man may have been transferred, his original battalion will appear on all documents as will his service number. Your soldier may have enlisted in a different military district from where he actually lived. Rupert Hinds, for instance, enlisted in Smiths Falls, Ontario, with the 80th Battalion, but listed his next-of-kin as his mother, living in Toronto. A check of the 1901 census confirms that he was living at this address with the rest of his family. As Rupert worked for the railroad he may have gone to Smiths Falls to work. Officer's attestation papers provide the same information except they do not include a serial number.

The next document will be the "casualty form — active service" that will provide you with a detailed summary of your ancestor's service and a record of any wounds sustained during active duty. Rupert Hinds's Casualty Form Active Service sheet shows that he joined the 80th Battalion, was transferred to 75th Battalion, and then the 54th Battalion. Eventually he assumed duty with the 11th Brigade, Trench Mortar Battery, and proceeded to England on 30 May 1916, still with the 75th Battalion. Rupert embarked for France 10 August 1916, but seems to have been selected for machine-gun training and eventually was posted to the 11th Canadian Machine-Gun Company. By 1918 his record shows that he went on leave, received a good conduct badge, was promoted to corporal, and was absorbed into the 4th Battalion Machine-Gun Battalion. On 28 October 1918 Rupert was reported as wounded in the field and the next recorded comment states that on 21 November 1918 he was SOS (struck off strength) Canadian Machine-Gun Corps.

Medical reports found in Rupert's file show that he had reported to hospital with shrapnel wounds to his right foot, right leg, and right arm. He was invalided to Canada on 19 April 1919 with a Distinguished Conduct Medal, the rank of sergeant, and minus a leg. Enlisted men would receive the DCM for acts of bravery; officers received the Military Cross (MC).

William Stanley's records show a similar pattern. He joined in 12 October 1916, indicating that he had previous experience with the 110th Battalion active militia. Upon enlistment he was assigned to the 208th Overseas Battalion and arrived in England on 14 May 1917, where he was recorded as "taken on strength" of the 102nd Battalion. William's record shows that by 1918 he was posted to France, had taken a course at gas school, and, on 30 April, received a face and scalp wound. He rejoined his unit, from hospital, on 22 June 1918 only to be "evacuated wounded" again on 6 November 1918. His medical record shows the wound resulted from a shell explosion that injured his face again. For the action in which he received his second wound, Lieutenant Stanley was awarded a Military Cross for bravery.

If you discover that an ancestor's Casualty Form — Active Service sheet indicates that a medal was awarded for bravery, you will not find a citation in their archive records. All bravery awards were issued with a special citation that detailed the action in which the recipient was involved as well as a simplified description of the action. A submission for a bravery award could only be granted to enlisted men if the action was witnessed by an officer. You will have to consult a separate record group at LAC, using a finding aid that is not online. At LAC you will find the citations after consulting finding aid 38-31, reference 2004-01505-5, boxes 1 to 75. Don't forget to check the London Gazette (www.gazettes-online. co.uk) for gallantry citations from both World Wars.

George Turcott's service file had the word "deserter" written on the front cover. He had two sets of attestation papers. It appears he joined the 134th Battalion, 16 January 1916, and was struck off strength 5 June 1916 because he was "illegally absent." I believe George had an affair of the heart and may have deserted to be with the woman who would eventually become his second wife. He may have even gone as far as Saskatchewan to start his new life because this is where the first child of that second marriage was born. During the war, soldiers who were absent without leave were reported to the police but not much more action was taken. The war effort took precedence over everything else; enlisting, training, and moving new recruits to overseas postings took priority. After the war there was a general amnesty for any man who was absent without leave from his unit during the war. George, however, seems to have returned to Ontario and re-enlisted in the

205th Machinegun Depot. His medical report states that he was quite capable of performing his duties but was often absent for long periods because of his "lumbago." Finally, he was declared "medically unfit" for military service and released from duty, 14 March 1917. George's two sets of attestation papers provide the family historian some interesting information. His first form confirms his date and place of birth, address, and family contact as found on the 1901 census. When he re-enlisted he changed his place of birth to Cork, Ireland, from Frontenac County, Ontario. Everything else was correct except the name of family contact; that was his second wife. My previous research had discovered that George's father was of French-Canadian ancestry while his mother was Irish. Without realizing it, he had provided future family historians with a place to start the search for his family's Irish roots.

Two other documents you are likely to find is a pay list denoting any money due to your ancestor, although some of the files I have researched did not include this, and an official copy of a soldier's enlistment history. The last document is often a summary of the "casualty form-war service" record. You may find the summary easier to read than the casualty form but always cross-check the two for transcription errors. All of these records will supply you with enough information to place your First World War ancestor into context.

To really understand your ancestor's First World War record, consult *Canadians at War, 1914–1919: A Research Guide to World War One Service Records* by Glenn Wright (Milton: Global Heritage Press, 2010).

My Ancestor May Have Been a Prisoner of War

You may discover that your ancestor was a prisoner of war in one of the many German camps. I was once presented with a shoebox of items owned by a First World War veteran and passed on to the family following his death. In the box was a cap badge for the 15th Battalion, a collection of letters, and some very interesting postcards. The postcards had been sent to the family while the soldier was a prisoner and showed him posing with friends and camp guards. The letters provided information on conditions in the camp while the cap badge and an eventual search of his files in Ottawa enabled me to construct a family narrative.

At the beginning of the war the Canadian government had not given much thought to the problem of capture by the enemy. It was still common military practice to consider capture as the fault of the soldier: was he asleep on duty, was he a coward, or was his capture a dereliction of duty. During the South African (Boer) War, most of our soldiers captured by the Boers were relieved of their weapons, horses, and other equipment, then released. Usually there was a military trial (court marital) held for individuals captured and released by the Boers to establish whether or not their capture resulted from dereliction of duty.

As the First World War progressed and our country became more committed, the treatment of our soldiers held in enemy prison camps became an issue. By 1918, 132 Canadian officers and 3,715 men of other ranks had been captured and imprisoned.[10]

In 1899, Britain had signed the Hague Convention that defined the treatment of soldiers in captivity. In essence, prisoners could be put to work, they were to be paid for the task (less the cost of their maintenance), and were to be the responsibility of the government and not the unit that captured them. The convention also stated that the detaining power was to provide food, clothing, and accommodation that were at least equal to the depot troops (enemy soldiers assigned as guards) of the detaining power. An information bureau was to be established by each belligerent to respond to questions raised about

POWs and to maintain information about captures, transfers, hospitalization, and deaths. The responsibility for collating the lists of Canadian prisoners fell to the Information Department, Casualties and Prisoners, under the direction of the Canadian Red Cross Society.

Julia Drummond and Evelyn Rivers Bulkeley assumed the responsibility of examining nominal returns provided by the German government through the British Foreign Office and sorting out members of Canadian or British units who stated their next-of-kin lived in Canada. A card index was compiled by the Red Cross Headquarters in Toronto and a second list was maintained by the Department of Militia and Defence in Ottawa.

Surprisingly, the file cards prepared for the Department of Militia and Defence have not been found. The Red Cross Society records held in Geneva, Switzerland, concerning First and Second World War POWs, have just recently been released for research and hopefully will be available online in the years ahead.

The Canadian Government commissioned a *Report on Maltreatment of Prisoners of War — Report of the Royal Commission on Reparations Canada*, 1932, by Errol M. McDougall (commissioner), available through Amicus, which will give you the location of copies in Canadian libraries.

Life in a POW camp was particularly difficult for our soldiers. Following the German offensive against the Ypres Salient in April 1915, numerous Canadian Battalions (3rd Toronto, 7th B.C., 15th Toronto, 2nd Ontario, 13th Montreal) lost over 300 men each. On 2 June 1916, the Princess Patricia's Canadian Light Infantry and the 4th Canadian Mounted Rifles suffered heavy casualties at Mount Sorrel resulting in another 730 names added to the POWs lists. Most of these men spent the first few weeks of their capture in the clothes they had fought in. After interrogation they were sent to one of over forty prison camps. Each of the 260

German divisions were assigned one or two POW camps as the destination for enemy troops they captured.[11]

When they finally reached their destination, soldiers soon discovered that life in a camp involved boredom, lack of common amenities, and poor food. One soldier described his daily ration as black coffee made from acorns for breakfast; soup containing cabbage, black peas, and maybe twice a week tiny pieces of meat for dinner; and thin soup for supper. They could also purchase two pounds of bread, which was described as brown on the outside, khaki on the inside, and so putty-like that if thrown against a wall it would stick.

Lieutenant Stanley and Sergeant Hinds Were Awarded Medals

Lieutenant William Stanley's letter comments about the "action down south" and the amount of German rations and liquor they had liberated. This was the Canadian assault at Amiens, which completely took the Germans by surprise, resulting in a significant Canadian victory. Official accounts remark on the amount of resources captured. The 102nd Battalion and the 4th Battalion, Canadian Machinegun Corps, were both involved so Rupert Hinds and William Stanley were involved in the same action. The Canadian Corps was moved north following Amiens and assigned the task of capturing Arras, crossing the Canal du Nord, and capturing strong points at Bourlon Wood and Cambrai. Hinds and Stanley would again have faced the forced march north and the preparations for the assault on Arras.

On 27 September the Canadian Corps attacked across the Canal du Nord. This was accomplished by a massive bombardment, followed closely by the forward movement of the troops.

Twenty-four batteries of machine guns were employed at the Canal. During the attack they fired an amazing 320,000 rounds of ammunition. Actually, the Canal du Nord was taken with some ease and moderate casualties. The Germans were overwhelmed by the bombardment and the Canadian troops had moved so quickly that they soon overran the enemy trenches. In some cases the German units were annihilated. The fourth division was given the responsibility of capturing Bourlon Wood. These heights were described by one observer as just several hundred acres of trees, shattered, dark, and sinister. The Canadian plan called for a pincer movement rather than a frontal assault. The 102nd Battalion was one of those whose responsibility was to approach the heights from the south. By 27 September the woods were in Canadian hands, all objectives had been achieved, and Cambrai was taken.

Rupert Hinds received the wound that sent him back to Canada with a Distinguished Conduct Medal at Bourlon Wood. The citation for his DCM states:

> During the capture of Bourlon Wood he assisted materially in the good work of his battery which accounted for numbers of the enemy, besides a battery of field guns. After two days heavy fighting, he and four men were all that remained in action of the eight guns of those who started.[12]

Interestingly, nothing is mentioned of the loss of leg or any act involving saving the life of one of the officers. In all likelihood the citation for bravery at Bourlon Wood was submitted before the incident that Rupert Hinds referred to at the beginning of this chapter.

The Canadian Corps moved forward and on 6 November William Stanley won his Military Cross. His citation states:

> For conspicuous gallantry and fine leadership during the advance east of Valenciennes, on 6th of November, when in charge of a company. His wonderful rapidity of movement which completely demoralised the enemy and resulted in the capture of a large number of machine guns and prisoners. He showed complete disregard of personal safety, and at one point, when his advance was checked by a machine gun, he personally organised and led a party which captured it, being the first man in the position, the occupants of which were all captured or killed, without any loss to his party. Throughout he set his men a magnificent example.[12]

He too returned to Canada with a wound.

Now, back to those names on the plaque high on the wall of the school. The names are Private William A. Heal, 20th Battalion, Canadian Machine Gun Corps, who died 26 August 1918, age twenty-seven, at Cambrai, and Private William T. Heron, 3rd Battalion, CMGC, who died 29 September 1918, age twenty-two, also at Cambrai. They died in the same engagement in which Rupert Hinds and William Stanley were involved: the final push to Mons and the end of the war. Two came back with wounds and medals for bravery and two are buried in France.

As an interesting aside to the William Stanley research, you can find a picture of him with fellow officers if you check the website for the 102nd Battalion and an article in the *Toronto Star*, dated 1936, which reports on the death of Lieutenant-Colonel William Stanley after being struck by a streetcar while crossing Queen Street.

FIRST WORLD WAR RESOURCES

LAC

- RG 9 II F10, those who served with the British Expeditionary Force and received a gratuity.
- RG 9, III D3, vols. 4812-5075, unit war diaries for the army. Some can be viewed online and all can be borrowed through interlibrary loan.
- RG 9, series IIB 8, attestation papers, also online.
- RG 10, names of Aboriginal soldiers.
- RG 38, the names of Newfoundland soldiers. I would also recommend you check *www.ngb.chebucto.org*, if you're researching your Newfoundland ancestors who served during the First World War. Newfoundland was not part of Canada until 1949, so was not part of the C.E.F.
- RG 150, acc. 1992-93/166, box 2340-35, memorial cross recipient cards. Provides recipient's name and address of next-of-kin.
- R.G. 150, acc. 192-93/166, these boxes contain the attestation paper and other records pertaining to First World War service men and women.

LAC Records of POWs

- RG 9-III-D-1 (1914-1920), files on each C.E.F. unit and formation, interviews with repatriated prisoners of war, badges, colours, publications, etc.
- RG 25, the records on the treatment of prisoners of war in Canada and Great Britain.

- RG 38-D-9, the treatment of prisoners of war by the enemy — Royal Newfoundland Regiment.
- RG 150-9 (finding aid 150-4), daily casualty lists (1915–19). Each C.E.F. unit is assigned a separate page by month where its casualties are broken down by day. Prisoners of War are one category.
- MG 30 (E28, E33, E116, E292, E376, E525, E552), family records donated to the archives. Those listed usually hold information about life as a prisoner of war during the First World War.

Websites

Canada's War Museum, *www.warmuseum.ca/cwm/home*.

CBC Digital Archives, *archives.cbc.ca/war_conflict/first_world_war/ topics/2425*.

The Commonwealth War Graves Commission, *cwg.org*.

The Imperial War Museum, *www.iwmcollections.org.uk*.

London Gazette, *www.gazettes-online.co.uk*, for the mention of medal awardees.

The Long, Long Trail, *www.1914-1918.net*.

McGill University, *digital.library.mcgill.ca/warposters*.

National Army, U.K., *www.national-army-museum.ac.uk*.

Resources for teachers, *www.virtualmuseum.ca/English/Teacher/ world_war.html*.

Royal Flying Corps records held at the Directorate of History and Heritage, Department of National Defence, Ottawa, *www.airforce.ca*.

Toronto Star, *www.pagesofthepast.ca*.

University of Calgary, *www.library.ucalgary.ca*, for the *Official History of the Canadian Army and the First World War*, by G. W.I. Nicholson, commissioned by the Directorate of History and Heritage, Department of National Defence; plus regimental histories.

POW–related Websites

Archon, *www.nationalarchives.gov.uk/archon/default.htm*, a directory provided by National Archives U.K. that will direct you to other record repositories in the United Kingdom.

Beyond the Wire, *www.1914-1918.net/grandad/pow.htm*, a searchable database, gives you the document and page number. You may have to hire a researcher in England to search the records held in WO 161 for detailed information about your ancestor.

Imperial War Museum, *www.iwmcollections.org.uk/prisoners/essay.php*, provides researchers with some basic information about POW records.

National Archives, U.K., *www.nationalarchives.gov.uk/documentsonline/pow.asp*, search and download First World War interviews and reports of over 3,000 individuals who were prisoners of war.

Books

A number of these books will have names of medal recipients, information about the uniforms and weapons they used, and, in the case of the Wigney and Love books, a way of tracing the enlistment numbers you might find on a First World War document.

Abbink, H. *The Military Medal: Canadian Recipients, 1916–1922*. Calgary: Alison Pub., 1987.

Berton, P. *Vimy.* Toronto: Pen and Sword Books, 2003.

Bird, W. *Ghosts Have Warm Hands.* Toronto: Clarke Irwin & Co., Ltd., 1968.

Black, E. *I Want One Volunteer.* Toronto: Ryerson Press Ltd., 1965.

Dancocks, D.G. *Legacy of Valour: The Canadians at Passchendaele.* Edmonton: Hurtig Publishers, 1986.

Dancocks, D.G. *Spearhead to Victory, Canada and the Great War.* Edmonton: Hurtig Publishers, 1987.

Duguid, A.F. *A Question of Confidence: The Ross Rifle in the Trenches.* Ottawa: Service Publications, 2000.

Godfrey, A.B. *For Freedom and Honour: The Story of 25 Canadian Volunteers Executed in the First World War.* Nepean, ON: C.E.F. Books, 1998.

Greenfield, N.M. *Baptism of Fire: The Second Battle of Ypres and the Forging of Canada, April 1915.* Toronto: HarperCollins, 1969.

Hampton, B. *Canadian Flying Services, Emblems and Insignia (1914–1984).* Vancouver: B. Hampton, 1986.

Harper, J. *A Source of Pride: Regimental Badges and Titles in the Canadian Expeditionary Force, 1914–1919.* Ottawa: Service Publications, 1999.

Law, Clive. *Distinguishing Patches: Formation Patches of the Canadian Army.* Ottawa: Service Publications, 1996.

Law, Clive. *Uniforms of the Canadian Expeditionary Force.* Ottawa: Service Publications, 1997.

Love, David. *A Call to Arms: The Organization and Administration of Canada's Military in World War One.* Winnipeg and Calgary: Bunker to Bunker Books, 1999. This book contains everything a researcher would need to know about the C.E.F. An invaluable resource.

Melville, Douglas. *Canadians and the Victoria Cross.* St. Catharines, ON: Vanwell Publishing Ltd., 1987.

Nicholson, G.W.L. *Canadian Expeditionary Force, 1914–1918: The Official History of the Canadian Army in the First World War.* Ottawa: Queen's Printers, 1962. This history is a must for anyone serious about researching the war.

Riddle, David. *The Distinguished Conduct Medal to the Canadian Expeditionary Force 1914–1920.* Winnipeg: Kirby-Marlton Press, 1991.

Riddle, David. *The Distinguished Service Order to the C.E.F. and Canadians in the Royal Naval Air Service, Royal Flying Corps and R.A.F., 1915–1920.* Winnipeg: Kirby-Marlton, 1991.

Riddle, David. *The Military Cross Awarded to the Canadian Expeditionary Force, 1914–1920, with full citations.* Winnipeg: Kirby-Marlton Press, 1991.

Rosen, A.L. *Canadian Expeditionary Force Military Cap Badges of World War I.* Toronto: Alternative Graphics, 1985.

Skuce, J.E. *CSEF: Canada's Soldiers in Siberia 1918–1919.* Ottawa: Access to History, 1990.

Summers, Jack. *Tangled Web, Canadian Infantry Accoutrements, 1855–1985.* Canadian War Museum; no.26, Bloomfield, ON: Museum Restoration Service, 1992.

Swinnerton, I.S. *Identifying your World War I Soldier from Badges and Photographs.* London, U.K.: Federation of Family History Societies, 2001.

Walker, R.W. *Recipients of the Distinguished Conduct Medal, 1914–1920: Being a List Arranged Regimentally and Alphabetically of all those Awarded the D.C.M. Between August 1914 and June 1920.* Birmingham, U.K.: Midland Medals, 1981.

Wheeler, V. *The 50th Battalion in No Man's Land.* Nepean ON: C.E.F. Books, 2000.

Wigney, E.H, *Serial Numbers of the C.E.F.* Nepean ON: E.H.Wigney, 1996.

Books on POWs

Connes, G.A. *A POW's Memoir of the First World War: The Other Ordeal.* New York: Berg Publishing, 2004.

Cox & Co. *List of British Officers Taken Prisoner in the Various Theatres of War Between August 1914 and November 1918.* London, U.K.: Cox & Co. Publishing, 1988.

Dennett, C.P. *Prisoners of the Great War: Authoritative Statements of Conditions in the Prison Camps of Germany.* Boston: Houghton-Mifflin Co., 1919. This American book includes an excellent list of most German prison camps.

Harvey, F.W. *Comrades in Captivity: A Record of Life in Seven German Prison Camps.* London, U.K.: Sedgwick & Jackson, 1920.

Morton, D. *Silent Battle: Canadian Prisoners of War in Germany, 1914–1917.* Toronto: Lester Pub., 2004.

Strachan, T. *In the Clutches of Circumstance: Reminiscences of Members of the Canadian National Prisoner of War Association.* Victoria, BC: Cappis Press, 1985.

Vance, J.F.W. *Canadian Prisoners of War through the Twentieth Century.* Vancouver: UBC Press, 1994.

Wigney, H.E. *Guests of the Kaiser: Prisoners of War of the Canadian Expeditionary Force, 1915–1918.* Nepean, ON: C.E.F. Books, 2008. Names and descriptions of many of the Canadians who found themselves in German prisoner of war camps during the First World War.

CHAPTER SIX

The Second World War:
I Need Help Finding My Family's Records

"They gave up their tomorrows for our todays" was the caption above a group of pictures of former students of Riverdale Collegiate in Toronto who had made the ultimate sacrifice during the Second World War. Kenneth James Cox, although he didn't attend this school, was also one of those who gave up his tomorrows. He died in England on 26 November 1943 while serving with the Royal Canadian Air Force as a navigator in a Mosquito fighter/bomber. His brother, Leonard Gordon Cox, did return from the war after serving in Italy and northwest Europe with the Royal Canadian Army Service Corps. Ray Mecoy also made it home after serving in the North Atlantic and English Channel on board the minesweeper *Fort William* as a stoker with the Royal Canadian Navy. Ray was one of many men from central Canada who joined the Royal Canadian Naval Volunteer Reserve and went to sea. One died in a plane crash; another lived with the stress, lice, and the constant threat of death in Italy and Europe; the third swept the English Channel of mines early on the morning of 6 June 1944. Ray's story, and more details about Canada's Navy during the Second World War, can be found in Chapter Nine.

Kenneth James Cox (navigator) and John James Blanchfield (pilot), 410 squadron, England. Family photograph.

How did this happen when in 1919, after the "war to end all wars," the Treaty of Versailles was signed, severely limiting Germany's ability to wage war? And, if your ancestor stepped forward and volunteered for active service, what can we learn from their service records? Because of privacy concerns there will be limits to your research. If your ancestor died during the war you can find him or her on the Commonwealth War Graves site, in the Book of Remembrance, or via a request at *www. collectionscanada.ca*. If your ancestor is still alive or died within the last twenty-five years you can access the records through a special request, after you have proved your relationship. However, if you are requesting the service record of another, non-related individual, you will have to seek permission from the family. Be aware that LAC will send copies of the records only to the address of the next-of-kin.

Where Should You Start?

Spend some time researching the Great Depression (1929–39) and the Spanish Civil War (1936–39). The Great Depression had a worldwide impact. Jobs were scarce, governments withdrew money from the economy, high tariffs restricted international trade, and farmers watched helplessly as drought and winds destroyed their farms. Men moved across the country looking for employment, living in shantytowns, and seeking social justice. Many joined the trade union movement or any one of a variety of socialist organizations offering protection and support for the average worker. In Canada the Relief Camp Workers Union, Canadian Labour Defence League, Cooperative Commonwealth Federation, and the Communist Party of Canada were only a few of those organizations. Read about Tim Buck, J.S. Woodsworth, and Prime Minister R.B Bennett.

In 1936, civil war broke out in Spain. The monarchy had abdicated and elections were held but the eventual result was civil war between the Republican Party, which wanted social change, and the Nationalist Party (Fascist). The Fascist governments of Mussolini and Hitler (in Italy and Germany) sent troops to support the Nationalists while the Soviet Union under Stalin organized International Brigades for the Republicans. Approximately 1,600 Canadians volunteered to fight in Spain with the International (anti-fascist) Brigades, eventually forming the Mackenzie-Papineau Battalion. By the end of the civil war almost 400 had been killed or were missing in action. The Spanish Civil War ended with the victory of Francesco Franco's Nationalist Party. Many historians believe that the Spanish Civil War was a prelude to the Second World War. *Renegades*, by Michael Petrou, gives an almost complete list of the Canadians who fought in Spain with their home, ethnicity, date of birth, occupation, and final status.

As well as the usual sources of information you'll want to check RCMP files. The Government of Canada did not support the volunteers who served with the Mackenzie-Papineau Battalion, and even enacted legislation to hinder recruitment. Public support for the volunteers made the government ultimately soften its stand. Probably one of the greatest Canadian figures associated with the Spanish Civil War is Dr. Norman Bethune. He raised money for mobile medical facilities, served in Spain, and eventually died supporting the Chinese Communists during their own civil war in 1946. The Chinese erected a monument to Bethune and still honour his commitment.

THE SECOND WORLD WAR

The Second World War formally started in September 1939 after Germany invaded Poland and refused to accede to the demands by France and England to return the invaded territories. England declared war and a week later Canada followed suit. Library shelves have kilometres of material for you to consult. Read about Adolf Hitler and the rise of National Socialism in Germany, and/or the failure of the League of Nations.

Suffice to say that by 1940 the Canadian 1st Division was in England and, if you're going to understand your ancestors' war, you'll need to know something about the army they joined.

The Army in Which They Served

The only significant change from the organization of the army in the First World War was that your ancestors owed their allegiance to a regiment rather than a battalion. Many of the post–First

World War battalions had been perpetuated by affiliation with a regiment. Thus William Stanley's 102nd battalion was perpetuated by the North British Columbia Regiment, the 73rd battalion by the Black Watch (Royal Highland Regiment) of Canada, and the 78th battalion by the Winnipeg Grenadiers. Corps troops (artillery, engineers, ordinance, medical, service, signals, dental, forestry, provost, postal, pay, and chaplain), maintained their basic designation often having a variety of descriptive terms applied to specify their specialty. Artillery could be field, medium, heavy, or rocket; the service corps could be army transport, motor ambulance, tank transporter, or motor ambulance and the medical corps — casualty clearing, general hospital, or convalescent depot.

Your ancestor's regiment was composed of almost 900 men and officers. Each regiment had four rifle companies, consisting of three platoons. Each platoon was normally divided into three sections of ten men led by a corporal. The military referred to the four rifle companies as Able, Baker, Charlie, and Dog and their sole purpose was to be a strike force. In addition to the rifle companies, the regiment had support and headquarters units. Each of these contained various specifically trained companies of men expected to support the fighting units. Finally, there was battalion headquarters, which was the directing force during a battle.

The Canadian Army that fought in northwest Europe looked approximately like this:

- Army group — 600,000 men, under command of a field marshal
- Army — 150,000 men, under command of a general
- Corps — 60,000 men, under command of a lieutenant-general

- Division — 15–18,000 men, under command of a major-general
- Brigade — 3,500 men, under command of a brigadier
- Regiment — 850 men, under command of a lieutenant-colonel
- Company — 130 men, under command of a major
- Platoon — 37 men, under command of a lieutenant
- Section — 10 men, under command of a corporal

There were approximately sixty-four regiments of infantry each designated as armour, machine gun, infantry, light anti-aircraft, reconnaissance, or headquarters defence. Each was assigned to either the 1st or 2nd armoured brigade or 1st, 2nd, 3rd infantry division or 4th or 5th armoured division. Each infantry division had approximately 18,000 personnel.

For example, if your ancestor served in the 1st Canadian Infantry Division in March 1945 he or she would have recognized the following organizational structure:

Headquarters
1st Canadian Infantry Division
(Defence platoon Lorne Scots, Intelligence Corps, Pay and Chaplain Corps)
(Provost Corps, Corps of Signals, Postal Corps)
Canadian Armoured Corps: 4th Princess Louise Dragoon Guards
Canadian Infantry Corps: The Saskatoon Light Infantry (m.g.)
Attached Headquarters for each of: Artillery, Engineers, Service, Electrical/Mechanical, Medical and Ordinance Corps
Canadian Infantry Corps

1st Infantry Brigade
> The Royal Canadian Regiment
> The Hastings and Prince Edward Regiment
> 48th Highlanders of Canada

2nd Infantry Brigade
> Princess Patricia Canadian Light Infantry
> The Seaforth Highlanders of Canada
> The Loyal Edmonton Regiment

3rd Infantry Brigade
> Royal 22nd Regiment
> The Carlton and York Regiment
> The West Nova Scotia Regiment

As in the First World War, the members of each division wore a distinctive coloured patch on the shoulder to help identify the unit to which they belonged. The 1st Infantry Division wore a red one, the 2nd Division blue, and the 3rd grey. The 4th Canadian Armoured Division's patch was green and the 5th Armoured wore red/maroon. If you discover your ancestor's uniform you can identify the division to which he or she belonged, because the name would be worn just above the divisional patch and, of course, any rank or skill at arms badges. Once you've done that it is an easy matter to research the engagements they were been involved in.

Upon joining the army, your ancestor was assigned a regimental number and sworn in as part of the Canadian Active Service Force (C.A.S.F.). Originally, officers were not assigned a regimental number but this changed in 1945. The numbers were assigned by corps (service, medical, engineers, postal, chaplain, etc.) or regiment (Hastings Prince Edward Regiment,

To Help With Your Research

Second Canadian Division, along with support corps, included the following regiments:

> the Lorne Scots (platoon), 14th Canadian Hussars (armoured), the Toronto Scottish (machine gun), (4th Brigade) Royal Regiment of Canada, Royal Hamilton Light Infantry, Essex Scottish, (5th Brigade) Regiment de Maisonneuve, Black Watch (Royal Highland Regiment of Canada), Calgary Highlanders, (6th Brigade) Les Fusiliers Mont Royal, Queen's Own Cameron Highlanders, and South Saskatchewan Regiment.

3rd Canadian Division, along with support corps, included:

> the Lorne Scots (platoon); 17th Duke of York's Royal Canadian Hussars (armoured); Cameron Highlanders of Ottawa (machinegun); (7th Brigade) Royal Winnipeg Rifles; Regina Rifle Regiment; Canadian Scottish Regiment; (8th Brigade) Queen's Own Rifles; Regiment de Chaudiere; North Shore (New Brunswick) Regiment; (9th Brigade) Highland Light Infantry; Stormont, Dundas, and Glengarry Highlanders; North Nova Scotia Highlanders.

Near the end of the war Britain asked Canada to supply more armoured divisions with supporting infantry brigades. By 1945 your ancestor may have served with one of:

4th Canadian Armoured Division, with supporting corps: Lorne Scots (platoon), South Alberta Regiment (armoured reconnaissance), Elgin Regiment (armoured delivery), New Brunswick Regiment (machine-gun company), (10th Brigade) Lincoln and Welland Regiment, Algonquin Regiment, Argyll and Sutherland Highlanders, (4th Armoured Brigade) Governor General's Foot Guards, Canadian Grenadier Guards, British Columbia Regiment, Lake Superior Regiment (motor, infantry corps).

5th Canadian Armoured Division, with supporting corps: Lorne Scots (platoon), Governor General's Horse Guards (armoured reconnaissance), Princess Louise's Fusiliers (machine-gun company), (11th Brigade) Perth Regiment, Cape Breton Highlanders, Irish Regiment of Canada (5th Armoured Brigade), Lord Strathcona's Horse, Royal Canadians, 8th Princess Louisa's New Brunswick Hussars, British Columbia Dragoons, Westminster Regiment (motor, infantry corps).

As well as these armoured divisions, two independent armoured brigades were created: 1st Armoured Brigade: Ontario Regiment, Three Rivers Regiment and Calgary Regiment.

2nd Armoured Brigade: 1st Hussars Regiment, the Fort Garry Horse, and Sherbrooke Fusiliers Regiment. Each of these independent armoured brigades had support corps.[1]

Essex Scottish Regiment, Sherbrooke Fusiliers, etc.) with blocks
of numbers assigned to the various militia districts. Your Second
World War ancestor was also issued with two identity disks that
included name, branch of service, religion and regimental number and CDN for Canada or, in the case of officers, rank. In
the event of death, one disk remained with the soldier and the
other was collected for recording. One disk was suspended from
a neck cord and the second was suspended from the original.
This wasn't much different from your ancestor's First World War
identity disk, with the exception of a revised list of religions.

If you know your ancestor's regimental number, where he or
she enlisted and the design of the identity disk, consult Clive Law,
Regimental Numbers of the Canadian Army 1936–1960 (Ottawa:
Service Publications, 2010).

These are some of key figures who had some responsibil-
ity for the life and death of your family member: General Harry
Crerar, General Andrew McNaughton, Major-General Chris Vokes,
Lieutenant-General Guy Simonds, and Major-General J. Roberts.
The politicians who had to finance the war and handle the situation
on the home front include: Prime Minister William Lyon Mackenzie
King, Minister of Militia and Defence J.L. Ralston, and C.D. Howe.

What Medals Would They Have Won?

You might expect to find any one of the following medals. The
ones I have listed are the most common. Bravery medals were
different — not necessarily in shape, size, or uniqueness of ribbon
— but because they had limited distribution. You may also discover a medal bar. Instead of wearing a full set of medals, veterans
could wear this bar just above the left pocket. The bar would display a section of the ribbon, about one centimetre high and three

centimetres wide. The length of the bar depends on the number of medals a recipient received. Veterans of the First World War who saw service in the Second, wore the ribbons of their First World War medals on the left of the bar followed by the ribbons of any Second World War medals they were issued. All medals are worn in a specific order and it is important to know this if you decided to frame them for display. The order is:

1. 1939–45 Star
2. Atlantic Star
3. Air Crew Europe Star
4. Africa Star
5. Pacific Star
6. Burma Star
7. Italy Star
8. France and Germany Star
9. Defence Medal
10. Canadian Volunteer Service Medal
11. War Medal 1939–45.

Gallantry medals were to be worn to the right of other stars or medals and thus farthest from the left shoulder of the wearer. These are the basic medals awarded:

- Canadian Volunteer Service Medal was granted to anyone of any rank who had volunteered for active service. The troops often referred to it as the "spam medal" because it "came up with the rations."
- 39–45 Star was awarded to air crew after two months and army/navy personnel after six months on active operations.

- France and Germany Star was granted for service in France, Holland, Belgium, or Germany for anyone serving after 6 June 1944.
- Italy Star was earned for service in Sicily and Italy between 3 September 1943 and 8 May 1945.
- Africa Star was awarded for service in North Africa between 10 June 1940 and 12 May 1943.
- Defence Medal was granted for six months service in England between 10 September 1939 and 8 May 1945.
- Atlantic Star could be earned by air crew who served for two months and naval personnel who served afloat for six months, between 3 September 1939 and 8 May 1945 in the European theatre and 3 September 1939 and 2 September 1945.

These are the most common set of Canadian Second World War medals and are shown in correct order of display. They were issued with a medal bar that displayed only a one centimetre by three centimetre piece of medal ribbon. Recipients were expected to wear the medal bar on their battle dress just above the left chest pocket. Author's collection.

- Pacific Star was earned for operational service in the Pacific between 8 December 1941 and 2 September 1945.
- Air Crew Europe Star was granted for two months flying from Britain over Europe from 3 September 1939 to 5 June 1944.
- War Medal (1939–45) was awarded to armed forces personnel and merchant marines after serving 28 days between 3 September 1939 and 2 September 1945.

Each of these medals has a unique ribbon that should help you to identify which medals your ancestors earned if you only have a ribbon bar. The only clasps awarded were a Dieppe clasp (instituted 1994) for those involved in Operation Jubilee in 1942; a bar with a small maple leaf awarded for volunteering for overseas service, both attached to the Canadian Volunteer Service Medal (CVSM); and, eventually, a Hong Kong bar for those involved in the Battle of Hong Kong. If your ancestor was "Mentioned in Dispatches" for some conspicuous action, he or she was entitled to wear an Oak Leaf on the War Medal (WM). Should a family member have paid the ultimate sacrifice the family was issued a Memorial Cross with the name, rank, serial number, and branch of service engraved on the back.

Where Did Your Ancestor Fight?

- Hong Kong, 18–25 December 1941. Two Canadian Battalions, the Winnipeg Rifles and Royal Rifles of Canada, were annihilated while defending the island against Japanese troops.

Twenty-three officers and 267 other ranks were killed or died of wounds while twenty-eight officers and 465 other ranks were reported wounded. The Japanese committed acts of brutality, often murdering wounded prisoners. Of the 1,975 Canadians who served in Hong Kong, 557 did not return. In 1943, 1,183 prisoners were taken to Japan and forced to work in the mines. The conditions that our soldiers faced in the camps were particularly atrocious: disease, lack of food, random beatings by the guards, and forced labour. If one of your ancestors served there and was taken prisoner read some of their diaries and research the "Kamloops Kid." You'll discover that Britain sent our troops to Hong Kong knowing that the island and territory could not be defended from the land side. All the major guns (artillery) faced the sea and could not be brought to bear on the Kowloon side of the island, where the Japanese attacked from. As well, the major British naval vessels, formerly stationed in Hong Kong, had been ordered to sea.[2]

To learn more about the Battle of Hong Kong, read N.M. Greenfield, *The Damned: The Canadians At the Battle of Hong Kong and the POW Experience, 1941–1945* (Toronto: HarperCollins, 2010).

- Dieppe: Operation Jubilee, 19 August 1942. This was the first engagement of the Canadian Army in Europe and is considered another planning disaster. It was supposed to be a "raid in strength" to test enemy defences, capture a limited objective, and then withdraw to waiting transport craft. However, lack of naval bombardment, not enough air force involvement, poor intelligence or refusal to believe what was shown on photographic missions, the selection of a site totally unacceptable for the use of tanks, and a seawall that prevented our 4,963 men from entering Dieppe. Of these, 907 were killed, 584 wounded, and 1,874 spent the rest of the war as prisoners. Canadian Major-General Roberts became the scapegoat for the raid when it was obviously the fault of the key planners. Even British General Bernard Montgomery refused to have any part in the organization of the attack on Dieppe. If you're interested in reading more about Dieppe, check out the role played by Lord Louis Mountbatten. The Canadian Second Division fought at Dieppe and with corps troops of the RCA (artillery), RCE (engineers), RCCofS (signals), RCASC (service), RCAMC (medical), RCAOC (ordinance), C. Prov. Corps (provost), and the following regiments:

4th Infantry Brigade
Royal Regiment of Canada
Royal Hamilton Light Infantry
Essex Scottish

5th Infantry Brigade
Black Watch of Canada
Regiment de Maisonneuve
Calgary Highlanders

6th Infantry Brigade
Fusiliers Mont Royal
Cameron Highlanders of Canada
South Saskatchewan Regiment

The 14th Army Tank Regiment, the Calgary
Regiment, was also involved.[3]

- Invasion of Sicily, Operation Husky, 10 July–
  17 August 1943 and the War in Italy, 3–4
  September until the end of the campaign 2 May
  1945. Operation Husky involved the Canadian
  First Division (names of the regiments are on
  page 189). There are a number of excellent
  books about the fighting in Sicily and Italy
  but one that will give you a feel for what our
  troops faced is Farley Mowat's *And No Birds
  Sang.* Mowat was a lieutenant with the Hastings
  Prince Edward Regiment and was involved
  in some of the major actions of this campaign.
  The first division suffered 2,227 casualties during the invasion of Sicily and eventually the 5th
  Canadian Armoured Division (15,000 troops),
  1st Canadian Corps (8,500 troops), and General
  Headquarters and line of Communication
  troops (3,700) were sent to Italy. If your ancestors
  served in Sicily and Italy, research the following
  major engagements: Moro River and Ortona
  where there were 2,605 casualties; the Liri Valley
  (3,713 casualties); the taking of the Gothic Line
  and Battle of the Remini Line with 4,511 losses;
  and the advance from the Montone to the Senio

where we suffered another 2,581 casualties. All told, we sent 92,757 personnel to Italy, which includes the 1,178 Canadians who served with the 1st Special Service Battalion. The Battalion was a joint U.S.-Canadian effort commonly referred to as the Devil's Brigade. The Brigade trained in Montana, wore American uniforms, and saw action at Anzio and northwest Europe. A film starring William Holden was made about the brigade.

Of all the Canadians who fought in Italy, almost 25 percent were casualties: 408 officers and 4,991 men killed; 1,218 officers and 18,268 men wounded; and 62 officers and 942 men taken prisoner. Approximately 365 Canadians died of other causes. Eventually men from the First Division were withdrawn from Italy and sent to northwest Europe as part of the D-Day invasion. The Canadians who remained in Italy to complete the job were often referred to as "D-Day dodgers."[4]

• D-Day, 6 June 1944 (Operation Overlord) to the surrender of Germany, 8 May 1945. We've all seen the images of the allied army arriving on the beaches of Normandy, France, on that morning in June. Of the ninety divisions available to General Eisenhower only five were Canadian with a total personnel establishment, by the end of the war, of 170,000. Canada eventually had 237,000 men and women serving in northwest Europe by the end of hostilities. Once we had cleared the beaches of Normandy, code named

Juno, our job was to swing left and north freeing the important ports of France and then driving the Germans out of Holland. The fighting was not easy. During its ten months of operation First Canadian Army, under the command of Lieutenant-General Crerar, faced almost sixty divisions of the German forces — some of the most fanatical, best-trained troops available to the enemy. Over 11,000 Canadian soldiers fell in action on the beaches of Normandy (6 June to 31 July); during the action at Caen and the Bourguebus Bridges (1–23 July); at the battle of the Falaise Pocket (1–23 August 1944); during the clearing of the coastal belt and the ports (September 1944); at the battle of the Scheldt (September–November 1944); and during the battles of the Rhineland (8 February–10 March 1945) and the Rhine Crossing (23 March–22 April 1945). They rest in graves in France and Holland. If your ancestor has a France and Germany Star or an Air Crew Europe Star in his possession, he was part of the Canadian Army that fought some of these battles or was a member of the lines of communication troops that supported the men at the front. To really get a flavour of their experiences, read some of excellent biographies written by the men and women who "put boots to the ground" and actually faced the horrors of war.[5] Start with your ancestor, if you can.

I Have a Photo of My Ancestor. How Do I Know If It's from the Second World War?

Second World War battledress changed considerably from the First World War. The "08" pattern webbing worn in 1916 was replaced

Waiting for the artillery barrage to lift somewhere in Normandy. Photograph depicts a typical Canadian Second World War uniform. PA163403.

with "36" pattern webbing. The latter had a narrower belt as well as narrower straps. It also had a different means of attaching the large or small packs in which soldiers carried their personal items. The battle jacket was waist-length instead of mid-thigh. Rank, trade, and skill-at-arms badges hadn't changed that much from the previous war except there were many more of them. Eventually the military authorities replaced all the trade badges with a simple letter *T* with or without a wreath to indicate that the soldier had specific training. When recruiting became a problem any serviceman who volunteered for overseas service wore what became known as a "mars" badge. This badge was similar to the medical symbol for male and was worn with a small GS badge. The conscription issue again divided the country and was only settled when the government of Mackenzie King held a plebiscite. The vote accepted conscription but King agreed that men conscripted would not have to serve in northwest Europe unless they volunteered. During training a great deal of pressure was put on conscriptees to agree to serve overseas. Part of this pressure was to refer to them in the newspapers and generally in public as "zombies." Needless to say, the men who were already fighting in Europe and who had volunteered for overseas service when they originally enlisted were not happy about the whole conscription issue or the conscripted recruits. There certainly was a lack of trust when these men reluctantly appeared as reinforcements in active regiments.

You may also discover a hat badge with your ancestor's medals or uniform. Second World War hat badges are unique to the particular regiment in which your ancestor served. If your ancestor kept his regimental hat badge you have an excellent means of identifying which brigade or division he belonged to. Knowing this allows you to identify where the regiment served using regimental war diaries and museums. When you acquire your ancestor's service record, check the date of enlistment and compare it to the dates in regimental histories to ascertain where he might have served. Don't forget that if he served in specific theatres he should also have the appropriate medal(s). If the family has lost or misplaced medals, you can apply for replacements, providing you can prove a relationship.

What Can I Expect to Find in My Ancestor's Records?

The military had its own set of abbreviations and general reference terms. These can sometimes be confusing to anyone unfamiliar with the military mind. To start, there are the general categories used by the three branches of service to define a recruit's military fitness.

Army

A.	General Service.
B1.	Service Abroad (not G.S.)
B2.	Service Abroad (not G.S.)
C1.	Home Service (Canada only)
C2.	Home Service (Canada only)
D.	Temporarily Unfit
E.	Unfit for A,B,C,

Navy

A.	General Service
D.	Temporarily Unfit
E.	Unfit for category A

RCAF

A1B.	Fit for full flying and ground duties anywhere and under any conditions
A1HBH.	Fit for full flying and ground duties in Canada

A2B.	Fit for limited flying duties and all ground duties in Canada
A3B.	Air Crew (other than pilot) fit for their full flying duties and full ground duties anywhere and under any conditions
A3HBH.	Ditto but Canada only
A4B.	Fit for passenger flying and full ground duties anywhere and under any conditions
A4HBH.	Ditto but Canada only
ATB.	Unfit for flying temporarily but fit for full ground duties anywhere
ATBH.	Ditto but only in Canada
ATBT.	Temporarily unfit for any form of duty
APB.	Permanently unfit for flying, fit for ground duties anywhere
APBH.	Ditto but only in Canada
APBT.	Permanently unfit for flying, temporarily unfit for ground duties
APBP.	Unfit for any form of duty.[6]

When you acquire the records expect the following forms:

- Attestation Papers — these contain vital statistics concerning the volunteer: regimental number, physical description, address of next of kin, general health, and signed agreement to serve.
- War Service File — this is really a statement of service. The file contains qualifications of individual, record of promotions, reductions, transfers, casualties, reports from "date taken on strength of field force."

- Discharge Certificate — includes vital statistics, date of enlistment, medals awarded and any marks or scars.
- Service Gratuities Certificate — provides more detailed information about service.
- Occupational History Form — this form requests details of work experience and asks volunteer if employer has promised employment following war service.
- Department of National Defence Summary of Enlisted Personnel — another personal history.
- D.N.D. Statement of War Service Gratuity — here you'll find the amount of the gratuity paid to the returning serviceman/woman. There were options available other than cash.
- Medical History of Invalid — this is a medical board review that reports on any disabilities reported during basic training.
- Proceedings of Discharge — includes medal card, medical and dental reports, pay settlement.

You'll also discover that Second World War records contain more details than First World War files. At the end of the First World War soldiers returned to Canada, were thanked by their local politicians, and then sent home. There was no gratuity for war service and very little support for those who were mentally or physically damaged by their war experience. Ex-soldiers often met during reunions and the Great War Serviceman's Association was soon formed, eventually becoming the Legion we know today. When the Second World War ended many of the elected representatives serving in Parliament had served in the First World War. They insisted that returning service personnel would receive some support from a "grateful government." Thus, your ancestor had the option of receiving a one-time cash gratuity, a low interest mortgage on one of the houses built specifically for returning veterans, or subsidies to return to university and complete their education. Leonard Cox's file shows that he accepted the one-time cash gratuity.

The service records confirmed that Leonard Cox was entitled to the Italy Star, France and Germany Star, War Medal, and Canadian Volunteer Service Medal for War Service. They also confirmed that he had successfully passed basic training but was rated as B1 because a medical board discovered that he had a problem with his feet that made it difficult for him to march any distance. He was transferred to the Canadian Army Service Corps, trained as a truck driver, and sent to England. In July 1943 he was part of operation Husky, the invasion of Sicily. Following the invasion of France, Len was transferred to support the invasion of northwest Europe and ended his war with the liberation of Holland. Not mentioned in the records is what he told family and friends about his wartime experiences. Unfortunately, he never wrote anything about the years he spent in Italy and Europe, and family members have only a few recollections: ships blowing up during the arrival off the coast of Sicily, the terrible conditions in Italy, seeing the starvation in Holland after the Germans departed, and how much he liked the Dutch people.

Personal letters will give you some insight into the attitudes your ancestor had about what he or she was doing in a faraway land, fighting a war from which they may not return. The letters of Flying Officer Cox show that he slowly became convinced that he may have not made the right choice joining, that he may not see his home again, and that he felt the people in England didn't really appreciate what the Canadians were doing for them. Enlisted men's letters were censored so you may not find such sentiments expressed in their notes home.

My Ancestor Was a Prisoner of War

In 1929 the Geneva Convention redefined some of the rules governing the treatment of prisoners of war. It was clearly stated that the "detaining powers" were responsible for rations, clothing, living arrangements, and other necessities at least equal to the garrison troop guards. The sections dealing with work, relief operations, punishment, and repatriation were all expanded. Neither Japan nor Russia signed the agreement. Their refusal to accept the rules of the Convention had considerable impact on our troops held in Japanese prison camps and Russian prisoners held by Germany.

If your ancestor spent time in a German, Italian or Japanese camp, there are a number of important details you can include in your family narrative. For instance, in the European theatre of war 7,088 members of the Canadian Army, 2,482 aircrew, and ninety-two naval personnel were captured. In the Pacific theatre 1,689 army, forty-two aircrew, and two naval servicemen spent time in POW camps. Of these numbers 380 Canadians in European camps and 290 in the Pacific theatre camps died of injury, disease, wounds, or were killed by the enemy. Their names are on the Commonwealth War Graves website.

Our country suffered two major wartime shocks: first in December 1941 when Hong Kong fell and 1,689 Canadian soldiers were captured, and again in August 1942 during the ill-conceived Dieppe raid when 1,948 of our soldiers marched into captivity. If your ancestor was captured at Dieppe, somewhere in his records or personal effects will probably be mention of Stalag VIIIB (Lamsdorf, enlisted men) or Stalag VIIB (Eichstatt, officers). These were the two camps that held prisoners from that raid. The Germans established a variety of camps, each with a specific responsibility. You may discover reference or abbreviations in your family records for anyone of the following:

Dulag or Durchgangslager — a transit camp to process prisoners

Ilag/Jlag or Internierungslager — for civilian detainees

Marlag or Marine-Lager — naval personnel POW camp

Milag or Marine-Internierten-Lager — held merchant seamen

Oflag or Offizier-Lager — officer's camp

Stalag Luft or Luftwaffe-Stammlager — for aircrew personnel

Stalag or Stammlager — a base camp for enlisted men

Japanese and Italian camps were organized differently. If your ancestor was a prisoner in a Japanese camp he was treated very harshly — worked very hard with very little food to eat. Canadians captured at Hong Kong were at first held in North Point Camp on the Island of Hong Kong and later at Sham Shui Po Camp on the Kowloon mainland. Officers were held at Argyle Street Camp. Later in the war the Canadian prisoners were sent to six camps in Japan: Omine, Oeyama, Narumi, Yoshima, Tsurumi, and Niigata-Rinko. Following the war many of the Japanese camp commanders and guards were tried for war crimes. On 1 September 1947, the Supreme Command for the Allied Powers Legal Section stated the following concerning the trial of one of the guards "… between 1943 and 1945 at Tokyo No. 3-D Camp, Yokohama, Honshu, Japan; Tokyo POW Branch Camp No. 5-B Niigta, Honshu, Japan, and Tokyo POW Branch Camp No. 16,

Kanose, Niigata, Honshu, Japan. American, British and Canadian Prisoners of War were interned at these Camps. There were numerous instances of brutal treatment of prisoners by [*name of guard*]. The death rate of Canadian Prisoners at Camp No. 5-B at Niigata was nearly thirty percent …"[7]

When you visit LAC you will discover a significant number of records related to prisoners of war. The government had learned a lesson from the First World War and in some sense was slightly better prepared to deal with the treatment of Canadian service personnel held by enemy belligerents. Four major committees were established: the Red Cross Enquiry Board, the Department of National Defence Director of Internment Operations, the National War Services POW Next of Kin Division, and the Committee for the Protection and Welfare of Canadian Prisoners of War in Enemy Hands. As well as these government agencies, there were at least three other major private organizations involved: the Canadian Red Cross, the War Prisoners' Aid of the World's Committee of YMCAs, and the Canadian POW Relatives Association.

To further your knowledge about Canadians captured during the war, research the military trial of German 12th S.S. Commander Kurt Meyer for his part in the murder of Canadian troops during the Normandy invasions.

Good luck with your search for your Second World War ancestors. Incidentally, if you ever find a Victory Nickel among your ancestor's possessions, the one from 1942/43 that looks like it's made of copper, check the rim because the government stamped in Morse code: "we win when we work willingly." This was obviously a propaganda effort at a period in the war when things weren't going too well. Also, check your ancestor's collection of memorabilia because you may find one of the folding service pocket knives issued to all navy and army personnel. Often they ended up in tool boxes.

SPANISH CIVIL WAR RESOURCES

LAC

- MG 10-K2, fonds 545, file list 1 — records, reports and lists of personnel wounded and repatriated, demobilization, proof of identity.
- MG 10-K2, fonds 545, file list 6 — rosters, including lists of wounded, killed in action, missing in action, troublemakers, deserters, and some short biographies. Here you'll find master lists of all members of the Mac-Paps and other Canadians who served in other units of the Spanish Republican Army. The originals are in Moscow.
- RG146 (CSIS)–(R929-0-4-E), Vol. 4183 — RCMP files from the 1930s that contain information related to individuals in the labour movement. Volume 4183 contains information about recruiting for the Spanish Army.

Websites

Wikipedia, *www.wikipedia.org/wiki/Mackenzie-Papineau_Battalion*, *www.wikipedia.org/wiki/Norman_Bethune*.
CBC Archives, *archives.cbc.ca*.

Books

Beeching, William. *Canadian Volunteers, Spain, 1936–1939.* Regina: Canadian Plains Research Centre, University of Regina, 1989.

Hoar, Victor. *Mackenzie-Papineau Battalion: Canadian Participation in the Spanish Civil War.* Toronto: Copp-Clark Publishing, 1969.

Peck, Biggar, Mary. *Red Moon Over Spain: Canadian Media Reaction to the Spanish Civil War, 1936–1939.* Ottawa: Steel Rail Publishing, 1988.

Petrou, Michael. *Renegades: Canadians in the Spanish Civil War.* Vancouver: UBC Press, 2008.

Zuehlke, Mark. *The Gallant Cause: Canadians in the Spanish Civil War, 1936–1939.* Vancouver: Whitecap Books, 1996.

SECOND WORLD WAR RESOURCES

LAC

RG 24 series C3, Canadian Army war diaries — reels T1847-T1882; T6668-T6698; T7071-T7114; T7599-T7620; T10528-T10664; T10869-T10900; T11021-T11078. The finding aid is 24-60.

RG 24 holds service files for the Second World War.

RG 24-C-25 holds casualty lists.

National Defence

Canadian Military Headquarters in London records are held in the Directorate of History and Heritage, reference DHH, document number 713,065, D1 and D2.

Websites

Besides the sites below, there are also interesting sites dedicated to the Axis powers (Germany, Italy, Japan, and their allies). Don't forget to use AMICUS to search for regimental/air force/navy museums and archives that can prove useful in adding interest to your research.

Air Force Association of Canada, *airforce.ca*.

Airborne Museum at Sainte-Mere-Eglise, Normandy, *www.musee-airborne.com*.

The Caen-Normandy Memorial Centre for History and Peace, *www.memorial-caen.fr*.

Canada's Juno Beach Memorial, *www.junobeach.org*.

Canadian Military Heritage Project, *www.rootsweb.ancestry.com/~canmil*.

Canadian War Museum, *www.cwm.ca*.

CBC Archives, *archives.cbc.ca/war*.

D-Day Ancestors Portal, *www.ddayancestors.com*.

D-Day Museum, Portsmouth, U.K., *www.ddaymuseum.co.uk*.

Department of National Defence, *www.dnd.ca*.

Imperial War Museum, *www.iwmcollections.org.uk*.

National Archives, U.K., *www.nationalarchives.gov.uk*.

The National D-Day Memorial Foundation (U.S.), *www.dday.org*.

Olive Tree Genealogy Gateway, *www.olivetreegenealogy.com/mil*.

Royal Canadian Legion, *www.legion.ca*.

Toronto Star, *pagesofthepast.ca*, and other newspapers online for obituaries.

Book of Remembrance, *www.veterans.gc.ca/remembers/sub.cfm?source=collections/books/7thbook*.

Veterans' Affairs: Canada Virtual War Memorial, *www.veterans.gc.ca/remembers/sub.cfm?source=collections/virtualmem*.

Commonwealth War Graves: Debt of Honour Register, *www.cwgc.org/debt_of_honour.asp*.

Books

Resource Guides and Historical Accounts

Bouchery, J. *The Canadian Soldier, From D-Day to VE-Day.* Histoire & Collections, translated from the French by Alan McKay, Paris France, circa 2001. Here you will discover a complete description of the "organisation, uniforms, insignia, equipment, armament, tanks and vehicles" of the Canadian Army during the Second World War.

Christie, N. *The Suicide Raid: The Canadians at Dieppe, August 19th 1942.* Nepean, ON: C.E.F. Books, 2001.

Ellison, K. *The Canadian Army's Hong Kong Story, 1941–1945.* Surrey, BC: British North America Philatelic Society, 2005.

Miller, J. *Forgotten Heroes: the Canadians at Dieppe.* Toronto: Methuen Press, 1975.

Nicholson, G.W.L. *The Canadians in Italy, 1943–1945.* Ottawa: R. Duhamel, 1966.

Oliver, L. *The Battle for Hong Kong, 1941–1945: Hostage to Fortune.* Montreal: McGill-Queen's University Press, 2006.

Roland, C. *Long Night's Journey into Day: Prisoners of War in Hong Kong and Japan, 1941–1945.* Waterloo, ON: Wilfred Laurier University Press, 2001.

Saunders, T. *The Dieppe Raid: 2nd Canadian Division.* Barnsley, South Yorkshire, U.K.: Pen & Sword Military, 2005.

Stacey, C. P. *Six Years of War: The Army in Canada, Britain and the Pacific,* Volume 1. Ottawa: Queen's Printers, 1966. This and the following two texts are the official histories of the Canadian Army in Second World War and a must read for any serious historian/researcher.

Nicholson, G.W.L. *The Canadians in Italy, 1943–1945,* Volume 2. Ottawa: R. Duhamel, 1966.

Stacey, C. P. *The Victory Campaign: The Operations in North-West Europe, 1944–1945*, Volume 3. Ottawa: Queen's Printers, Ottawa, 1966.

Veterans' Affairs. *Canadians in Hong Kong.* Ottawa:Veterans' Affairs Canada, Ottawa, 2005.

Personal Accounts

Harvey,J.,D. *Boys, Bombs and Brussels Sprouts.*Toronto: McClelland & Stewart, 1981.

Mowat, Farley. *And No Birds Sang.* Toronto: Key Porter, 2003.

POWS

LAC

- MG 10–D1 (R12087-0-8-E) — Canadian Prisoners of War in Germany 1942–1945. Four hundred files on persons whose family name started with D,L,R,W, or Z — files contain the name, place of birth, rank, religion, occupational background, names of parents, photographs, finger prints, and medical record (the archives have not yet identified the location of the other surnames).
- MG 30 (R2463-0-8-E) — fonds contain material (diaries, etc.) of Canadian prisoners of war in Germany and Japan.
- RG 18-F-3 (R196-154-1-E) finding aid 18-24 — lists enemy aliens and prisoners of war from

the U.K., German and Italian prisoners sent to Canada, and nominal rolls.

- RG 24-C-1 (1942-1946, R112-552-8-E) finding aid 24-8 — holds material on repatriation plans, escapes/shooting of escaped prisoners, shackling of POWs in Canada, the official reports on camp conditions in Europe, treatment of prisoners in the Far East, as well as the records of the Prisoner of War Associations.
- RG 24-D-1-b, finding aid 24-85 — contains information on the capture and detention of enemy subjects: Italian and German POWs.
- RG 25-A-3-b finding aid 25-5 — holds the report on repatriation of Canadian Prisoners of War.

Books

Allister, W. *Where Life and Death Hold Hands: The Long Road to Forgiveness.* Don Mills, ON: Stoddart, 1989.

Carter, D. *POW, Behind Canadian Barbed Wire: Alien, Refugee and Prisoner of War Camps in Canada, 1914–1946.* Elkwater, AB: Eagle Butte Press, 1998.

Chater, L.H.E. *Behind the Fence: Life as a POW in Japan, 1942–1945, the Diaries of Les Chater.* Transcribed and edited by Elizabeth Hamid. St. Catharines, ON: Vanwell Publishing, 2001.

Greenfield, N. M. *The Damned: The Canadians at the Battle of Hong Kong and the POW Experience, 1941–45.* Toronto: HarperCollins, 2010.

LeGrandeur, P. *We Flew, We Fell, We Lived: Stories from RCAF Prisoners of War and Evaders, 1939–1945.* St. Catharines, ON: Vanwell Publishing, 2006.

Prouse, A. R. *Ticket to Hell via Dieppe: From a Prisoner's Wartime Log, 1942–1945.* Toronto: Van Nostrand, Reinhold, 1982.

Lists of the Camps

Center for Research Allied POWs under the Japanese, *www. mansell.com/pow-index.html*, will provide you with the location of around 250 Japanese camps.

POW camp Stalag VII A, *www.moosburg.org/info/stalag/laglist. html*, German camps giving camp number, military district, place name, and period the camp was open.

Wikipedia, *en.wikipedia.org/wiki/List_of_POW_camps_in_Italy*, approximately eighty Italian camps listed.

Wikipedia, *en.wikipedia.org/wiki/Wifi/List_of_POW_camps_in_ Japan.*

Lists of Names and Prisoner Narratives

All-Japan POW Camp Group History, *www.home.comcast.net/ ~winjerd/CmpGroup.htm*, an American site, contains an excellent description of the types of Japanese camps.

CBC Archives, *archives.cbc.ca*, search keywords "Prisoners of War."

Children of Far East Prisoners of War, *www.cofepow.org.uk*.

Hong Kong Veterans Commemorative Association, *www.cforce. hkvca.ca*, a list of casualties following the capture of Hong Kong.

For a list of this regiment's POWs taken at Dieppe, *cap.estevan. sk.ca/SSR/documents/pows.html*.

For a list of killed and captured during the Dieppe Raid, *cap. estevan.sk.ca/SSR/Casualty/notes.html*.

International Committee of the Red Cross, *www.icrc.org/eng*, resource centre, the ICRC Archives Information Sources, and request for personnel data.

Prisoner of War and Internment Camp lists by country, *en.wikipedia. org/wiki/list_of_concentration_and_internment camps.*

Loyal Edmonton Regiment Museum, *www.lermuseum.org/ler/mh/ wwii/pows.html.*

Royal Air Force Ex-POW Association, *www.rafinfo.org.uk/rafexpow.*

Royal Hamilton Light Infantry Regiment, *www.rhli.ca/dieppe/ dieppemain.html*, a list of POWs.

U.K. National Ex-Prisoner of War Association, *prisonerofwar.org.uk.*

CHAPTER SEVEN

Women in the Military: Great-Grandma Has a Set of Medals! I Didn't Know She Served

On 20 February 2000, a plaque was unveiled at the Canadian Forces Base Esquimalt, British Columbia, dedicated to the significant role played by the Canadian Women's Army Corps during the Second World War. In part it states: "The Corps contributed to the Allied victory, paved the way for future generations of Canadian service women, and raised questions about the equality of women in the civilian world."[1] The plaque is a small reminder of the significant role played by women in the military throughout the centuries.

When researching your female ancestors you may be surprised to discover that you have a heroine who challenged the hardships of colonial life, an ancestor who appears on a regimental "married" muster role, someone who became a nurse and served during the North-West Rebellions (1885) or Boer War (1899), accompanied the Yukon Field Force to Dawson (1899), or served during the First World War as a driver or mechanic with the Royal Flying Corps. You may discover a female ancestor who joined the Canadian Women's Army Corps (CWAC), Women's Auxiliary Air Force (WAAF), or Women's Royal Canadian Naval Service (WRNS) during the Second World War. It is also possible that one of your female relatives stepped forward and supported the war effort by learning a trade that was usually reserved for men or worked as a volunteer in one of the many organizations that supported the men at the front.

Women of the Navy, Army, and Air Force Women's Corps. An excellent example of the uniforms worn by each branch of the service. PA 208583.

If your relative served, her documentation will be on file at Library and Archives Canada under the same Record Group or Manuscript Group as her male counterparts. You can find information on your female ancestors at the same sites you used for any male ancestors: LAC, Veterans' Affairs, the Commonwealth War Graves Commission, the Canadian War Museum, and your provincial archives and local libraries. As well, your female ancestor may be entitled to medals.

WHERE TO BEGIN?

What do you need to know about your female military ancestors? You should start your search with a study of some of the Canadian heroines who played some kind of military role in our history.

Begin with Madeleine de Verchères who, in 1695, saved her family from an Iroquois attack by taking command of the fort on her father's seigneury and organizing the defences. Her bravery saved the inhabitants from certain death.

Flora MacDonald originally settled in North Carolina with her husband, Allan. On 18 February 1776 she mounted a horse and rode up and down the ranks urging the men to defend their homes against the rebel troops. The couple eventually came to Canada as Loyalists.

Of course, there's the story of Laura Secord and her part in the defeat of the American forces at the battle of Beaver Dams in the War of 1812.

In 1863, FitzGibbon wrote a letter in support of Laura Secord's brave actions:

> I do hereby certify that Mrs. Secord, wife of
> James Secord, of Chippewa, Esq., did, in the

month of June 1813, walk from her house, near the village of St. David's, to De Cou's house in Thorold by a circuitous route of about twenty miles, partly through the woods, to acquaint me that the enemy intended to attempt, by surprise, to capture a detachment of the 49th Regiment, then under my command, she having obtained such knowledge from good authority, as the event proved. Mrs. Secord was a person of slight and delicate frame, and made the effort in weather excessively warm, and I dreaded at the time that she must suffer in health in consequence of fatigue and anxiety, she having been exposed to danger from the enemy, through whose lines of communication she had to pass. The attempt was made on my detachment by the enemy; and his detachment, consisting of upwards of 500 men and a field-piece and 50 dragoons were captured in consequence.

I write this certificate in a moment of much hurry and from memory, and it is therefore thus brief.

(Signed) James FitzGibbon,
Formerly Lieutenant,
49th Regiment.[2]

Even if you don't discover any connection to some of the significant female heroines of Canadian history, you should still be aware that your female ancestors who settled in British North America faced some serious challenges during periods of military instability. I've already mentioned that women like

Susanna Moodie were often left on the family bush farm while their husbands served with the militia during the rebellions of 1837 or the Fenian Raids of 1860. Some of them even may have picked up a musket and defended their farms against enemy forces. The only way you'll ever know about these challenges may be through family stories, such as the one in my wife's Teal family that records how during the Fenian Raids the mother took the children to hide in the woods while the husband put a cooking pot on his head, picked up his rifle, and managed to keep the Fenians away from the family farm.

If you have traced your family history back to one of the British regiments that served in this country, from the Conquest of New France through to the final withdrawal of their Regiments in 1870–71, you will have learned about the hardships married women faced as their husbands prepared to depart England. Being married to a man who served in a British regiment was not an easy life. Soldiers were expected to seek permission from their commanding officer before considering marriage. They had to have had earned the requisite rank and good conduct record and the woman had to be "morally unimpeachable." Even if everything was acceptable to the commanding officer there was still a chance that there may not be a vacancy on the "married roll." Only about 6 percent of the men in a regiment were allowed to marry and have their families carried "on strength." If a soldier elected to marry without permission, his wife and family were considered "off the strength" and not allowed to sleep in barracks or earn extra money by cooking, cleaning, or doing laundry for the officers and men of the regiment. Most importantly they were not allowed to travel abroad with the regiment when it was posted overseas. This could mean destitution for your ancestors.

Military authorities did not want the added imposition of caring for wives and children so standing orders often stated: "It cannot be too often repeated to the men that they are on no account to marry without leave and their marriage must at all times be discouraged as much as possible."[3] Officers' wives were exempt from these restrictions and were quite at liberty to follow their husbands on overseas postings. Of course they were expected to pay for their own passage, food, and other necessities.

When a regiment was sent abroad, selecting which wives went was done by ballot. As the regimental band played and the men were marched on board ship, the wives were given the chance to draw from a hat or ballot box, usually placed on a drumhead. The choice was simple: "to go" or "not to go." Selecting a "not to go" ballot often meant the parish workhouse for the soldier's family. Finally, in 1818 an act of Parliament was passed that required parishes to provide travelling expenses and food to soldiers' wives who were left behind and were (the parish hoped) going home to their parents. These women were issued with a pass certifying their identity.[4]

Even women who were allowed to accompany their husbands did not have an easy life. They and their children were given only a fraction of the food allowance provided for an enlisted man. If barrack space was available the best a married couple could expect was one bunk with only a blanket surrounding the bed for privacy. Children were expected to sleep on the floor underneath the bed. They would, of course, be surrounded by the other men of the regiment who shared the same living quarters. One can only imagine the conditions on board troop ships or when the regiment moved by land from one post to another.

On marches the women and children were delegated to the baggage train near the back of the column. Some commanders refused to allowed soldiers' families to ride on the wagons or be supported if they fell behind during the march. At all times the women were subjected to the same military discipline as their husbands. They were severely punished for anything that threatened the functioning of the regiment. Insubordination, immoral behaviour, slowing the progress of the regiment while on march, looting, robbery, excessive consumption of alcohol, or encouraging desertion could all result in being taken off strength and denied any of the privileges allowed to married couples by the regiment.

Usually the task of supervising the baggage train fell to the quartermaster but in some instances a regular line officer was assigned to the duty. In his journal, Lieutenant John Le Couteur, 104th Foot, recounts how he was assigned this task even though he felt it "a capacity below that of an officer."

> So instead of having to march, I took charge of all the women, children, sick, sorry, or lazy, besides all the heavy luggage of a strong Regiment on a permanent move. Never was I so pestered. "Mrs. Le C.," the officers' wives imploring, some commanding, "See to my luggage. Do place an awning to the bateaux. See to my children. See to the Baby." Now, let no one imagine it was a pleasant duty, tho, I had some very nice women in my boat....[5]

A discharged British soldier and his family could have elected to stay in Canada and accept a land grant as part of his service or they may have deserted the army and started a new life in a new land. After the battle of Plattsburg, during the War of 1812, a large percentage of British veterans, many of whom had seen extensive service in Europe, deserted the army and sought a new life in the United States. Thus, one of your female ancestors may have been part of a British regiment, followed her husband on his posting to British North America or even the Thirteen Colonies, elected to remain following the hostilities and started a new life in North America.

The Crimean War marked the last time families were allowed to accompany their husband's regiment overseas. Interestingly, it was during the same war and the horrors that the public read about in the English newspapers, that Florence Nightingale established the first nursing order. For many women, this was a logical and professional way of serving in the military.

What About Your Great Grandmother's Medals?

Canadian researchers need to begin by learning about the history of women in the armed forces. Many of us will discover that an ancestor was a nursing sister, simply because this was, historically, the first stepping stone to entering the Canadian military. Here's a useful timeline from LAC:

- 1885 — North-West Rebellions. Minister of Militia and Defence Adolphe Caron appointed Lieutenant-Colonel Darby Bergin as medical director-general and invited women across Canada to form Red Cross Societies. Eventually twelve women were employed as nurses under the direction of Loretta Miller.
- 1898 — the Yukon Field Force. No medical component was planned but four members of the Victorian Order of Nurses did accompany the unit: Georgina Powell, Margaret Payson, Rachel Hanna, and Amy Scott.

- 1901 — The Canadian government decided to create a permanent nursing service, with eight of the ten nurses who served in South Africa as the first official recruits. On 2 July 1904 the number was increased to twenty-five.

Nursing Sister Deborah Hurcomb, who served with the Canadian Contingent during the Boer War. PA 057334.

- 1899–1902 — South African/Boer War. Georgina Pope is placed in charge of the first Canadian military nurses sent overseas during the war. The first nurses left Canada on 30 October 1899 with the 2nd battalion, Royal Canadian Regiment: Minnie Afflick, Sarah Forbes, Fane Pope, and Elizabeth Russell. A second group sailed on 21 January 1900: Margaret Horne, Deborah Hurcomb, Margaret Macdonald, and Marcella Richardson. Militia Order No. 20, 25 January 1900, states that they were to be "accredited as Lieutenants with the pay and allowance of that rank." All nurses were provided with military uniforms. The third group of Canadian military nurses set sail on 28 January 1902: Sarah Forbes, Deborah Hurcomb, Margaret Macdonald, and Georgina Pope had already seen service in South Africa. Florence Cameron, Eleanor Fortescue, Amy Scott, and Margaret Smith were going for the first time. All were issued the Queen's and King's South African Medals and Georgina Pope was awarded the Royal Red Cross Medal for conspicuous service in the field.

- 1914–18 — First World War. Well over 2,800 women of the Royal Canadian Army Medical Corps serviced with the Canadian Forces overseas in field hospitals and on board hospital ships in combat zones and in various theatres of war. Many were with ambulance units. In total, 527 were employed in Canada while 1,901 went overseas. Of those, 313 served with British forces while others joined the American medical corps or Red Cross. Because of "manpower" shortages, the Royal Air Force employed almost 1,200 women as clerks and transport drivers. Eventually 750 women worked as mechanics for the RAF in Canada. During the war a number of women joined military-style organizations and trained in small arms, drill, first aid and vehicle maintenance just in case they are required as home guards. Veterans' Affairs has a list of the Canadian nurses who died during the war. You can view your ancestor's attestation papers online at LAC. Women who served with

A group of Canadian Nurses during the First World War. Canadian nursing sisters where given Officer's Commissions, something that often rankled their British nursing colleagues who were not granted the same honour. PA 008142.

rank were also issued the British War Medal and Victory Medal at the end of the war.

- 1939–45 — Second World War. Almost 5,000 women served as nurses with the army, navy, and air force medical corps during the war. They were also called to serve in factories, voluntary organizations, and the armed forces. The Canadian Women's Auxiliary Air Force (CWAAF) was formed July 1941 and renamed a short while later to the Royal Canadian Air Force (Women's Division). The Canadian Women's Army Corps (CWAC) was formed in August 1941 and the Women's Royal Canadian Naval Service (WRCNS) in July 1942. Eventually, 20,497 women served in the CWAC, 16,221 in the RCAF Women's Division, and 6,655 in the WRCNS. Almost 4,000 women from the various forces served in the United Kingdom, and in May 1944 a select group of CWACs was sent to combat areas in Italy and then in France and Germany. The National Selective Service Board was established in March 1942 and by September a registration of single or married women without children was initiated to fill the need for workers in industry. By 1944 over 1,000,000 women were working full-time as paid employees in industry. By 1943 the NSSB was recruiting married women with young children. The government also called on women to work in volunteer organizations.

In 1941 the National War Services set up a Women's Voluntary Service Division, which assumed responsibility for local Women's Voluntary Services Centres across the country. If your ancestor served with the Medical Corps or in any of the armed forces, she would have been entitled to the medals issued for service during the war.

You will soon come to realize that many of the events they voluntarily supported or joined in played a significant role in gaining the equality for women we have today.

WOMEN IN THE MILITARY RESOURCES

LAC

British Army Records

Where they survive, married lists can be found among the regular muster rolls for the British Army in WO 12 and WO 16. Visit the British National Archives at *www.nationalarchives.gov.uk* to learn more about these resources; however, if you discover something of interest you may have to hire an on-site genealogist to do further research for you. Some of the War Office records have been purchased by our archives and are available in the WO fonds, 1713–1940 collections. Use finding aid 90. There is no guarantee that you will find "married rolls" in any of these collections because it is not something that most genealogists/family historians have really spent time researching.

- MG 13–WO 12 — Muster Books and Pay lists, Regiments.
- MG 13–WO 10 — Muster Books, Royal Artillery.
- MG 13–WO 17 — Monthly Returns for British Troops in Canada, (originals B-1556-B1585, B1587-B1604, and B-1606-B1613).
- MG 13–WO 67 — Depot Description Books.
- MG 13–WO 73 — Monthly Returns, Distribution of the Army (reels, B-1750-B1770).

After 1870

In general, check the following:

- MG 13–WO 100 — copied extracts of the medical staff and nursing sister entitled to campaign medals, 1793–1912.
- MG 28-1471, R2925-05-E, photographic material — Naval Service.
- RG 8 — British Military and Naval Records.
- RG 9 — Canadian Militia and Defence.
- RG 9-II B 1, Vol. 263, AG Docket 1840/02 — war diaries of the 10th Field Hospital.
- RG 9-II B8, Vols. 1–1256 also has attestation papers.
- RG 9-III-C-10, Canadian Army Medical Corps historical records.
- RG 150 contains attestation papers — available online.
- RG 24, National Defence Records.

- RG 24-C-2, Canadian Women's Army Corps — 52 Co., Occupation force plus related topics.
- RG 24-E-1-a, related to W.D. RCAF, regulations and recruitment, "b" contains enlistment in the U.K. and University Air Training Corps, "c" contains history of the Division, Ottawa.
- RG 24, R112-109-2-E, holds photographs of the various corps.
- RG 24, Vol. 6309, file HQ 63-16-4, nursing sisters in the Boer War.
- RG 38 — Veterans' Affairs Records.
- RG 44 — National War Service Records.

Websites

Canadian Forces, *www.forces.ca/en/page/women-92#history-1,* for a general history of women in the armed forces.

Canadian Military Gateway, *www.cmhg-phmc.gc.ca,* references to women in the military.

Canadian Military Heritage Project, *www.rootsweb.ancestry.com/~canmil/ww1/women/index.html,* a list of women nurses during the First World War with pictures and archival references.

Canadian War Museum, *www.warmuseum.ca,* recently had a display on the role of women in the military.

Canadian Women Who's Who, *www.canadianstudies.ca/NewJapan/womenbios7.html.*

CFB Esquimalt Naval & Military Museum, *www.navalandmilitary museum.org/info_pages/about_index.html*

Famous Canadian Women, *www.famouscanadianwomen.com/timeline/timeline%20introduction.htm,* has a series of timelines you might find informative.

InternetArchive,*www.archive.org/details/CEF_NursingSisters_1914*, nominal rolls, 1914–15.

LAC, *www.collectionscanada.gc.ca/nursing-sisters/025013-2302-e.html*, if you suspect one of your ancestors may have been a nursing sister.

McMaster University, *pw20c.mcmaster.ca/women-and-war*, excellent resources on women's role during the Second World War.

National Film Board, *www3.nfb.ca/ww2/home-front/women-and-the-war.htm*, "On All Fronts" material primarily related to Canadian Women and the Second World War.

Naval Museum of Alberta, *www.navalmuseum.ab.ca/WRCNS.html*, where you can find a history of the Women's Royal Canadian Naval Service.

Queen's University, *archives.queensu.ca/Exhibits/archres/wwi-intro/women.html*, Women's Auxiliary Air Force.

Women in the Air Force, Bomber Command Museum, *www.bombercommandmuseum.ca/s,womenairforce.html*, has some information about the WAAF.

Books

Bates, C., D. Dodd, and N. Rousseau. *On All Frontiers: Four Centuries of Canadian Nursing.* Ottawa: Ottawa University Press, 2005.

Bruce, J. *Back the Attack! Canadian Women During the Second World War — at Home and Abroad.* Toronto: MacMillan of Canada, 1985.

Coates, C. and C. Morgan. *Heroines and History: Representations of Madeleine de Vercheres and Laura Secord.* Toronto: University of Toronto Press, 2002.

Dundas, B. *A History of Women in the Canadian Military.* Ottawa: Art Global and the Department of National Defence, 2000.

Page, F.C.G. *Following the Drum: Women in Wellington's Army.* London, U.K.: Andre Deutsch Limited, 1986.

Pierson, R. R. *Canadian Women and the Second World War.* Ottawa: Canadian Historical Association, Historical Booklet No. 3, 1983.

Robinson, C.R. *Mistress Molly: The Brown Lady, Portrait of Molly Brant.* Toronto: Dundurn Press, 1980.

Toman, C. *An Officer and a Lady: Canadian Military Nursing and the Second World War.* Vancouver: University of British Columbia Press, 2007.

Venning, A. *Following the Drum: The Lives of Army Wives and Daughters Past and Present.* London, U.K.: Headline Book Publishing, 2005.

CHAPTER EIGHT

Discovering Your Canadian Air Force Ancestors

THE FIRST WORLD WAR

On 4 February 1915, William Frederick Nelson Sharpe died in an airplane crash at Shoreham, England. Sharpe was twenty-two years old and was in the 1st Battalion, Canadian Contingent, of the Royal Flying Corps. He is considered the first Canadian aviator to die during the First World War. He certainly wasn't the last. Major Frederick Wanklyn is credited as the first Canadian to join the British Royal Flying Corps and the first to see combat in France. Beyond the stories of these two men were thousands of Canadians who made the decision to escape the mud of Flanders and train as an aviator. Perhaps your ancestor is listed by the Canadian Armed Forces Directorate of History and Heritage as one of the 18,653 Canadians who served with the Royal Flying Corps. Lieutenant Reginald Hershey VanRensselaer Scherk (the grandfather of a family friend) was one of these Canadians. He started the war as a young officer with the 220th Battalion, CEF, before transferring to the Royal Flying Corps as an observer. His attestation papers show his year of birth as 1896, but his actual birth year was 1898. He had obviously lied about his age!

Photograph of 2nd Lieutenant R. Scherk, 220th Battalion, First World War, taken shortly before embarkation. Family collection.

When the war started in August 1914, Canada did not have an air force. Britain started the war with two air services: the Royal Flying Corps was the army service, and the Royal Naval Air Service fell under the authority of the admiralty. These two services were amalgamated on 1 April 1918, forming the Royal Air Force.

The Royal Flying Corps arrived in France at the start of the war with four squadrons of sixty-three aircraft and approximately 900 personnel. By 1915–16 there were almost 421 aircraft in twenty-seven Squadrons. Between 1917 and 11 November 1918 the Royal Flying Corps/Royal Air Force reached a total of 188 squadrons, 22,000 aircraft, and approximately 300,000 personnel. It is also estimated that almost 25 percent of those who served were Canadians. By 1 November 1918, the RFC/RAF had 5,972 killed,5,813 wounded, 1,873 missing in action, and 1,093 reported as prisoners of war or interned. Canada's contribution was approximately 1,500 casualties.[1] It was often stated that the life expectancy of a pilot or air observer was just a matter of weeks. This had to do mostly with the type of aircraft they flew. British aircraft technology did not equal the quality of machines produced by Germany until at least 1918. Visit the Canada Aviation and Space Museum at Rockcliffe Airport in Ottawa, in person or at *www.aviation.technomuses.ca*, to view some of the aircraft flown by your air force ancestors.

Interestingly, and perhaps unfortunately for your ancestor, Anthony Fokker, a Dutch inventor in the employ of the German government, was the first to develop a synchronizing gear that allowed a pilot to fire a machine gun through the propeller without shooting off the blades. This gave the German flyers a huge advantage over their British or French adversaries. Fokker also went on to develop perhaps one of the best airplanes to serve in either air force, the Fokker DVII. When the war ended, one clause of the Treaty of Versailles stated that Germany had to destroy all its Fokkers. You can view an actual Fokker DVII in the museum at Knowlton, Quebec. It is one of a very few still in existence and on display.

In his history of the Royal Flying Corps in Canada, *Dancing in the Sky*, C.W. Hunt states that "at the battle of the Somme, manpower losses in the air war averaged 300 percent a year. By September of 1916, the casualty rate had risen to 400 percent. During March and April of 1917 the situation reached crisis proportions; Allied pilots were being killed, captured, or wounded faster than they could be replaced."[2]

Canadians served in the Royal Flying Corps or Royal Naval Air Service with distinction in almost every theatre of war; three won the Victoria Cross for conspicuous gallantry: William Avery Bishop, Alan Arnett McLeod, and William George Barker. Barker is considered the most decorated Canadian aviator while Bishop had the highest number of combat victories, seventy-two confirmed enemy aircraft destroyed.

Most of us who discover an ancestor in the flying corps will find that he was just one of the many who served as a pilot, an observer, or an aircraft mechanic/airframe fitter. Start by learning how your ancestor acquired his wings, if he was air crew, or where he was stationed if he was ground crew.

Your aviator ancestor had to volunteer for service with the Flying Corps, often after having seen service in one of the other branches of the military. If his application was accepted, a candidate was interviewed by an officer at the Air Ministry. Some of the questions were: Can you ride a horse, bicycle, or handle a motorcycle? Have you ever sailed a boat or do you play tennis? If you appeared to be of "gentlemanly" character and were so considered a possible flying candidate, you were sent for a medical exam. Some pilots don't remember ever receiving a medical exam, but future Canadian Prime Minister Lester Pearson stated that his exam consisted of picking out strands of coloured wool to test for colour blindness and then being spun around on a swivel chair to see how quickly he recovered from dizziness.

After passing the medical, your ancestor would have been assigned to what would later be referred to as ground school. In six weeks the candidate was instructed in Morse code and how to conduct a simulated artillery shoot, assemble and rig an airplane, dismantle and reassemble an engine, and splice steel wire. At the end of the training a potential pilot would know enough to go into Army Co-operation, Reconnaissance, Bombing, or Scout Flying. They could also find themselves in training for artillery observation or kite balloon observation.

In Canada, the RFC had training camps at Borden, Deseronto, North Toronto, Beamsville, and Long Branch, Ontario. Candidates could also receive instruction at Fort Worth, Texas, and the Wright School in Dayton, Ohio. In England, advanced training was provided at Gosport and Upavon.

Every candidate really hoped to become a scout pilot in a single-seat fighter aircraft. The newspapers often referred to these pilots as the "knights of the air" and propagandized their exploits.

These were the pilots that flew protection for observation/ bomber aircraft and engaged in one-on-one aerial conflict with the enemy. As the war progressed, both sides attempted to produce fighter aircraft that could outperform the opponent in aerial combat. Arthur Could Lee, a fighter pilot, states that "because these craft were, by later standards, so slow, so small, so responsive in control and so tight in manoeuvre, a pilot could come to such close grips with an opponent that if goggles were lifted, as they often were, he might see an enemy's features, even his grimace, or when he was attacked from astern the death jerk of his helmeted head as bullets struck between the shoulders."[3] In reality every man who flew as a scout or fighter pilot in either war had one thought: kill or be killed.

A Royal Flying Corps brigade consisted of several scout squadrons grouped into an army wing, along with a corps cooperation and balloon observation wing. Thus, your flying officer ancestor could find himself flying a single-seat fighter or a reconnaissance aircraft employed in bombing or artillery spotting and carrying an air-observer, or perhaps doing reconnaissance from a small basket suspended beneath a large gas filled balloon.

Before being posted to a specialist squadron he had to pass Initial Flying Training. This consisted of learning to fly a Maurice Farman "Shorthorn" aircraft. Candidates were expected to get the machine into the air, fly a certain distance under control, and bring the aircraft successfully to the ground. Often they would be sent up solo after only rudimentary instruction, so training casualties were quite common. After a few hours of flying the Maurice Farman, a pilot was sent to Central Flying School.

At Central Flying School the novice pilot was introduced to three types of planes: the BE2c, a rather ugly two-seater biplane with a 70hp, V8 engine; the 504 Avro, with either an 80hp or 100hp rotary engine; and the Sopwith two-seater with a 110hp motor. All three aircraft were generally incapable of achieving more than 100 miles per hour in flight. The student would be expected to pass tests on cross-country flying, forced landings, handling of controls during specialized air manoeuvres, recovery from a spin, and a height test. They would also learn the fine points of army co-operation, bombing, photography, artillery observation and air fighting. At the end of training, and if the pilot hadn't killed or injured himself, he would be granted his "wings" and be assigned to a specialist squadron for advanced operation flying training. He would also be commissioned as a 2nd Lieutenant in the Royal Flying Corps and his pay would increase from $1.00 per day to approximately $7.00 with an allowance for uniforms.

At AOF training your ancestor would have had training at gunnery school and experienced flying more advanced aircraft: the Bristol Scout, Sopwith Pup, or SE5. These were front-line machines and all had unique characteristics that had to be mastered successfully if your ancestor expected to get them off the

ground, fight in the air, and return safely. After advanced training, a new pilot was either posted to a new squadron going out
to France or sent to the pilots' pool at St. Omer, France, ready
to replace a casualty. Once posted, training in formation flying, ground strafing, and map reading continued. Your ancestor
probably arrived in France with fifteen to twenty hours of flying
experience, about ten to twelve of those solo.

Even with this training, there was a very good chance
that the new pilot would not survive very long at the Front.
C.W. Hunt mentions that in May 1917 eighteen cadets were
sent to England to complete their training, "of the eighteen
who survived the training and got to England, fifteen had met
the enemy by year's end. Of these fifteen, five had been killed,
three were missing in action, three were seriously wounded,
and two were prisoners of war. Only two survived the combat
unscathed."[4] Generally, fatalities represented 10.5 percent of
the RFC pilots, 10.8 percent of the RNAS, and 10.9 percent
of the RAF enlistments.[5]

The stress of operational flying must have been incredible.
Often pilots flew above 20,000 feet without oxygen in unheated,
open-cockpit aircraft. They were exposed to the freezing air-
stream from the propeller, fumes from the engine, and numbness
in hands and feet that could result in frostbite. Pilots tried to
protect themselves by wearing layers of clothing, fur-lined gloves,
and boots. Many designed face masks and covered any exposed
parts of their body with whale oil. The loud noise created by the
propeller and the firing of the machine guns would certainly
have resulted in some loss of hearing. Also, no First World War
pilots had parachutes even though a suitable product was available
and issued to observers in the balloon corps. It was considered
cheaper to replace a pilot than an aircraft. The RCAF (created 1
April 1924) didn't include parachutes in their aircraft until 1925.

It is easy to image some Canadian pilots suffering from nervous breakdowns or resorting to alcohol to calm their nerves after a flight. Read some of the autobiographical accounts left by First World War pilots concerning the celebration held in the officers' mess after a day of flying. It is said that one Canadian ace lived on a mixture of milk and rum because he was having trouble keeping food in his stomach.

Many Canadians joined the Royal Naval Air Service and were stationed anywhere the British Navy had a presence. They served in France, Mesopotamia [Iraq], and Africa, patrolling the Red Sea, the Adriatic, and the Mediterranean. Most, however, flew over the North Sea, the Atlantic, or the English Channel and even staffed fighter and bomber squadrons in northern France. By December 1916, there were approximately 300 Canadians serving in the RNAS, and by the end of the war 936 served with naval air force squadrons.[6]

Some of the famous Canadian aces whose exploits you can read about are Raymond Collishaw, William Avery Bishop, Alan Arnett Mcleod, William George Barker, Arthur Roy Brown, Donald Roderick MacLaren, Andrew McKeever, and Alan McLeod. Then there are the German aces: Max Immelmann, Oswald Boelcke, Manfred von Richthofen, and Hermann Goering; the French aces: Georges Guynemer, René Dorme, Jean Marie Dominique Navarre, Charles Nungesser, and René Paul Fonck; and the British aces such as Albert Ball and Lance George Hawker.

Where Do You Search for First World War Pilot Records?

Your aviator ancestors would have enlisted into either the Royal Flying Corps or Royal Naval Air Service or been seconded from some other branch of the service. What records are available have been gathered from a variety of sources in the hope this would provide some biographical details about who enlisted, where and when they served and how many gave their lives. Many First World War records held in the National Archives U.K. were destroyed by the German Air Force during the Battle of Britain in the Second World War. What remains have recently been put online. I found Reginald Scherk's flying records.

The Department of Defence, Canadian Directorate of History and Heritage, has cards prepared for each identified Canadian who served in the British Flying Service. The computer files contain 13,160 names of which 6,904 are identified as Canadians, 1,736 non-Canadians (mostly Americans who joined or were trained in Canada), and 4,520 of unknown origin. Of these, 5,241 joined the Royal Flying Corps, 936 the Royal Naval Air Service, and 6,709 the Royal Air Force. The records also show that 7,453 joined the air force as mechanics directly recruited in Canada.

What Can You Expect to Find Once the Records Arrive?

Recently I acquired three sets of records for Lieutenant Reginald Hershey VanRensselaer Scherk. These records are interesting because they are typical for that conflict.

First there are the inherited treasures, often ignored for some time and then rediscovered in the basement or under the bed. These are often a collection of medals, diaries, letters, certificates, or other ephemera. Included in the family records I received were actual reports of bombing operations undertaken by Lieutenant Scherk and his pilot.

Family treasures can provide a wealth of information that may not be found in the service files held at the archives. Lieutenant Scherk's family had his First World War medals, photographs of him in uniform as a young infantry officer, his officer's commission, pictures of the airplanes he flew when he joined the RFC, and various other memorabilia.

Scherk started the war as an officer with the 220th Battalion, and was later transferred to the 12th Battalion and then the 1st Central Ontario Battalion, before applying for a transfer to the Royal Flying Corps. His first assignment was as an observer; eventually he applied for retraining as a pilot.

Also discovered among the family's records were his observer's wings, identity bracelet, and war medals. Other treasures included another family member's cap badge, pictures, and a large collection of greeting cards sent home during the war.

The second set of important documents is that provided by LAC. In the case of Scherk (born 25 May 1896) his service records can be found in RG 150, Accession 1992-93/166, box 8691-40. Of course, his attestation papers can be downloaded from the LAC website and are the first source of information any family historian should consult. Once you discover these papers it becomes relatively easy to check census records to confirm your discovery. In the case of 2nd Lieutenant Reginald Hershey VanRensselaer Scherk, the uniqueness of his middle names certainly helped the search. The 1911 census showed that he had two siblings and that his father, Frederick, was a medical doctor. The family lived in east end Toronto. It also indicated that he had perhaps lied about his age on his attestation papers. You can confirm this by checking Ontario birth records.

The records you acquire from Ottawa will often have an official cover page that lists the contents of the files. This list can prove more valuable than just acting as an outline of the contents. Next to each heading is the code used by the military to distinguish different forms. For instance, attestation papers are recorded as M.F.W. 23, 133, or 51; M.F.W. 51 is the form used for officers.

You can also expect: casualty form; training history sheet; field, regiment, or company conduct sheets; medical, dental sheets; pay certificates; and, should your ancestor be involved in any court of enquiry, a list of documents concerning the proceedings of the court. Not all these items will be found in the folder but enough should be available for you to prepare a fairly accurate picture of his training and service in England or France.

Be prepared for some interesting discoveries. Your ancestor's medical history might record an indiscretion. There may be demotion in rank or even court martial records. If your ancestor deserted the military and then for some reason rejoined or was given a general amnesty, the envelope containing the files will be stamped in large letters with the word "deserter." You may also find some mention of the term "Field Punishment." This means he had committed some form of indiscretion, often late for parade or talking back to his sergeant, for which he would incur some kind of punishment not leading to a court martial.

Because Canada did not then have an air force you'll have to apply to both LAC and National Archives U.K. Fortunately, First World War officers' records are available online through the National Archives in England through their "documents online" website. When you receive these records you will find documents outlining training and postings as well as other important dates. These records are different from those held by LAC and should not be overlooked.

The Royal Flying Corps records for Lieutenant Scherk show his training as an air observer. They are rather limited because he joined the flying corps late in 1917 and did not receive any recommendation-for-gallantry awards. What aided in writing his family narrative were the mission reports he had brought home as souvenirs. These are not readily available for many of our flying corps ancestors.

Do not forget to search for the squadron war diary. Royal Flying Corps, Royal Naval Air Service, and Royal Air Force squadron war diaries are available for download through National Archives U.K. The diary contains the history of the squadron, the names of medal recipients, the location of aerodromes in France where the squadron was stationed, and a variety of statistics. Often the names of specific flying officers are mentioned in relation to noteworthy patrols as are encounters with enemy aircraft. They certainly make for interesting reading as the following excerpt from Lieutenant Scherk's squadron diary shows:

> On the 22nd April, when returning from a Raid, on THOUROUT, the pilot of machine D.H.9 C.6138, No.7655 Sergtr. (Pilot) Oliver S.J. and his observer Sergt. Kelsall, had a very unnerving experience, from which both emerged with slight injury, by using supreme skill, and resource in the manipulation of his controls. A piece of "Archie" burst his propeller and before he could switch off, his engine had almost raced itself from its bearing and caught fire. He at once shut off the petrol supply and side slipped about 1,000 feet. The fire went out, and he then glided the machine very steadily. He had just crossed over our lines at about ten thousand feet, when the engine fell completely out of the machine. The machine fell into a left hand spiral, and by keeping full right rudder and holding his control lever right forward and over to the right, he managed to keep the machine in a slow spiral, from which he was not able to pull out. He landed about two miles from

the spot where the engine fell, escaping with a broken nose and his observer with a broken leg. The machine was completely destroyed.[7]

To acquire the correct war diary you will have to know the RFC/RNAS/RAF squadron number. Interestingly, Lieutenant Scherk and his pilot are mentioned in the squadron diary after completing a successful bombing raid in support of the British Army's attempt to stop the German advance at Arras. Family historians will want to connect all of the events recorded in the squadron war diary with what was happening in Russia, the subsequent release of German troops from the Eastern to the Western Front, and the battle of Arras.

THE SECOND WORLD WAR

On the Second World War Bomber Command Memorial, *www. bombercommandmuseum.ca*, are the following words, written by Father J.P. Lardie (Chaplain 419, 428 Squadron RCAF):

> Three thousand miles across a hunted ocean they came, wearing on the shoulders of their tunics the treasured name, "Canada," telling the world their origin. Young men and women they were, some still in their teens, fashioned by their Maker to love, not to kill, but proud and earnest in their mission to stand, and if it had to be, to die for their country and freedom.
>
> One day, when the history of the 20th century is finally written, it will be recorded that when human society stood at the crossroads

and civilization itself was under siege, the Royal
Canadian Air Force was there to fill the breach
and help give humanity the victory. And all those
who had a part in it will have left to posterity a
legacy of honour, of courage, and of valour that
time can never despoil.[8]

*Royal Canadian Air Force wings issued upon completion of training as
a pilot. Author's collection.*

Recently, I had the opportunity to talk to a veteran of Bomber
Command. He had enlisted in the Royal Canadian Air Force, done
his basic training through the British Commonwealth Air Training
Plan, received his pilots' wings, and been assigned to Bomber
Command. Arriving in England he had gone to Bournemouth
and reported to the Royal Canadian Air Force manning pool for
assignment to an Operational Training Unit. Eventually he had
been teamed up with a Lancaster Bomber crew who had already
finished one operational tour of duty (thirty missions). Needless
to say they were not impressed with the fact that their previous
pilot was reassigned to a desk job, having completed two tours of
duty (sixty missions), and now they were expected to place their
lives in the hands of a "sprog" (inexperienced) pilot.

Readers should understand that on average 36 percent of bomber crews did not complete a "tour of duty"; receiving "the chop" by being killed, wounded, or becoming a prisoner of war while on active flying duty. Earlier in the war the rate had been over 50 percent![9] Fortunately, the fellow I spoke to had been assigned to further training before being placed on active duty and during that time the war ended. What was particularly interesting was that he turned twenty-one years of age the month after Germany surrendered, 8 May 1945. He had been eighteen when he joined the Royal Canadian Air Force.

Personally, I couldn't imagine myself flying anything at that age, assuming responsibility for the lives of other crew members, especially while someone else was trying to kill me. But thousands of our ancestors did just that and survived to return home. Some, however, paid the ultimate price and are resting in war cemeteries in England and Europe or have no known grave and are commemorated on the walls of monuments.

Why did our ancestors elect to join this branch of the service? Where are their records of service? And what do we need to know to complete this page of our family narrative?

Your air force ancestor could have been with Fighter Command, Coastal Command, Bomber Command, Army Co-operation Command, South East Asia Command, or Transport Command, or even seen action with No. 331 Wing during the invasion of Italy. He could have become a flying or pilot officer (F/O, P/O) and as a flying officer might have seen duty as a navigator, flight engineer, wireless operator, air gunner, or an air training instructor. He or she could have also been one of the thousands who were assigned as ground crew: air craft mechanics, wireless operators, radar technicians, or any of the hundreds of other skills needed to keep the air craft flying and administrative duties in order.

They would have received their initial instruction as part of the British Commonwealth Air Training Plan (BCATP) and then been assigned to either Home War Establishment (HWE) or Overseas War Establishment (OWE). As a Canadian in the air force, your ancestor might have seen service with our own Royal Canadian Air Force (RCAF), joined the British Royal Air Force (RAF), or been a member of the RCAF who was assigned to a RAF squadron. All this makes it an interesting challenge when trying to discover service records.

What Do You Need to Know about Your Ancestor's Air Force?

If you're sure your ancestor served in the Royal Canadian Air Force overseas (OWE), he would have belonged to a Squadron with a "400" designation. In Army Co-operation Command these were numbers 400, 414, and 430 squadrons, until 1943 when Army Co-operation Command was disbanded and the crews absorbed by Second Tactical Air Force. In Fighter Command there were eight day-fighter and three night-fighter squadrons and one intruder squadron. For instance, RCAF 126 Wing was home to Spitfire squadrons: 411, 412, 416, and 443.

Fourteen RCAF squadrons served with No. 6 (RCAF) Bomber Group: 405 "Vancouver" squadron, 405 (Pathfinder) squadron, 408 "Goose" squadron, 415 "Swordfish" squadron, 419 "Moose" squadron, 420 "Snowy Owl" squadron, 424 "Tiger" squadron, 425 "Alouette" squadron, 426 "Thunderbolt" squadron, 427 "Lion" squadron, 428 "Ghost" squadron, 429 "Buffalo" squadron, 431 "Iroquois" squadron, 432, "Leaside" squadron, 433 "Porcupine" squadron, and 434 "Bluenose" squadron. When you visit the Canadian War Museum you can see examples of the nose art taken from some of the Canadian bombers that flew with No.6 Group.

If your ancestor was a member of 404, 407, or 415 squadrons, he was part of Coastal Command and was shore based. If with 413, 422, 423, or 162 he would have flown or serviced flying boat aircraft. Three squadrons saw service with South East Asia Command: 413 was a coastal reconnaissance squadron, and 435 and 436 were transport squadrons. The RCAF supplied one squadron to RAF Transport Command — 437.

Each squadron was assigned to a Wing and each Wing to a Group. As an example, on D-Day, 6 June 1944, 83 Group, 2nd Tactical Air Force, contained 126 Wing — 401, 411, 412 Squadrons; 127 Wing — 403, 416, 421 Squadrons; 144 Wing — 441, 442, 443 Squadrons; 143 Wing — 438, 439, 440 Squadrons and 39 Wing — 414, 430 Squadrons. Eighty-five Group contained 409 and 410 Squadrons while 10 Group (Fighter Command) had 406 Squadron and 11 Group (Fighter Command) held 402 and 418 Squadrons.

Canadian squadrons not part of the overseas war establishment did not have the 400 designation. For a complete list of Canadian squadrons, both Overseas and Home War Establishments, consult *The Royal Canadian Air Force At War, 1939–1945*.[10] Each of these squadrons maintained a war diary, most of which are available on microfilm and interlibrary loan from LAC.

Where Did It All Begin for My RCAF Ancestor?

Family historians whose ancestors joined the RCAF, or for that matter any of a number of Commonwealth Air Forces, should spend time reading about British Commonwealth Air Training Plan (BCAPT). Consult the books listed in the resource section.

This will help you understand what your air force ancestor faced when first accepted.

Between 1940 and 1945 the plan graduated 131,553 air crew. Almost 50,000 became pilots in bomber command, fighter command, air transport, or coastal command.[11] For those who had not been considered appropriate for pilot training, there were many other occupations. Your ancestor could have trained as a navigator (Nav.), wireless operator (WO), air gunner (AG), air bomber (B), or even a flight engineer (E). A wireless operator could also find himself as either air crew or ground crew. Your male or female ancestor could have also been trained as an aircraft mechanic, radar operator, or any of the other occupations required to keep the planes flying and the administration functioning.

What Did Your Ancestor Experience During Training?

Your ancestor had to volunteer for the air force and pass a stringent medical. My wife's father often explained how he was turned down for service because he was underweight and had a nasal condition. He paid for his own surgery to correct the breathing problem and then gained weight. When he reapplied, he was accepted for training. His first stop was one of the Initial Training Schools (I.T.S.) and indoctrination at an RCAF Manning Pool.

Bill Olmstead of North Bay, Ontario, recounts how upon arriving at No. 2 Manning Depot, Camp Shilo, Manitoba, the recruits were housed in the former Cow Palace.

> Twenty-five hundred recruits painfully made
> the transition from civilian to military life,

quickly learning that as Aircraftsmen, Second Class (AC2), we were the lowest forms of life made to be verbally abused by drill instructors who used the most crude and graphic — but effective — language we would ever hear. We became used to line-ups and endless waiting — waiting to use the twenty-four toilets, waiting to wash, waiting in a shift line of twelve hundred men for meals three times a day, waiting for pay parade or sick parade.

We learned to march. We learned to drill, to salute properly, to become regimented and obedient. From raw, unruly recruits we slowly developed some semblance of military bearing. We endured route marches and long cross-country runs ... Everything was done to a meter: rise and shine, PT, breakfast, drill, lunch, drill, dinner, route march, and then bed, so tired that the orchestra of noises created by twenty-five hundred men bunked in one enormous room couldn't stop deep sleep from taking over.[12]

From there, candidates were shipped to an elementary flying training school (EFTS) where they spent eight weeks being given ground school training as well as 50 hours of flying. At the end of this period, following exams and assessment of flying potential, the candidate could be designated as air crew or assigned pilot training. If he was successful and considered potential pilot material, he progressed to a service flying training school (SFTS) for a further ten to sixteen weeks and seventy-five to one hundred hours of flying instruction. Eventually the school decided to train pilots on either single-engine or twin-engine aircraft.

Those assigned single-engine training were destined for fighter command while those on twin-engine knew they were going to bomber command, coastal, or transport operations. Of course, they still had to achieve passing grades to be awarded their wings.

Those considered not suitable for pilot training, or with special skill in mathematics, went to initial training school where they had more training on aerial photography, reconnaissance, and air navigation as well as practical experience in the air. The program took approximately twelve weeks and, if a candidate was successful, he took another ten-week course at a bomber and gunnery school. Following this, he moved on to a four-week program at an air navigation school. Upon graduation, he received his half wing and the "O" to wear on his tunic as an air observer. After 1942, the observer designation was redefined as air bomber, navigator, wireless operator, or air gunner. Eventually some of these trades were further redefined as wireless operator/ air gunner, navigator/bomber, etc. All entailed specific training and instruction. Flight engineer was a trade that was added to heavy bomber crews. He was an aero-engineer knowledgeable in all mechanical aspects of the bomber and had received enough instruction to replace the pilot if the latter was killed or wounded during a flying operation.

There were four training command centres: Number One was in Toronto, Number Two was in Winnipeg, Number Three Command was in Montreal, and Number Four was in Regina, later moved to Calgary. Your ancestor received his initial training (elementary flying training) at one of thirty-six schools, the majority of which were in western Canada. Here they flew Tiger Moths, Fleet Finch, Stearman, or Cornell aircraft. Upon successful completion of this stage, they moved to one of forty-one service flying training schools where they were trained on Harvard, Yale, Anson, Crane, or Oxfords. If your ancestor was not considered for pilot training he was assigned to one of ten air observer schools, four air navigation schools, two general reconnaissance schools, eleven bombing and gunnery schools, four wireless schools, or, later in the war, one flight-engineer school. Eventually, instruction was provided at specialty schools in radar, armament, teaching (instructor school), aeronautical engineering, aviation medicine, and cookery.

Your ancestor's air force had an interesting method of assigning rank. For flying personnel it seemed to be based on a quota; some pilots were officers while others were flight sergeants, as were some navigators or air bombers. So, a pilot in command of a bomber could find himself outranked by his navigator — at least on the ground. Thus, in your ancestor's service files and providing he was aircrew, you could discover the designation P/O (Pilot Officer), S/P (Sergeant Pilot), F/O (Flying Officer), or Flt.Sergeant (Flight Sergeant). I'm sure this purely British system must have rankled those who qualified as a pilot but were randomly assigned the rank of sergeant and found themselves sleeping in the sergeant's dorm, excluded from the officer's mess, wearing a different style of uniform, and not having the luxury of a "bat man" to maintain his living quarters if he was assigned to an RAF squadron, while his navigator, an officer, had all these privileges. Interestingly, the Canadian Ace George "Buzz" Beurling, who won distinction for his outstanding contributions during the Battle for Malta (June 1940 to December 1942), was originally granted sergeant rank. When he started to win recognition for his great accomplishments, the Air Force Command wanted to immediately grant him officer status. Beurling refused this promotion on many occasions because he felt the whole system of assigning rank was typically British and unfair. Eventually he was strongly encouraged to accept the change in rank whether he wanted it or not.[13]

Surprisingly, very little has been written about the nearly 45,000 Canadians who served as ground crew. These are the men and women who kept the planes flying and handled hundreds of other behind-the-scenes jobs. If they were not accepted for air training, for any number of medical reasons or administrative, your ancestors might have found themselves sent to the Air Force's Technical Training School at St. Thomas, Ontario, perhaps after a stop at No. 5 Radar School at Clinton, Ontario. At St. Thomas, a twenty-five-building former sanatorium situated on 197 hectares, your ancestors received twelve weeks of training. Here they learned about hydraulics, various aspects of mechanical theory, how to guide aircraft from the ground, how to place chocks, and everything else associated with air frame. Robert Collins recounts how "we sanded and varnished more wood, patched more fabric, relearned the structure of aircraft and the myriad kinds of tools. Words like 'spars-and-ribs,' 'stressed skin,' 'geodetic frame,' and 'micrometer' danced in my head, equilibrium, relative airflow, lift and drag, angles of yaw and roll. I met more rivets than I ever wanted to know."[14]

Upon graduation, ground crew were assigned to a squadron either in Home War Establishment or Overseas War Establishment. Flying personnel referred to ground crew as "Erks," a term that must have seemed derogatory to anyone who had wanted very much to be in aircrew but because of education or medical reasons could not. If you were designated as ground crew, your tour of duty was the duration of the war.

Lloyd Turcott, my wife's father, was trained as a wireless operator (sparks) and ended up as an Erk stationed in St. John's, Newfoundland, with Coastal Command. He applied on a number of occasions to train as an air gunner, hoping to be reassigned to Bomber Command. There was a shortage of tail gunners in Bomber Command because of the high loss of life in that profession and he figured this would get him posted to England and reassigned to aircrew. His wish was never granted.

By the end of the war, British Commonwealth Air Training Plan had graduated approximately 73,000 RCAF candidates: 10,000 personnel for the Royal Australian Air Force, 7,000 New Zealanders, and 42,000 Royal Air Force personnel. Included in the RAF figure are Poles, Norwegians, Belgians, Dutch, Czechs, and Free French air crew. Interestingly, by 1941 almost 9,000 Americans had joined the Royal Canadian Air Force; 800 were killed on service. The names of 379 of these are on Canada's Bomber Command Memorial Wall. Even after the United States entered the war, in December 1941, approximately 5,000 Americans elected to complete their tour of duty with the RCAF.[15]

When pilots arrived in England they received further training at an Advanced Flying Unit (AFU), and an Operational Training Unit (OTU). Those in Bomber Command were teamed up with their new crew. All the trades casually mingled in a large hall and formed crews. This was a democratic means of organizing individuals into a team that had to work together during bombing operations where everyone's life depended on the skill of crew mates. The new team then received further training at a Heavy Conversion Unit (HCU) before being posted to an Operational Squadron.

It is estimated that of the 40,000 RCAF aircrew serving with Bomber Command approximately 10,000 became casualties. Various sources claim that 32.67 percent of RCAF Bomber Command aircrew became statistical casualties. On the Runnymede Memorial in Britain, 3,072 Canadians are listed as having no known graves.

What Was My Ancestor's Rank?

Like the Canadian Army, the air force had its own command structure. From bottom to top, your ancestor would have been assigned to one of the following ranks:

AC2:	aircraftsman, second class
AC1:	aircraftsman, first class
LAC:	leading aircraftsman
CPL:	corporal
Sergeant and S/P:	sergeant and sergeant pilot
F/S:	flight sergeant
WO2:	warrant officer, second class
WO1:	warrant officer, first class

Officers held the following ranks (from bottom to top):

P/O:	pilot officer
F/O:	flying officer
F/L:	flight lieutenant
S/L:	squadron leader
W/C:	wing commander
G/C:	group captain
A/C:	air commodore
A/V/M:	air vice marshal
A/M:	air marshal
A/C/M:	air chief marshal

If your air force ancestor served in Fighter Command and you have a picture of him in uniform, check to see if he has the top button of his tunic undone. This seems to have been a symbol adopted by members of Fighter Command to show their privileged status.

The air force command structure was based on the group led by a group captain, responsible for a number of wings. Each wing had from two to five squadrons and was commanded by a wing commander. Each squadron was commanded by a squadron leader who was responsible for about twenty-six pilots and eighteen aircraft. A squadron was further divided into A and B flights, each commanded by a flight lieutenant responsible for the men and machines in his flight.

In his autobiography, Bill Olmstead describes a sortie flown by a squadron as,

> ... normally having twelve aircraft ... in three sections, or flights of four aircraft. The CO would lead the center or red section with a number 2 flying one hundred yards behind and to one side. The other two aircraft in the section would fly farther behind and to one side. Yellow section would fly a similar formation but five hundred yards to one side, either higher or lower than red section depending on the location of the sun. The third, or blue, section flew a comparable pattern on the other side of the CO. This was known as the "finger four" formation, and had been developed as the war progressed as the best of the many types of flying formation tested.[16]

You should also be aware that no matter which air force (RCAF or RAF) your ancestor joined, it was totally voluntary. Being a pilot was a particularly stressful occupation and some found it impossible to complete the thirty operations. A pilot could report to his commanding officer and refuse to fly, effectively relinquishing his wings. He would immediately be removed from the base, transferred to another branch of the service, and have his record stamped "LMF" (lacking moral fibre). Because all men on flying duty were under tremendous pressure from high losses, this limited the effect on crew morale by quickly removing anyone who could not endure the stress. Sometimes aircrew members who couldn't handle the stress of operational flying seemed to just disappear from the base. Other flying personnel were not informed of why someone chose to quit or where they had gone. There were no goodbyes.

What Medals Can You Expect to Find?

If you have a ribbon bar or set of medals, you should check what your ancestor had been awarded. Should you discover

The Air Crew Europe Star issued to flying personnel for active service. Author's collection.

only your ancestor's ribbon bar, remember that all medals had unique ribbons. Expect to find the regular service medals issued to all combatants in the Canadian military during the Second World War: the Canadian Volunteer Service Medal (CVSM), the Defence Medal (DM), and the War Medal (1939–45).

If your ancestor saw service in any theatre of war, expect to find one or more of the 39–45 Star, France and Germany Star, Italy Star, Africa Star, Atlantic Star, Pacific Star, or even the Burma Star. Descriptions of each of these can be found online at *www. vac-acc.gc.ca*. You may also find an Air Crew Europe Star, which was awarded to personnel who were on active duty for at least two months and had flown from Britain over Europe between 3 September 1939 and 5 June 1944.

There were a wide variety of medals for conspicuous service or gallantry. These were awarded under a specific quota system. Group or squadron leaders were expected to submit lists of candidates for approval on specific dates throughout the year. These were approved or denied based on a set of specific expectations and the quota system. If your family member received a medal for conspicuous service or gallantry while on flying duty, it could be one of the following:

- Victoria Cross (VC): presented to all ranks for acts of valour, self-sacrifice, or extreme devotion to duty. It is the highest award for bravery with many awarded posthumously. The following Canadians received this award while on flying operations: Andrew Charles Mynarski, David Ernest Hornell, Ian Willoughby Bazalgette, and Robert Hampton Grey.
- Distinguished Service Order (DSO): usually awarded to squadron leaders and above for

distinguished service under enemy fire. Most individuals receiving this award had also been mentioned in dispatches for conspicuous duty.

- Conspicuous Gallantry Medal (CGM): presented to personnel below the rank of officer for conspicuous gallantry while on active flying duty against the enemy.
- Distinguished Flying Medal (DFM): awarded to non-commissioned officers and aircraftsmen for devotion to duty while flying against the enemy.
- Air Force Cross (AFC): officers and warrant officers were awarded this medal for valour or devotion to duty, while flying though not on active duty against the enemy.
- Air Force Medal (AFM): awarded to all non-commissioned officers (sergeants, corporals) or aircraftsmen for valour or devotion to duty, while flying though not on active duty against the enemy.

If your ancestor served as ground crew, he or she may have been awarded one of the following medals for an act of bravery usually not directly against the enemy:

- George Cross (GC): issued primarily to civilians or personnel for acts of valour for which other honours were not granted.
- George Medal (GM): awarded for acts of great bravery performed by nursing sisters, officers, or airmen.
- Order of the British Empire (OBE): for gallantry on the ground but not in conflict with the

enemy. Usually to senior officers and matrons of the nursing service.

- Member of the British Empire (MBE): presented for gallantry on the ground and presented to officers, warrant officers, and nursing sisters.
- British Empire Medal (BEM): granted to non-commissioned officers, aircraftsmen, and women for bravery on the ground but not in direct conflict with the enemy.

For long-time service, consistent devotion to duty, or various acts of bravery, but not entailing any physical risk, your ancestor might have received one of the following:

- Order of the Bath (OB): usually awarded to the rank of group captain or above.
- Order of the British Empire (OBE): again to group captains or above.
- Member of the British Empire (MBE): presented to flying officers, warrant officers, senior staff nurses of the nursing service.

Only twelve Conspicuous Gallantry medals were actually issued to personnel who served with the Royal Canadian Air Force. Two of those twelve also received the Distinguished Flying Cross. If you suspect one of your ancestors might have won a gallantry award, search the *London Gazette* where all citations were listed in abbreviated form. The citation recorded in the *Gazette* is considerably different from the original recommendation made by your ancestor's commanding officer. The National Archives U.K. holds the recommendations for Canadians who flew with the RAF, while our own LAC has those for the RCAF.

Check your local library for books listing air force personnel who received gallantry awards. You can also check the Air Force Association of Canada.

If your air force ancestor happened to be involved in some ground action against the enemy, including enemy aircraft, he could have been entitled to the same bravery medals as military personnel in other branches of the service: the Victoria Cross (VC), Distinguished Service Order (DSO), Military Cross (MC), Distinguished Conduct Medal (DCM), Military Medal (MM), or even a Mentioned in Dispatches (MiD). A "Mentioned in Dispatches" did not entitle the recipient to a medal but did allow him or her to attach an oak leaf pin to the ribbon of his or her service medal. Similarly, if an individual was recognized for an act of bravery entitling him or her to a duplicate award, he or she was allowed to attach a "bar" to the original medal. When you read about RCAF personnel being awarded a bar, this person had performed an exceptional act of bravery and was recognized for it, on more than one occasion.

If your ancestor completed a tour of duty, he was entitled to wear the operational small sterling silver wings with an "O" in the middle. These wings were worn on the left pocket of the tunic.

If your ancestor was a member of a prestigious pathfinder squadron, he wore a small air force eagle on the left pocket of his battledress or sometimes just under the ribbon bar. The path-finder squadrons were composed of highly experienced, capable pilots and crew whose job was to fly ahead of the bomber stream and mark the target with coloured flares or incendiaries. Often they remained near the target, directing the bomber stream on to the objective.

Where Do You Begin?

Start with a LAC and your local library. The books you research will provide you with the foundation to put your ancestor in context. For Second World War air force records, consult the LAC. Remember that personnel records are only available to next of kin and must be requested by application accompanied by proof of death or written permission from your ancestor.

These abbreviations will help you decipher your ancestor's records:

AASF	— Advanced Air Striking Force
A/C 2	— Aircraftsman, Second Class
AFDU	— Air Fighting Development Unit
AFTS	— Advanced Flying Training School
AOC	— Air Officer Commanding
BCATP	— British Commonwealth Air Training Plan
BCDU	— Bomber Command Development Unit
BPD	— Base Personnel Depot
CFI	— Chief Flying Instructor
CO	— Commanding Officer
EFTS	— Elementary Flying Training School
Erk	— Amy ground crew airman or technician
F/O	— Flying Officer
G/C	— Group Captain
HCU	— Heavy Conversion Unit
IO	— Intelligence Officer
ITS	— Initial Training School
LAC	— Leading Aircraftsman rank
LMF	— Lack of Moral Fibre

ORB	— Operation Record Book
ORS	— Operational Record Section
OCU	— Operational Conversion Unit
Ops	— Combat Operations or Missions
OTU	— Operational Training Unit
PDC	— Pilot Disposal Centre
P/O	— Pilot Officer
PRO	— Public Relations Officer
SFTS	— Service Flying Training School
S/L	— Squadron Leader
Sprog	— Inexperienced Pilot
WAAF	— Women's Auxiliary Air Force
W/C	— Wing Commander
PFF	— Pathfinder Force
VE-Day	— Victory in Europe Day, 8 May 1945
VJ-Day	— Victory over Japan Day, 15 August 1945

As you read more about the experiences of your pilot ancestor, you'll become familiar with some of the following air force terms:

A/A	— Ack-Ack, anti aircraft gun
Ace	— a pilot with five destroyed enemy aircraft to his credit
Ammo	— ammunition
Bail out	— parachute from an aircraft
Bank	— steep turn
Beat up	— to attack a target continuously
Bogey	— an unidentified aircraft
Boost	— power applied to an aircraft engine by throttle setting
Briefing	— instructions before a mission or sortie

Buster	—	to push engine to maximum power
Clock	—	refers to airspeed indicator
Crate	—	slang for aircraft
Dead Stick	—	to fly without engine power
Deck	—	the ground
Dog Fight	—	aerial combat
Duff Gen	—	incorrect information
Flak	—	enemy anti-aircraft gun fire from the ground
Flamer	—	aircraft on fire
Flight	—	two to six aircraft, not squadron strength
Gaggle	—	a group of enemy aircraft
Gong	—	medal
Hun	—	German aircraft
Jerry	—	slang term to identify any German
Kite	—	any aircraft
Mae West	—	inflatable life jacket
Mayday	—	distress call
Mission	—	sortie, trip, operation
Ops Room	—	operations room used to assemble crews to provide information
Prang	—	crashed or damaged aircraft
Pukka Gen	—	correct information
Recce	—	armed reconnaissance
Ramrod	—	squadron strength, low level attack on a larger target
Ranger	—	night attack similar to Rhubarb, covering a wide area
Rhubarb	—	low-level, search and destroy conducted by two aircraft
Roadstead	—	squadron strength on a shipping convoy
Stooge	—	to fly aimlessly

Strafe	—	to attack ground targets
Tallyhoo	—	signal given to attack
Tannoy	—	loudspeaker system at air force base
Vector	—	to direct an aircraft on to a target
Vic	—	formation of aircraft, flying in a 'V'
Winco	—	Wing Commander
Wing	—	number of flying squadrons, usually two to four

You'll often hear or read in a pilot's biography the following terms used to describe aircraft or to identify aircraft to ground controllers responsible for organizing landing procedures. You may read that a bomber pilot flew "Q" for Queenie or "V" for Victor. The British phonetic alphabet was used from 1943 to 1945 with call signs like "G for George" or "O for Oboe."

The call sign on your ancestor's aircraft was preceded by the national roundel and two more letters that indicated the squadron. Check this if you have a picture of your ancestor standing next to the aircraft in which he might have flown or perhaps she serviced as ground crew.

Why Did Your Ancestor Join the Air Force?

Perhaps, it was for the thrill of learning to fly and being selected to wear that special dark-blue uniform that told others that you had volunteered for specialized training and hazardous duty. Pilot Officer John Gillespie Magee, an American serving in the RCAF, summed it up in his often-quoted poem "High Flight," written shortly before his death at age nineteen:

> Oh! I have slipped the surly bonds of Earth
> And danced the skies on laughter-silvered wings; ...
> Put out my hand, and touched the face of God.[17]

It certainly must have had something to do with the thrill of learning to fly and the prestige that came with wearing the distinct uniform, to "thunder up the clouds to glory" from another of Magee's poems, "Per Ardua." Or, maybe it was just more attractive than marching in the army or being seasick in the navy.

Our ancestors paid a significant price for our freedom. My father's brother, Kenneth James Cox, died in England in 1943 while serving with 410 Squadron. My wife's uncle, John Murchie, died during a training accident in 1941 and is resting in a grave in Ayr, Scotland.

A few years ago I received a letter addressed to my deceased father from a boyhood friend who didn't know that he had died twenty years previously. When I contacted Laurie Middlemiss, he was able to tell me something of their life growing up in east end Toronto, the uncle I never knew, and my father as a young boy, but not much about his wartime experiences. Later I discovered that Laurie had served in Bomber Command as a tail gunner, and had suffered a nervous breakdown before being returned to Canada to spend most of his life in a mental hospital.

The first Canadian to die in the Second World War was Sergeant Albert S. Prince. He died in an attack on a German battleship the day after war was declared. The last to die, six years later, was Flying Sergeant William Holowaty who was killed when the Lancaster Bomber he was flying back to Canada crashed. Between those years many more Canadian flyers and ground crew personnel served with distinction; some paid the ultimate price.

L.D. Bashow provides some significant figures in his history of the Canadians and the Bomber Command experience, *No Prouder Place*. If your ancestor was assigned to Bomber Command there was a one in four chance he would become a casualty. Bashow writes that in six years of war, Bomber Command lost 55,573 airmen, mostly on operations. Aircraft losses totalled 12,330, of which 8,655 were lost over Europe, Germany, or Italy. Of every one hundred airmen, thirty-eight would be killed on operations, eight would become prisoners of war, three would be wounded, seven killed in training accidents, and three wounded while training. He further states that of the 91,166 RCAF aircrew trained through the BCATP almost 83 percent graduated to one of the aircrew trades. The majority of graduates, approximately 40,000 Canadians, served with Bomber Command and of these 9,919 became casualties of war — killed, wounded, taken prisoner.[18]

If your ancestor was assigned to Fighter Command or any of the other commands, statistics were a little less frightening but their service was no less challenging. In fighter command a tour of duty usually consisted of thirty-five sorties that were followed by an assignment as an instructor or in operational planning at group headquarters. A second tour might consist of twenty-five sorties before being considered "tour expired" and being sent home. Sometimes a pilot might not be expected to complete all sorties if it was noticed he had developed "the twitch." This meant a pilot's nerves were becoming a little frayed.

If you want to know what it was like to attack enemy bombers, strafe ground targets, or engage enemy fighters in the air, read one of the excellent biographies I have listed. These men, alone in the cockpit of a Hurricane, Spitfire, Tempest, or any other aircraft, would have known what it was like to face death every time they left the ground. Many Canadians achieved the magical number of five enemy aircraft shot down to achieve Ace status. Some of these men — George Beurling, Russell Bannock, Robert Barton, Edward Charles, James Edwards, Donald Gordon, Ross Gray, George Hill, George Keefer, John Kent, Robert Kipp, Henry McLeod, John Mitchner, John Turnbull, and Vernon Woodward, to name just a few — became highly decorated pilots. Many more received bravery medals for conspicuous gallantry or meritorious service and some — Andrew Charles Mynarski, David Ernest Hornell, Ian Willoughby Bazalgette, Robert Hampton Grey — were awarded the Victoria Cross for some outstanding act of bravery.

Bill Olmstead sums up his experience as fighter pilot when, following the war, he described his Wing's contribution:

> The Wing expended 3,422,527 rounds of ammunition and lost 325 Spitfires and seventy-nine pilots, of whom twenty-one escaped or became prisoners of war. In 20,000 sorties our loss was one pilot for every 25 trips flown. 126 Wing flew more sorties than any other wing in the Second Tactical Air Force with a top-scoring record of 360 enemy air-craft destroyed, fifteen probables and 153 damaged. On the ground the pilots destroyed and damaged 4,468 enemy vehicles, blew up or disabled 496 locomotives, rendered 1,569 rail cars useless, and made 426 cuts in rail lines.[19]

What Can We Learn About Our RCAF Ancestors?

You probably already know if your ancestor was a pilot officer, flying officer, or served in some capacity as ground crew.

Perhaps you can also provide a service number and other pertinent information.

When your ancestor's records arrive you may be surprised by the quantity of material in their file. What you receive will depend on the extent of service, whether your ancestor was killed, or if there was a court of enquiry or even a court martial. The file may also contain letters from next of kin to authorities in Ottawa and, in the event of death, notification from both the government and squadron. The most significant document will be the record of training and service.

This document will give you important information about when they were Taken on Strength (TOS) and Struck off Strength (SOS) for each phase of their training. As well, you will be able to discover specific dates and locations of postings and promotions. According to Pilot Officer Blanchfield he started his training as an AC2, progressed to LAC, then Flt.Sgt, then Pilot Officer (P.O.).

If your ancestor was air crew but not a pilot officer, the Record of Service will show you the movement from initial training school to elementary flight training school and then on to air observation school or something else. Refer to the list of abbreviations on page 158, as well as LAC to help you understand the records.

If your air force ancestor died on service, his or her documents will also include a letter noting the fact and providing some basic information about the event. The next of kin also received notification from Ottawa and were issued a Memorial Cross and Operational Tour Wings. Any air crew member who died on active duty was considered as having completed a tour of duty and was entitled to this award. If the incident occurred in England there is a very good chance pictures of the funeral service, as well as photographs of the grave site, will be included in the service file.

Included in F.O. Cox's and P.O. Blanchfield's documents were transcripts of the court of enquiry conducted into the incident that resulted in the death. They had been scrambled to intercept enemy aircraft and, upon returning to base, instructed to practise an interception on another Mosquito. The planes made contact in the fog and both crashed.

In Cox's personal family album were letters of regret from former employers and friends, as well as a copy of his last letter written to his parents. All air crew were encouraged to write a letter and will, kept on file by the RCAF command in the event of death, to be forwarded to parents or significant others following the event.

Remember to check your local newspaper. It was a common practice to record military deaths and, in many cases, a picture was included. The *Toronto Star*'s webpage, *www.pagesofthepast.ca*, yielded four obituaries for F.O. Cox, all with pictures.

Lloyd Garnet Turcott served as a Wireless Operator, ground crew, stationed in St. John's, Newfoundland. Newfoundland was considered "overseas" by many of the military personnel stationed there during the war. In Lloyd's personal files were various pieces of memorabilia related to his war experiences, which helped start the family narrative before his service files arrived from Ottawa.

This first discovery allows you to identify the command headquarters Lloyd was assigned to during his posting. No. 1 Group Headquarters was responsible for submarine patrols and the aerial protection of those convoys leaving Newfoundland for England. Searching the archival records of this group gives researchers some idea of Turcott's part in the role of this unit. The autographs were probably Turcott's associates.

Also in the family album was the original certificate of discharge, which provides Lloyd's service number, date of release from the air force and the medals he was awarded. The service number was certainly helpful when requesting copies of the complete records from the archives.

Because Lloyd did not serve in England or northwest Europe he was not entitled to any of the Stars. He was, however, entitled to the overseas clasp for his CVSM because Newfoundland was not part of Canada until 1949. Upon discharge, Lloyd was issued a War Service Badge, which this document proves he received. A good description of the recipient is provided on the back of the discharge certificate along with specific years of service and a signature.

Readers may remember reading about Reginald Scherk in the previous chapter. Family historians should check if any members of the Sherk family served in the RCAF in the Second World War and received gallantry awards. I found P/O Walter Scott Sherk and P/O Raymond John Frederick Sherk.

The *Gazette* entries recorded that Walter Sherk was awarded the Distinguished Flying Cross, 17 March 1943, and a bar (equal to a second award) to his DFC on 31 May 1943. Raymond Sherk was Mentioned in Dispatches, 1 January 1945.

> Pilot Officer Sherk (W.S.), as captain of aircraft, was detailed to attack Cologne in February 1943. When about 70 miles short of the target the port engine failed. This officer, with great determination, pressed on, however, and successfully completed his mission. On all his operation sorties this officer has displayed the same fine fighting spirit and his determination and courage have been a source of inspiration to the whole squadron.[20]

And when he was granted a bar to his DFC, the *Gazette* printed the following:

One night in April 1943, Pilot Officer Sherk, Flying Officers McGladrey and Morrison and Sergeant Bebensee were pilot, wireless operator, navigator and flight engineer respectively in an aircraft which attacked Stettin. Whilst over the target area, the bomber was struck by falling incendiary bombs. One of them, which lodged behind the pilot's seat, jammed the aileron and rudder controls. Flames and smoke rapidly filled the cockpit and Pilot Officer Sherk's clothing caught alight. The aircraft began to lose height, diving steeply. Pilot Officer Sherk endeavoured to regain control, whilst Flying Officer McGladrey attempted to subdue the flames. Meanwhile, Sergeant Bebenbsee struggled to free the locked controls. Just as the situation appeared hopeless, the pilot regained control, and a course was set for home as Flying Officer McGladney extinguished the fire. Much of the navigational equipment had been lost but Flying Officer Morrison, displaying great skill, was able to plot accurate courses. Sergeant Bebensee, who worked untiringly for three quarters of an hour, succeeded in freeing the controls. Eventually, Pilot Officer Sherk flew the badly damaged bomber back to this country. In circumstances fraught with great danger, these members of the crew displayed great courage, skill and determination. [21]

F.O.s Roy Glover McGladrey and Roy Gordon Morrison with P/O Sherk received the Distinguished Flying Cross while

Sergeant Douglas Glenn Bebensee was awarded the Distinguished Flying Medal. These Canadians flew with No. 35 Squadron, which was part of the Britain's Royal Air Force Bomber Command.

Flying Officer Raymond Sherk's recommendation for a Military Cross (MC) reads:

> During the last two years this officer has shown continuous determination and devotion to duty. After participating in the destruction of an enemy aircraft in the Quattara Depression on 29 September 1942, he crashed landed 30 miles inside enemy territory. He was captured after walking to within a mile of the British lines. He remained a prisoner in enemy hands for almost a year during which time he made several unsuccessful attempts to escape. On one occasion after being at large for four days he was recaptured by the Germans but by a subtle ruse escaped again the same day and finally reached the 1st Canadian Division on 26 October 1943.
>
> He came to No. 401 Squadron in February 1944 and has taken part in over 70 operational trips. On 15 March 1944 while escorting Marauders over the Pas de Calais area his engine failed and he bailed out. Again showing fine determination he evaded capture and rejoined his squadron about a month later.[22]

If you do discover an ancestor in the *London Gazette*, you can follow up your discovery at Canadian air force website, *www. airforce.ca*, where you will find more details about your ancestor, including an outline of his training record. The original citation made by your ancestor's commanding officer will contain much more detail than the printed recommendation. You should always check the archives for the location of these documents.

Another avenue of discovery occurred when a Sherk family member mentioned that there had been a family reunion years ago. This often means that someone has assumed responsibility for collecting family records. Because two members of the family had been awarded gallantry medals, I contacted a publisher of Canadian aviation books, Larry Milberry, who was able to provide the telephone number of Raymond Sherk and Raymond was able to provide the email address for the Sherk Family genealogist in Pennsylvania. This contact produced an article, "Walter (Rocky) Scott Sherk (E1422202) Canadian Pilot and War Hero."[23]

The family newsletter article certainly adds an interesting dimension to Sherk family history. The pictures that accompanied the article show Walter as a sergeant pilot with his wife, probably shortly after his marriage, and later as a pilot officer wearing the ribbon bar for his DFC and the small wings of a Pathfinder pilot.

Pathfinder pilots were only issued with one set of these wings and forbidden to wear them during bombing raids. It was common knowledge that Pathfinder crews were not given the same courtesy by the enemy as regular bomber crews.

Canadians who were assigned to Bomber Command generally flew three types of aircraft: The Hanley-Page "Halifax," sometimes called the Hali-Bag; Vickers-Armstrong "Wellington," often called the Whimpy: and the A.W. Roe and Co. (Avro) Lancaster or "Lanc."

FIRST WORLD WAR AIR FORCE RESOURCES

LAC

- MG 30 — papers and diaries of individuals who have donated their personal files to the archives. Here you will find the records of flying aces Billy Bishop, William Barker, Raymond Collishaw, and others.
- MG 30-A72 — contains Lloyd Rochester's diaries, 1912, 1916–19 while he served in the RFC.
- MG 30-E280 — Raymond Collishaw fonds. Contains squadron rosters, lists of officers, information regarding Numerical listings of the squadrons of the RFC and RNAS, and the German Jastas (squadrons) that opposed them. Finding aid 1490. An attempt has been made to list the personnel who served with every squadron in the RFC, RNAS, and RAF during the war. Also included is material related to topics including the death of German pilots and the nominal rolls of many of the German Jastas.
- RG 9-II-B-7 — non-permanent active militia files, 1919.
- RG 9-III-D-3 — war diaries, RFC, 1916/06/16–1916/06/22, Vol., 5074, microfilm reel T-11353.
- RG 9-III-C-1 — commissions, RFC, candidates, 1917–18.
- RG 9-III-C-1 — operations, Vimy Ridge, commissions, RFC.

- RG 9-III-C-5 — applications for transfer, RFC, 1916.
- RG 9-III-C-14 — Air Force historical records 1915–20, Canadians in the RFC/RAF/ Royal Naval Air Service/Canadian Air Force.
- RG 24-C-25 — ledgers of CEF officers to RFC, 1918/19.
- RG 24-C-6 — fatal casualties of New Brunswick officers seconded to the RFC.
- RG 24-C-6 — nominal roll of Canadian airmen serving in the RFC and RAF.
- RG 24-C-8 — Royal Flying Corps, overseas aircraft flotilla — general — volumes 1–9, boxes 4506–4507 (1915–21). Files contain information related to training, discharges, drafts, application of enlistment, transfers of officers.
- RG 150-7 — Canadians serving with the RFC, nominal lists of officers.
- RG 150-1 — 1914–20, lists produced regularly of officers and men taken on strength, struck off strength, promoted, demoted, punished, pay withheld, decorated, absent, killed, wounded, and sick.

Websites

National Defence, Canadian Directorate of History and Heritage, *www.cmp-cpm.forces.gc.ca/dhh-dhp/index-eng.asp*, holds cards prepared for each identified Canadian who served in the British Flying Service.

Grenadier Bookstore, *www.grenadiermilitaria.com*.

National Archives U.K., *www.nationalarchives.gov.uk/documents online*, RFC/RNAS/RAF officer's records. Search the catalogue at *www.nationalarchives.gov.uk/records/looking-for-person/default.htm*. Select Military and scroll down through army, navy, and air force records. They provide a very useful guide for searching their military collection. However, to access many of their records you may have to either visit the archives or hire a researcher in England or for a small fee the archives will copy the documents and send them as a jpeg file to your computer.

Books

Barker, R. *The Royal Flying Corps in France: From Mons to the Somme*. London, U.K.: Constable, 1994.

Edwards, S. *From Up Above: My Fathers Letters from the Royal Flying Corps, World War One*. Owen Sound, ON: Susan Edwards Publisher, 2004.

Lee, A.S. *No Parachute: A Fighter Pilot in World War One*. London, U.K.: Jarrolds Publishing, 1968; reprinted by New York: Time-Life Books, 1991.

McInnes, I., and J. Webb. *A Contemptible Little Flying Corps*. London, U.K.: London Stamp Exchange, 1991.

SECOND WORLD WAR AIR FORCE RESOURCES

LAC

- RG 24, vol. 23195: E to H and I to M, vol. 32196: A to D and N to W. Air force nominal rolls for RFC and RAF can be found in RG 24, (air force) acc. 1995-96/670, box 1: Acland to Luxton.

- RG 24, (air force) acc. 1995-96/670, box 2: Macaskill to Zieman.
- RG 24, 1992-93/169, will provide service files. Use finding aid 24-167.
- RG 25 — Royal Canadian Air Force Squadrons in the United Kingdom, 1939–45.
- RG 24-E-7 — RCAF Operations Record Books (ORB), Squadron Diaries. Finding aid, 24-104(a) includes volume, number, name, and geographical location of the unit and dates of the Operational Record Book. Finding Aid 24-104(b) provides a typed list of O.R.B. by RCAF unit in microfilm reel order.
- RG 24-E and RG 24-C-2 — Second World War court martial records. Including charge sheets, correspondence, investigative material, proceedings, and evidence.
- RG 24-C-1 — records of RCAF personnel who were prisoners of war, next of kin, and related correspondence.
- RG 24-C-3 — war diary of the 2nd Canadian Parachute Battalion, within 1st Special Services Force.
- RG 24-G-20-3 — Second World War military personnel files, predominately 1939–45. Personnel files contain records of those men and women serving in the army, navy, or air force. At present the files are of those individuals who died during the war, through or as a result of enemy action, accidental death, or from natural causes.

- Accession Number 1992-93/314 GAD — finding aid 150-6 (paper), former RGs 150-4, 24-C-25-d,e,f,g,h, War Graves Registers, and related documents
- Containers 1–38 hold applications for burial of ex-CEF personnel to be buried in Canada or U.S. with a military marker paid for by the Government.
- Containers 39–144, "Black Binders" are the registers of death and location of the body or memorial in Belgium, France, or United Kingdom.
- Containers 145–238, "Brown Binders" focus on the circumstances of death with information about the initial grave.
- Containers 239–274 cover deaths and burial of personnel in Canada and the United States during and after the First World War.
- Containers 275-278, ledgers covering groups killed in First World War not mentioned in any of the other records. Included are those lost at sea, members of the Siberian Expeditionary Force, enemy aliens interned in Canada, and miscellaneous personnel of the CEF and Royal Canadian Navy.
- Container- 279–302, records of Second World War personnel killed in Canada, including British Commonwealth Air Training Plan.

Websites

Air Force Association of Canada, *www.airforce.ca.*
BCATP Museum in Calgary, *www.airmuseum.ca.*

Bomber Command Museum of Canada, Nanton, Alberta, *www.
bombercommandmuseum.ca*, covers excellent overview of
Canada's role in bomber command and particularly 6 Group.

Canadian Warplane Heritage Museum, Hamilton, Ontario, *www.
warplane.com*.

CanMilAir, *www.canmilair.com/RCAFhistory.htm*, where there is
an excellent historical overview of the RCAF.

Eastern Townships Heritage Museum, Knowlton, Quebec, *www.
townshipsheritage.com/Eng/Articles/Outings/knowlton.biplane.
html*.

Fleet Air Arm, *www.fleetairarmarchive.net*, search the archives at this
site.

Imperial War Museum, Duxford, *duxford.iwm.org.uk/server.
php?show=nav.00d*, where you can find images and archives
of the Air Force.

Juno Beach, *www.members.shaw.ca/junobeach/juno-4-20.htm*. Here
you can check the list of squadrons that were involved in
D-Day.

Luft Stalag I, *www.merkki.com*.

Metro Toronto Branch of the Aircrew Association, *www.torontoair
crew.com*. If you select from the list of air crew occupations
this site will eventually lead you the biographies of the veterans who belong to the association.

National Collection of Aerial Photography, *www.aerial.rcahms.
gov.uk*. Here you will find photographs of the effects of the
Second World War bombing campaign and excellent photos
of the Normandy landings.

RAF Bomber Command Memorial, *www.rafbombercommand.com*.
Great links to the RAF's Battle of Britain Memorial and
RAF museums at Hendon and Cosford.

Royal Air Force Organisation, *www.rafweb.org/index.html*. Find
those who have been awarded the Victoria Cross, and lots more.

Veterans' Affairs Canada, *www.vac-acc.gc.ca*.
WWI William Barker, VC, *www.constable.ca/caah/barker.htm*.

Books

Allison, L. H. Hayward. *They Shall Grow Not Old: A Book of Remembrance*. Brandon, MN: Commonwealth Air Training Plan Museum, 1992.

Barris, T. *Behind the Glory: The Plan that Won the Allied Air War*. Toronto: Macmillan of Canada, 1992.

Bashow, D.L. *None but the Brave: The Essential Contributions of RAF Bomber Command to Allied Victory During the Second World War*. Toronto: Canadian Defence Academy Press, 2009.

Bashow, L.D. *No Prouder Place: Canadians and the Bomber Command Experience 1939–1945*. St. Catharines, ON: Vanwell Publishing Ltd., 2005.

Dunmore, S. *Wings for Victory: The Remarkable Story of the British Commonwealth Air Training Plan in Canada*. Toronto: McClelland & Stewart, 1994.

Greenhouse, B., S.J. Harris, W. Johnston, and W. Rawling. *The Crucible of War 1939–1945: The Official History of the Royal Canadian Air Force*. Volumes 1, 2, 3. Toronto: University of Toronto Press, 1980.

Hendire, A. *Canadian Squadrons in Coastal Command*. St. Catharines, ON: Vanwell Publishing Ltd., 1997.

Hunt, C., W. *Dancing in the Sky: The Royal Flying Corps in Canada*. Toronto: Dundurn Press, 2009.

Milberry, L. *Canada's Air Force: At War and Peace*, Volumes One, Two, and Three. Toronto: CANAV Books, 2000.

Murray, Peden. *A Thousand Shall Fall*. Toronto: Stoddart Publishing, 1997; one of the best concerning bomber command.

Wise, S.F. *Canadian Airmen and the First World War: The Official History of The Royal Canadian Air Force*, Volume 1. Toronto: University of Toronto Press, 1980.

Uniforms and Insignia

Blatherwick, F.J. *Royal Canadian Air Force: Honours, Medals, Badges, 1920–1968*. Ottawa: Pelorus Publishing, 1992.

Brown, G. *The Conspicuous Gallantry Medal*. Vancouver: Pacific Publishing, 1977.

Carroll, W.H. *Eagles Recalled: Air Force Wings of Canada, Great Britain and the British Commonwealth, 1913–1945*. Atglen, PA: Scheffe, 1997.

Halliday, H. *Not in the Face of the Enemy: Canadians Awarded the Air Force Cross and Air Force Medal, 1918–1961*. Toronto: Robin Brass Studio, 2000.

Hampson, B. *Canadian Flying Service Emblems and Insignia (1914– 1984)*. Vancouver: B. Hampson Publishing, 1986.

Linden, R. *Canadians on Radar: Royal Canadian Air Force, 1940– 1945: Honours and Awards*. Ottawa: Canadian Radar History Project, 2000.

Martin, A. *The Canadian Medal Rolls: Distinguished Flying Medal 1939–1945*. Toronto: Charlton Press, 1984.

Nelson, K.J. *Royal Air Force Awards, 1918–1919: Being the Distinguished Flying Cross, Air Force Cross, Distinguished Flying Medal, Air Force Medal*. Whitby, ON: Kenneth James Nelson Publishing, 2000.

Riddle, D. *The Distinguished Service Order to the Canadian Expeditionary Force and Canadians in the Royal Naval Air Service, Royal Flying Corps and Royal Air Force, 1915–1920*. Winnipeg: Kirby-Martlor Press, 1991.

Tavender, I.T. *The Distinguished Flying Medal: A Record of Courage, 1918–1982.* Suffolk, U.K.: J.B. Hayward, 1990.

Biographies

Beurling, G. *Malta Spitfire, The Buzz Beurling Story: Canada's World War Two Daredevil Pilot.* Toronto: Penguin Books, 2002.

Bishop, W.A. *The Courage of the Early Morning: The Story of Billy Bishop.* Toronto: McClelland & Stewart, 1965.

Collins, R. *The Long and the Short and the Tall: An Ordinary Airman's War.* Saskatoon: Western Producer Prairie Books, 1986.

Harvey, D. *Boys, Bombs and Brussels Sprouts.* Toronto: McClelland & Stewart, 1982.

Harvey, D. *The Tumbling Mirth: Remembering the Air Force.* Toronto: McClelland & Stewart, 1983.

Hewer, H. *In for a Penny in for a Pound: The Adventures and Misadventures of a Wireless Operator in Bomber Command.* Toronto: Stoddart Publishing, 2000.

McCaffery, D. *Billy Bishop: Canadian Hero.* Toronto: James Lorimer & Company, 1988.

McIntosh, D. *High Blue Battle: The War Diary of No. 1 (401) Fighter Squadron, RCAF.* Toronto: Stoddart Publishing, 1990.

McIntosh, D. *Terror in the Starboard Seat, 41 Trips aboard a Mosquito: A True Story of 418 Squadron.* Toronto: Stoddart Publishing, 1998.

Nolan, B. *Hero: The Buzz Beurling Story.* Toronto: Penguin Books, 1987.

Peden, M. *A Thousand Shall Fall.* Toronto: Canada's Wings Publishing, 1979.

Ralph, W. *Barker VC: William Barker, Canada's Most Decorated War Hero.* Toronto: Doubleday Canada, 1997.

Soward, S.E. *A Formidable Hero: Lieutenant R. H. Gray, VC, DSC, RCNVR.* Toronto: Canav Books, 1987.

Medal Resources

Air Force Association of Canada, *www.airforce.ca/honours-awards/ search-awards-database.*

LAC, *collectionscanada.ca,* for the RCAF.

London Gazette is where abbreviated versions of all citations can be found. At *www.london-gazette.co.uk/search*, select Advanced. The citation is quite different from the original recommendation made by your ancestor's commanding officer.

National Archives, U.K., *nationalarchives.gov.uk*, holds the recommendations for Canadians who flew with the RAF.

CHAPTER NINE

War on the Water: My Ancestors May Have Served with the Navy

MY ANCESTOR MAY HAVE SERVED IN THE PROVINCIAL MARINE

The formation of the Provincial Marine was a direct result of the need for Britain to maintain control of the Great Lakes after the defeat of France following the Seven Years War (1756–63). Naval depots were established on Lakes Champlain, Ontario, Erie, and eventually the upper lakes. They were charged by the admiralty with maintaining a small fleet of ships. For many years, the marine was responsible for the transport of men and supplies along all the great waterways of this country. In time of emergency, it was expected that the Provincial Marine could be called upon to man armed gunboats, frigates, or even larger warships. Control of the Provincial Marine fell under the direction of the Quartermaster General's Department of the British Army stationed at Quebec.

As war became imminent in 1812, the British realized that they would have to supplement the marine with trained seamen from England. This was especially urgent as ever larger vessels were built to maintain control of the Great Lakes.[1]

Any participation of an ancestor in the war on the lakes is certainly worth mentioning. At one point, the United States and Great Britain built ships as large as any sailing the oceans of the world. If you suspect an ancestor served on the Great Lakes, check the records of the following vessels: *Queen Charlotte, Niagara (Royal George), Montreal (Wolfe), Charwell (Earl of Moira), Star (Lord Melville), Netley (Beresford), Magnet (Sir Sidney Smith), Hunter, Prevost, Prince Regent, Princess Charlotte,* or *Duke of Gloucester.* If you suspect your ancestor served on Lake Erie, August 1813, check the musters of: *Detroit* (crew 160), *Queen Charlotte* (crew 110), *Lady Prevost* (crew seventy-six), *General Hunter* (crew thirty-nine), *Chippewa* (crew twenty-five), and the *Little Belt* (crew fifteen).[2] (The names in parenthesis show the former names of ships whose designation changed when the British Admiralty took over command of the Great Lakes Squadrons. While researching, you may find the names of other ships.)

The British also manned these vessels with marines. These seagoing soldiers were used to help maintain order on board the vessel and to act as sharpshooters during naval engagements. In the early years of the war the Royal Newfoundland Fencibles served as marines. Later, British Royal Marine regiments were employed.

There were a number of major naval engagements fought on the lakes. Both American and British ships were used to transport troops during various invasion attempts, such as the naval battles of Put-in-Bay, 10 September 1813 on Lake Erie; the Burlington Races, 23 September 1813 on Lake Ontario; and the Battle of Plattsburgh, 11 September 1814 on Lake Champlain. The story of the American ships *Hamilton* and *Scourge* will certainly highlight some of the naval action on the lakes as both ships floundered during a particularly violent storm on Lake Ontario and recently have been discovered relatively intact on the lake bottom. Read about the *Nancy* if you want to discover something of the naval action on the upper lakes and the establishment of Penetanguishene as a naval base. You can also add to your family narrative by reading about men such as James Lucas Yeo, John Schank, Alexander Grant, John Steel, Thomas Macdonough, Hugh Earl, Charles Frederic Rolette, Robert Irvine, and Robert Barclay.[3] All served in the Provincial Marine or Royal Navy leading up to or during the War of 1812.

The war ended with the Treaty of Ghent and a formal redrawing of the border between Canada and the United States. The Treaty of Rush-Bagot, signed in 1817, severely limited the size of ships built on the lakes.

During the War of 1812, British naval services on the lakes fell under the jurisdiction of the Admiralty Lake Services. The depots at St. Jean, Quebec, Amherstburg (Fort Malden), Kingston, Ontario, and eventually Penetanguishene, Ontario, were all established as a result of the need to maintain warships on the Great Lakes. The Provincial Marine were again called upon to patrol the lakes during the Rebellions of 1837 and the Fenian Raids of 1866 and 1870.

Where Do You Begin Your Search?

If you suspect your ancestor may have served in the Royal Navy between the end of the War of 1812 and the beginning of the official Canadian Navy in 1910, start your search at the National Archives U.K. website. Search Military, then First World War. Scroll down to Naval Forces where you will find two very important subtitles: "List of Service Numbers and Volume Numbers" and "Royal Navy: Registers of Seamen's Services (1853 to 1923)."

On the first page is a chart giving you the volume in which you can locate the pay ledger sheets and service files for your ancestor. You will need to know his service number to access the correct volume. The pay ledger sheets (RG 150, 1992-93/170) will provide you with details about your ancestor's service, rating, etc., while the service files (RG 24, 1992-93/169) are more administrative.

The second source you'll want to access is the Royal Navy: Registers of Seamen's Service. When you select this option it will link you to the National Archives U.K.: *www.nationalarchives. gov.uk/records/looking-for-person/default.htm*. Click on the navy link you are interested in. Here you will gain access to the Admiralty records (ADM 139). Spend some time reading this site because it contains some very important information about naval records.

What if You Discover a Picture of a Navy Ancestor in "Square Rig"?

Not much changed over the years in seamen's naval dress and tradition, other than slight variations in clothing and the addition of new trade badges as technology influenced ship design. When Canada established a navy in 1910 it simply adopted British uniforms and traditions. It wasn't until the unification of the armed forces in the 1960s that Canada broke from this tradition, adopting a uniquely Canadian uniform.

The majority of us who had an ancestor in the navy will discover that he was a rating rather than an officer. Rating is a term used to describe other ranks and refers to his level of proficiency or rank. The basic rating was an ordinary seaman followed by able seaman, leading seaman, petty officer, and chief petty officer. Leading seamen would wear a "fouled anchor" badge while petty officers wore crossed "fouled anchors," and chief petty officers "fouled anchors" with a crown above.

As your ancestor achieved these ratings he wore the appropriate badge on the left sleeve. On your ancestor's right sleeve was his non-substantive rating recorded on his official papers as "sub-ratings." If your ancestor is wearing stripes on the sleeve of his left arm, usually just under the substantive rank/rating, these are not rank badges but good conduct stripes awarded for years of service with a conduct assessment of "very good." One stripe was awarded for over three years with a good conduct sheet, two for over eight years, and three for over thirteen years. Your navy ancestor received extra pay for these stripes. The non-substantive badges worn on the right sleeve denote a sailor's training. These could be for armourer, electrical engineer, shipwright, stoker, artificer, gunner's mate, signaler, or any of the multiple trades needed to keep a ship seaworthy.

If you are fortunate enough to discover a photograph of a navy ancestor, check the cap tally worn around his seaman's cap. The issue of these tallies was officially introduced in 1858 and will help you learn about the ship in which an ancestor served. During the Second World War these tallies did not include the name of the ship, just HMCS for Canadian sailors or HMS for British seamen.

After you access your pre–First World War Royal Navy ancestor's service record, you should familiarize yourself with the abbreviations in the musters and pay ledgers. An excellent chart is provided in *Tracing Your Naval Ancestors* on the National Archives U.K. website.

If your ancestor is dressed as an officer, check the hat badge to see if he was a petty or commanding officer and the sleeves of the uniform to identify the weave of the braid to establish rank and service: Royal Canadian Navy, Royal Canadian Naval Volunteer Reserve, Royal Canadian Volunteer Reserve, or Merchant Marine.

Discovering Your First World War Canadian Navy Ancestors

On Saturday, 30 January 2010, during a hockey game between the Vancouver Canucks and the Toronto Maple Leafs the announcement was made that Canada's Navy was celebrating its hundredth year. I'm sure this came as a surprise to many of the fans sitting in the arena. Many of us today really don't give much thought to the history of our armed forces and just assume that they have been in existence forever.

Finding Canadian First World War Navy ancestors can present something of a challenge. The search for Emory Fitzgerald, Royal Naval Canadian Volunteer Reserve, was just such a challenge. I found a postcard online that showed a picture of Emory. On the back was written: "O. Sea. Emery Fitzgerald, R.N.C.V.R # 2748, H.M.S. *Swiftsure*, c/o G.P.O. London England."

Where Did it Begin?

In 1907 the British Government transferred responsibility for the naval dockyard at Halifax to the Canadian government. In 1910 the base at Esquimalt, British Columbia, was handed over. On 12 January 1910, the Naval Service Bill was introduced in our Parliament followed by assent 14 May 1910, creating the Naval Service of Canada (Canadian Naval Forces). Prime Minister Sir Wilfred Laurier (1896–1911) envisioned a permanent navy with five cruisers and six destroyers, a naval reserve of experienced merchant officers to be called up when needed, and a volunteer reserve that could be mobilized during periods of emergency, and a naval college. The initial steps involved the transfer of two destroyers from the Royal Navy: HMS *Rainbow*, which arrived on the West Coast on 7 November 1910, and the HMS *Niobe*, stationed at Halifax, 21 October 1910. The concept of a Canadian Navy met with some opposition in Parliament and was part of the reason for the defeat of the Laurier's Liberal government in 1911. When Sir Robert Borden's Conservatives took office they immediately modified the Naval Service Act. The result was the opening of a small naval college in 1911, a name change to Royal Canadian Navy (29 August 1911), and the 1913 formation of the Royal Naval Canadian Volunteer Reserve. The navy had to make-do with the two old destroyers as training vessels.

On 7 August 1914, the government acquired two submarines, C.C.1 and C.C.2, from British Columbia. They had originally been purchased from Chile for use on the west coast but with war imminent Ottawa requested their purchase and transfer to Halifax.[4]

When war was declared, Canada's two warships and two submarines were transferred to the British Admiralty. At first, Canada was asked to concentrate on providing troops for the western front and not in building or manning warships. Our coastal defences consisted of a Naval Control Service to inspect and control the movement of shipping in Canadian ports and the Naval Control and Radio Telegraph Services to control radio stations ashore and afloat. However, the increase in enemy submarine activity forced the British Admiralty to change its mind about Canadian support. In 1916, Canada was asked to create a coastal patrol force of thirty-six vessels.

By 1918, the Canadian Patrol Service had 112 ships under the command of a retired Royal Navy officer, Captain Walter Hose. In August 1918, the Royal Canadian Naval Air Service was formed with pilots and airplanes provided by the United States government.

By the end of hostilities there were approximately 5,500 officers and men serving in the Royal Canadian Navy. Many more Canadians joined the Royal Navy. Canada's shipyards eventually built sixty anti-submarine trawlers, one hundred wooden drifters, and 550 anti-submarine motor launches, plus various ships for France.

Almost 1,700 officers and men served with the Royal Navy through the Overseas Division of the Royal Naval Canadian Volunteer Reserve. This number included 264 naval officers, 635 pilots in the Royal Naval Air Service, 107 surgeons, and 112 chief mechanics. These men served anywhere in the world that the British Navy had ships. Rowland Richard Louis Bourke, a Canadian commanding a Royal Navy motor-launch, received the Victoria Cross for his part in an attack on the port of Ostend.

When Your RNCVR Ancestor's Service Records Arrive What Can You Expect to Discover?

Photograph of Emery Fitzgerald, RNCVR, HMS Swiftsure, acquired from an online auction. Author's collection.

287

After I received the postcard of Emery Fitzgerald I started to search for his service records. He was one of those Canadians who served on board a Royal Navy vessel. We know this because his postcard notes his ship was HMS *Swiftsure*. A check of British naval vessels proves that the *Swiftsure* at one time had served with the Royal Navy's Pacific Squadron and was on station in Esquimalt Harbour in 1889. Later records show *Swiftsure*, launched 12 January 1908, served with the Home Fleet until 1906 and with the Channel Fleet until 1908. In November 1914, she was assigned convoy duty to India and then stationed near the Suez Cannel. In February 1915, she was part of the Dardonelles' Squadron supporting the unsuccessful invasion of Turkey and in February 1916 was part of the 9th Cruiser Squadron in the Atlantic. Eventually she was placed on reserve in 1917 at Chatham England.

We can surmise from the postcard that Emery must have joined the ship after 1910 because the note on the back of the picture states that his rating is ordinary seaman, the lowest rating, and he enlisted in the Royal Naval Canadian Volunteer Reserve. There was no RNCVR until after the establishment of the Canadian Navy in 1910 and if he had served earlier he would have been rated at least able seaman.

Emery Fitzgerald's service number, found on the back of the card, allowed me to order his service records from LAC. The records contained his Application to be Enrolled, Statement of Service sheet, Demobilization Form (overseas), various documents from the Department of Pensions and National Health, and letters Emery had written to the Department of National Defence concerning Naval Prize money. Included in the package were also the usual documents concerning the awarding of the British War and Victory Medals as well as his war badge number, 1531.

Just the fact that Emery had claimed prize money indicates that he was on board during specific naval engagements involving enemy shipping. The Admiralty granted prize money according to a scale from commanding officer down to the lowest seaman. It was granted when an enemy ship was captured and brought back to port. Using the Internet it was easy to trace the history of the ships on which Emery served. Interestingly, HMS *Swiftsure* is not listed on his service sheet. The rest of the information provided useful vital statistics about Emery.

Discovering Your Second World War Royal Canadian Navy Ancestors

I knew George Hunter Cree, Ray Mecoy, and Ed Parsons; all served in the Royal Canadian Naval Volunteer Reserve during the Second World War. Two, my uncle George and neighbour Ray, grew up in east end Toronto, while Ed, also a neighbour, was born and raised in Newfoundland.

They all would have been familiar with the terms "square rig," "rating," "fo'c's'le," "jimmy-the-one," "mess deck," "dog-watch," "mick," "red-lead," "tiddley," and "Newfyjohn." They may have even sung about the "Wavy Navy" and they were representative of the majority of Canadian sailors (97,600 men and 7,122 women) who came from central Canada with little knowledge of the sea. At the end of the war they would have been proud that Canada had the third largest navy in the world and that they had served in what was also referred to as the "Coca-Cola" navy.

All three of these men served at sea, perhaps on a town-class corvette, frigate, bangor minesweeper, tribal class destroyer, motor torpedo boat, armed trawler, or even a submarine. During their time in the navy they were an able seaman, a petty officer, or served as stoker, signalman, wireless telegraphist, gunner's mate, torpedo man, cook, or supply rating, all at different levels of rank or classification.

They could identify officer rank by checking the cap badge or braid on the sleeves of an officer's uniform and quickly note if he or she was Royal Canadian Navy (RCN), Royal Canadian Naval Reserve (RCNR), Royal Canadian Naval Volunteer Reserve (RCNVR), or even Merchant Navy (MN) just by the weave of the braid. They obeyed the command of a petty officer, warrant officer, sub-lieutenant, lieutenant, lieutenant commander, commander, captain, commodore, and admiral in that increasing order of rank.

There is a good chance that they received all the standard medals: Canadian Volunteer Service, Defence Medal, War Medal (1939–45), and 1939–45 Star at the end of the war. They may even have won medals for outstanding service or bravery in the face of the enemy, although those usually went to officers. The one exception, for those who served at sea, was the Atlantic

Ships' crew, HMCS Fort William *(Bangor class minesweeper). Ray Mecoy is second from left, row four. Group photos like this one provide excellent examples of the typical naval uniforms worn by Canadians during the Second World War. Family collection.*

Star. This one medal stated that your ancestors had fought in the longest engagement of the war: The Battle of the Atlantic, 1940–45. If they served on the West Coast, then they would have earned the Pacific Star.

Cree, Mecoy, and Parsons all saw sea duty on corvettes, minesweepers, or destroyers. As Canadians serving on Canadian ships, their family narrative might include convoy duty during the Battles of the Atlantic or St. Lawrence, or maybe patrol duty and action in the Mediterranean or English Channel. They experienced the fury and discomfort of the North Atlantic during winter, may have been part of Operations Neptune and Torch, and knew shore leave in Halifax, Londonderry, and New York City.

They may have experienced the shattering sound of depth charges exploding over a suspected submarine contact; the explosion of 4-inch guns during an attack on an enemy convoy off the coast of France; the detonation of enemy mines as their ship methodically swept enemy mine fields; or the thrill, stress, and perhaps horror of action in a motor torpedo boat as it swept in to attack enemy shipping in the pitch blackness of night. Or they might have been part of the navy administration that staffed shore-based installations in Canada and England.

If your ancestor was one of the 104,722 Canadian men and women who joined the Canadian Navy between 1939 and 1940, it is not enough to simply state that he or she earned the Atlantic or Pacific Star. You will want to learn about training, what life was like onboard a ship at sea, and, if your ancestor was one of 2,024 who died or 319 who were wounded while on active duty, you will want to research the circumstances.[5]

If your ancestor was one of those killed or wounded you'll want to discover the history of the ship and why it sank. Chances are good your ancestor served on one of the twenty-four Canadian warships lost during the Second World War or the five so severely damaged in action that they were declared unseaworthy for further service. Of these twenty-four ships, ten were corvettes, six destroyers, four bangor minesweepers, one an auxiliary cruiser, another a frigate, and two armed yachts.

Service records for naval personnel are held in Record Group 24 and, as is the case with all military records from the Second World War, there are some privacy issues. If your navy ancestor died during the war then their records are open to the public. If they died in the last twenty years only limited information will be released to immediate family. Of course, if your navy ancestor is alive today they can apply for their own records. The archives also hold all ships' records including logs, reports of action and ships' musters. You will have to access the finding aids (24-87 for instance contains ships' logs) to gather a complete set of information on the ship in which your ancestor served. Our archives also hold manuscript groups of collections donated by individuals. These sometimes include interesting information about life aboard naval vessels.

When you start to write your Royal Canadian Navy family narrative, you will need to understand some of the terms and references that your ancestor would have known, used, or been familiar with from their service documents. If your documents arrive without a list of explanations, the following will help:

AMC	— Armed Merchant Cruiser
A/S	— Anti-Submarine
Asdic	— Sonar or submarine detection gear
ASW	— Anti-Submarine Warfare
C-in-C, WA	— Commander-in-Chief, Western Approaches
CCCS	— Commodore Commanding, Canadian Ships (U.K.)

CCNF	—	Commodore Commanding, Newfoundland Force
CNS	—	Chief of Naval Staff, RCN
CO	—	Commanding Officer
COAS	—	Commanding Officer, Atlantic Coast, RCN
Coxswain (cox'n)	—	Senior CPO on the ship
CPO	—	Chief Petty Officer
EG	—	Escort Group
ERA	—	Engine Room Artificer
Fo'c's'le	—	forward part of the ship — seamen's mess
Galley	—	ship's kitchen
Heads	—	toilets
HF/DF	—	High-Frequency Direction Finding
HMCS	—	His Majesty's Canadian Navy
LS	—	Leading Seaman
MOEF	—	Mid-Ocean Escort Force
NSHQ	—	Naval Services Headquarters, Ottawa
OD	—	Ordinary Seaman
ON	—	Fast westbound convoy
ONS	—	Slow westbound convoy
PO	—	Petty Officer
RDFO	—	Radar Officer
R/T	—	Radio Telephone
SC	—	Slow eastbound Convoy
SOE	—	Senior Officer, Escort
SWIC	—	Surface Warning, First Canadian (Radar)
WA	—	Western Approaches
WESTOMP	—	Western Ocean Meeting Place

W/T	— Wireless Telegraphy
WLEF	— Western Local Escort Force
XO	— Executive officer

Your ancestor would have found his place in the basic command and administrative organization of any ship:

- Lieutenant Commander/Captain — regardless of rank, commander, or lieutenant commander, when at sea the officer in charge is referred to as the captain and is responsible for all aspects of the ship. There are a number of ways to discover who was the commanding officer of the ship(s) your ancestor would have served upon.
- Sub Lieutenant or Lieutenant — if the captain was killed, he took command. The XO was responsible for discipline, allocation of duties on the watch, and general organization of ships' duties. On a destroyer, he was a first lieutenant. The crew often referred to him as "Jimmy" or "Jimmy the one."
- Coxswain — senior chief petty officer is next in rank and aids the XO in keeping the roster of duties (the bill) up-to-date. During action, the coxswain took the helm, steering the ship. The chief bo'sun's mate is also a chief petty officer who helps the executive officer with the supervision of the crew and daily routines onboard.
- Medical, supply, and engineering officers — responsible for the men in these departments and report directly to the captain and the executive officer.

- Navigator — works directly with the captain in all matters concerning navigation. He supervises the operations room.
- Gunnery, anti-submarine, communications, and radar officers — handle all matters related to their branches and men under their command. Communications is divided into wireless and visual watches.
- Gunner — supervises the ammunition supply. Ordinary seaman might be assigned as gunner's mate.
- Supply department — includes writers, cooks, and stores men.
- Engineers/stoker — responsible for machinery, boilers (engines), etc. Often a chief petty officer who was highly trained was in command of the stokers. Stokers also had different levels of rank depending on their level of knowledge. The stokers often "messed" together and were exempt from regular watch duties. Their responsibility was the engine room, probably the most dangerous place on the ship. Torpedoes often struck "amid ship" right where the engine room was located.
- Shipwright — handled the general maintenance of the ship, checking for leaks, maintaining boats, etc.
- Midshipman — usually a very junior officer in training.
- Ordinary and able bodied seamen — the rank and file aboard a ship. All had some kind of specific training necessary to man their watches or when called to action stations.[6]

The number of officers and men on a ship depended very much on the size of the vessel. A corvette might have a crew (complement) of eighty officers and men, a frigate would have 135 crewmen, while a destroyer would muster 240 hands. Obviously, the larger the ship the larger the number of officers, specialty branches, and seamen required to operate it at sea and the more complicated the organization or "bill."

Your navy ancestor would have been assigned watches as part of his daily "station." The watches on board Canadian and British warships were the same:

- First Watch — 2000 to 2400 (8:00 p.m. to 12:00 a.m.)
- Middle Watch — 2400 to 0400 (12:00 a.m. to 4:00 a.m.)
- Morning Watch — 0400 to 0800 (4:00 a.m. to 8:00 a.m.)
- Forenoon Watch — 0800 to 1200 (8:00 a.m. to 12:00 p.m.)
- Afternoon Watch — 1200 to 1600 (12:00 p.m. to 4:00 p.m.)
- First Dog Watch — 1600 to 1800 (4:00 p.m. to 6:00 p.m.)
- Second Dog Watch — 1800 to 2000 (6:00 p.m. to 8:00 p.m.)

A sailor served watch on/watch off while on board his ship. Normally, he wouldn't have two consecutive watches. This scheduling meant that men were either on duty, trying to sleep, off duty, or messing (eating). It meant a very busy existence in the fo'c's'le where the ordinary seamen lived. At sea, the smell from the lower decks was a mixture of food, sweaty clothing drying, unwashed men (showers were turned off at sea to conserve fresh water for the boilers), and the smell of vomit from those who were seasick. There are stories of men who spent the whole time on deck — watch on/watch off because they couldn't control their seasickness.

Corvettes were particularly noted for their corkscrew motion while at sea in any kind of ocean swell.[7] One sailor on board a corvette described how, after a few hours at sea, the mess deck would be awash in three or four inches of water swishing back and forth as the ship rode up and down the ocean swells. The motion of the corvette caused cutlery and anything else not lashed down to end up on the floor floating back and forth with the motion of the ship. The mess deck doors were not shut for fear that if the ship were torpedoed the doors might warp and trap the men inside. A canvas tarp was stretched over the doors as blackout but this didn't stop sea water from entering. That, and the fact that the radiators were often shut off because when sea water hit heated radiators it gives off a sickening smell, meant that the temperature inside the fo'c's'le was only a few degrees warmer than outside. The navy was so short of men in the early years of the war that seasick men served their watch with a bucket between their feet or close by and only continually sick men were considered for shore duty.

When you discover the type of vessel your ancestor served on you'll want to research where the ship and crew saw action. Canada assumed a major role in the Battle of the Atlantic and was responsible for many of the convoys that became the lifeblood for England. Fast convoys sailed primarily from Halifax, while slow convoys mostly sailed from Sydney, Cape Breton Island. Escort groups (corvettes/destroyers) accompanied convoys from either of these ports or join from St. John's. In the early years of the war, ships had limited endurance and escorted a convoy to a mid-ocean point where it was met by an escort from England. Eventually, the escorts sailed from a Canadian port to Londonderry, Ireland, where they refuelled and provide escort back to Canada or the United States.

Family photograph of George Hunter Cree, telegraphist, HMCS Red Deer. The Red Deer saw service during the Battle of the St. Lawrence. Notice the naval service cap commonly worn by seamen during both wars. The cap tally was HMCS and never recorded the name of the ship. Family collection.

The air force could not patrol this mid-ocean area and it became known as the "black hole"; German submarines waited here. Only later in the war, when long-range escort groups and aircraft could cover the mid-ocean, did the U-boat war turn in favour of the Allies.

Your Canadian Navy ancestor was familiar with the "Triangle Run." This meant trips from Halifax or St. John's to Londonderry or New York City and back to Canada. Your ancestor's ship might have also been scheduled for repair or refuelling in Hvalfjordhur, Iceland. Duty on the Triangle Run meant being at sea in all four seasons.

George Hunter Cree always commented on how he enjoyed the time spent in New York City. Once the Americans realized the men were Canadian they never paid for a meal or a drink while ashore. All the shows, theatres, and dance halls were free to servicemen. Similarly, seamen stationed in St. John's commented on how friendly the citizens were, often inviting them home for dinner.

Duty in Halifax, Londonderry, New York City, Iceland, or even Jamaica was all part of the Battle of the Atlantic. Winter on the North Atlantic, hunting for submarines as they attacked the convoy, seasickness, and the reality of life on board a corvette must have been challenging. Knowing that your life expectancy, if you were torpedoed, was a matter of minutes during the winter and that the first responsibility of escorts on convoy duty was the safe and timely arrival of the convoy and not the rescue of shipwrecked sailors, must have made your ancestor's life at sea stressful. *The Cruel Sea* by Nicholas Monsarrat (New York: Knopf Publishing, 1950), or the movie of the same name, provide an accurate depiction of life on board a corvette.

If your ancestor served in the merchant marine on a basically unarmed ship carrying war supplies to England you can only imagine how they must have felt. Serving in a tanker with a cargo of high octane aviation fuel, while around you ships were being torpedoed, must have tested your ancestor's resolve. Pay in the merchant navy was certainly better than in the regular navy but the risks were greater.

You might discover that your ancestor served on a minesweeper, destroyer, or motor torpedo boat. All of these ships offered unique experiences and are worth reading about. Interestingly, the majority of men who served on the fast MTBs in the English Channel and Mediterranean were Canadians. Their stories of fast and furious action at night on board these small wooden ships, loaded with high octane gasoline for the motors, while attacking enemy convoys with torpedoes and small deck guns, are certainly exciting.

Ray Mecoy's family was able to produce a photograph of the crew of the minesweeper HMCS *Fort William* and had Ray's medals. Ray had told them about convoy duty and experiences in the English Channel and the D-Day landings.

George Hunter Cree's family didn't remember their father talking much about his experiences aboard ship but did seem to think that he had served on the *Red Deer*. HMCS *Red Deer* was a minesweeper built by Canada Vickers Limited (Montreal). It was launched 5 October 1941 and commissioned into the Canadian Navy 24 November 1941. It flew pennant J255 and served in the Battle of the St. Lawrence and the North Atlantic on the triangle run. A family historian writing about George Hunter Cree should certainly include information about the Battle of the Atlantic, the Battle of the St. Lawrence, and life on-board during convoy duty.

Many Canadians don't realize that German submarines sailed down the St. Lawrence River and torpedoed a number of merchant ships. From May to October of 1942, in September 1943, and from October to November 1944, the

U-boat war was on our doorstep. Eventually three Canadian warships: HMCS *Charlottetown*, HMCS *Shawinigan*, and the armed yacht HMCS *Raccoon* were sunk. The frigate HMCS *Magog* was severely damaged.

To learn something about our adversaries, read H.A. Werner, *Iron Coffins* (New York: Holt, Rinehart and Winston, 1969), a personal account of the U-boat battles of the Second World War. I would also suggest you watch the movie *Das Boot*. These two resources will certainly provide you with some appreciation of the dedication exhibited by our adversaries. Approximately 75 percent of those who joined the German submarine service perished during the war. Of the 41,000 men who served in the German submarine service (Unterseebooten, U-boat), 28,000 were lost at sea and 5,000 became prisoners of war. An excellent website, *www.uboat.net*, will provide you with an interesting assortment of information.

Remember to seek out newspaper archives for references to your ancestor. Many Second World War veterans' families record information about war service in obituaries. A recent death notice recorded that the individual had joined the Royal Canadian Naval Volunteer Reserve on 23 August 1940. It went on to record his service number, rating (A.B.), non-substantive rating (L.T.O.) and service on board HMCS *Prince Henry*, *Skeena*, *Chaudiere*, and *Saskatchewan* before being "demobilized," 23 July 1945. His was an interesting career because HMCS *Prince Henry* was an armed merchant cruiser, *Chaudier* and *Saskatchewan* were former Royal Navy River Class corvettes, and *Skeena* was a St. Laurent Class destroyer escort. The *Skeena* saw significant action during the D-Day landings and was eventually wrecked on the rocks near Reykjavik.

WAR OF 1812 RESOURCES

LAC

The records at LAC fall into three categories: Provincial Marine, Royal Navy, and Admiralty Lake Services.

- MG 12–ADM 1 — the returns of the Provincial Armed Vessels and Marine Force on Lakes Erie and Ontario in 1812. Microfilm C-12856.
- MG 12–ADM 36 — Muster Books, 1799–1807, Halifax. Listed are officers and men aboard His Majesty's Ships, Volumes 15490 and 17229.
- MG 12–ADM 37 — Ships' Musters, series II, 1757–1818. Muster books of various ships on Lakes Champlain, Ontario, Erie, and Huron, and at Halifax.
- MG 12–ADM 38, (R11630-0-0-E) — ships' muster books, predominantly 1813–34. These muster books contain the names of all persons forming the complement of the ship. Given is name, rank, place of birth, former ship, date of first entry, charges and deductions, and the number of days onboard. The archives holds the muster books for naval yards and depots at Île-aux-Noix, Holland Landing, Penetanguishene, Lake Erie, Lake Champlain, Quebec, Montreal, Niagara-on-the-Lake, and Kingston, 1813–34. Volumes 2294–2303 hold the muster rolls for various companies of Royal Marine Artillery. The muster rolls also contain information on women and children.

- MG 12–ADM 51, Finding Aid 90 — Admiralty fonds contain log books arranged by the name of the vessel. The archives has copies of log books of ships at Louisbourg in 1745 and 1758, Quebec 1759–60 and 1813, Halifax 1756–58 and 1813, and logs of service on Lake Champlain and the Great Lakes 1814–18.
- MG 24–F18 (R6351-0-6-E), the diary of David Wingfield, "Four Years on the Lakes of Canada in 1813, 1814, 1815 and 1816 by a Naval Officer Under the Command of the Late Sir James Yeo, Commodore and Commander-in-Chief of His Majesty's Ships and Vessels of War Employed on the Lakes."
- RG 8, I, C series — Records of the Royal Navy and Provincial Marine. Provincial Marine, 1821–29, 1830–45, 1808–12, 1813, 1815, and 1816. A description of the Provincial Marine, Royal Navy, and Admiralty Lakes Service records can be found in the inventory to RG 8 that prefaces Finding Aid 1800.
- RG 8, III A — the Admiralty Lake Service Records. Included are the records of Naval Commissioner and Naval Storekeeper on the Great Lakes 1814–33.

Websites

Napoleonic Miniatures Wargames Society of Toronto, *www. napoleonicminiatureswargame.com*, click on Naval Battles. An interesting site that details the history of the major naval battles on the lake in a game format.

National Archives U.K., *www.nationalarchives.gov.uk/records/looking-for-person/default.htm*, click on Navy.

Other Ships on the Great Lakes in the War of 1812, *www.hamilton-scourge.hamilton.ca/ships.htm*, a list of ships from the War of 1812.

The Provincial Marine at Amherstburg 1796–1813, *www.warof1812.ca/provmarine.htm*. Here you will find an excellent example of a Provincial Marine officer's uniform as well as a history of the facilities at Amherstburg on Lake Erie.

Books

Banford, D. *Freshwater Heritage: A History of Sail on the Great Lakes, 1670–1918.* Toronto: Natural Heritage Books, 2007.

Cooper, J.F. *Ned Myers: Or a Life Before the Mast.* Annapolis, MD: Naval institute Press, 1989.

Douglas, W.A.B. *Gunfire on the Lakes: The Naval War of 1812–1814 on the Great Lakes and Lake Champlain.* Ottawa: National Museum of Man, 1977.

Gardner, R. *The Naval War of 1812.* Annapolis, MD: Naval Institute Press, 1998.

Gough, B. *Fighting Sail on Lake Huron and Georgian Bay: The War of 1812 and Its Aftermath.* St. Catharines, ON: Vanwell Press, 2002.

Malcomson, R. *Warships of the Great Lakes, 1754–1834.* Edison, NJ: Knickerbocker Press, 2004.

Ministry of Defence, U.K. *The Navy List of Retired Officers Together with the Emergency List.* London, U.K.: Her Majesty's Stationary Office, 1979.

Nelson, L. *The Sixty Years' War for the Great Lakes, 1754–1814.* East Lansing, MI: Michigan State University Press, 2001.

Pappalardo, B. *Royal Navy Lieutenants' Passing Certificates (1691–1815).* Surrey, U.K.: List and Index Society, Kew, 2001.

Skinner, C.A. *The Upper Country: French Enterprise on the Colonial Great Lakes.* Baltimore: Johns Hopkins University Press, 2008.

Swayze, J.F. *The Rowboat War on the Great Lakes, 1812–1814.* Toronto: Macmillan Press, 1965.

Syertt, D. *The Commissioned Sea Officers of the Royal Navy (1660–1815).* Aldershot, Hants, U.K.: Scolar Press, 1994.

Wingfield, D. *Four Years on the Great Lakes, 1813–1816: The Journal of Lieutenant David Wingfield, Royal Navy.* Toronto: Dundurn Press, 2009.

FIRST WORLD WAR NAVAL RESOURCES

LAC

- RG-12-B-16, finding aid 12-74 — A list of naval trawlers and drifters built in Canada, 1914–39.
- RG 24-D-1-a — Construction of ships, trawlers, and drifters, First World War.
- RG 24-D-1-a — Submarines C.C.1 and C.C.2, complement of men.
- RG 24-D-2 (R112-491-3-E) — ships' logs. Finding aid 24–87 provides the box number, file description, identifies the name of the ship and type of log. You will find both First and Second World War logs.
- RG 24-D-25 (R112-778-3-E) — Naval pay accounting ships' ledgers, 1911–22. There are eighty-eight ships' ledgers that contain nominal lists. Against each name is information about individual rank, discharge date, period of full pay, remarks, etc.

- RG 38–Box 16 — War Service Badge number ledgers. First World War ledgers are box 16 and 17. These ledgers contain the names of the War Service Badge recipients for the First World War. They provide the name of the veteran, regimental number, serial number of badge, and date of issuance.
- MG 30–E444 — Frank Llewellyn Houghton fonds. Of particular interest are his memoirs about life in the navy: "A Sailor's Life for Me."

Websites

Canadian Navy, *www.navy.forces.gc.ca.*
CFB Esquimalt Naval & Military Museum, *www.navalandmilitary museum.org.*
LAC's photography database, *www.collectionscanada.gc.ca/02/020115 _e.html,* for information on photos of the ship.
Naval History, *www.naval-history.net,* Archived by British Library and Library of Congress Working with National Maritime Museum & Citizen Science Alliance/University of Oxford.
Naval Museum of Manitoba, *naval-museum.mb.ca.*
The Royal Canadian Naval Association, *www.hqrcna.com.*
The War at Sea, *www.gwpda.org/naval/n0000000.htm.* This is an excellent site that will provide a researcher with a wealth of information about the naval war.

Books

Fevyer, W.H. *The Naval General Service Medal, 1915–1962 to the Royal Navy and Royal Marines for the Bars Persian Gulf, 1909–1914, Iraq, 1919–1920, N.W. Persia, 1920.* London, U.K.: The Naval Military Press, 1995.

Gimblett, R. *The Naval Service of Canada, 1910–2010: The Centennial Story.* Toronto: Dundurn Press, 2009.

Gough, B.M. *The Royal Navy and the Northwest Coast of North America, 1810–1914.* Vancouver: University of British Columbia Press, 1971.

Hadley, M.L. *Tin-pot and Pirate Ships: Canadian Naval Forces and German Sea Raiders, 1880–1918.* Montreal: McGill-Queen's University Press, 1991.

Hurd, A. and H.H. Bashford. *The Heroic Record of the British Navy: A Short History of the Naval War, 1914–1918.* Toronto: F.D. Goodchild Publishing, 1919 (available on microform and as an e-book).

MacFarlane, J.M. *Commissioned and Warrant Officers of the R.C.N., 1910–1939.* Victoria: Maritime Museum of British Columbia, 1993.

Macpherson, K. *The Ships of Canada's Naval Forces, 1910–2010.* St. Catharines, ON: Vanwell Publishing, 2002.

McKee, F. *The Armed Yachts of Canada.* Erin, ON: Boston Mills Press, 1983.

Perkins, D. *Canada's Submariners: 1914–1923.* Erin, ON: Boston Mills Press, 1989.

Perkins, J.D. *The Canadian Submarine Service in Review.* St. Catharines, ON: Vanwell Publishing, 2000.

Tucker, G.N. *The Naval Service of Canada: Its Official History.* Ottawa: King's Printers, 1952.

SECOND WORLD WAR RESOURCES

LAC

RG 24 holds most of the records on Canadian ships serving during the Second World War. To discover these records use the finding aids provided by the archives. For instance, finding aids 24-176, 24-91, 24-86 and 24-292 proved particularly useful in discovering the records of HMCS *Red Deer*.

- RG 24, series D-1-c, vol. 6720, general information about HMCS *Red Deer*, 1941–60.
- RG 24, series D-1-c, vol. 6767, collisions and grounding.
- RG 24, series D-1-c, vol. 6818, ships movements — HMCS *Red Deer*, 1942–45.
- RG 24, series D-1-c, vol. 6888, salvage and towing — 1942–47.
- RG 24, series D-1-c, vol. 6905, submarine attacks — HMCS *Red Deer*.
- RG 24, series D-1-c, vol. 6914, working up programs — state of readiness and efficiency, 1943–44.
- RG 24-D-2 (R112-491-3-E) — ships' logs. Finding aid 24–87 provides the box number, file description, identifies the name of the ship and type of log. You will find both First and Second World War logs in this RG.
- RG 24, series D-10, vol. 11667, dockyards Halifax — movements and programs – HMCS *Red Deer*.
- RG 24, series D-10, vol. 11564, ship's complement, 1944–45.

- RG 24, series D-10, vol. 11574 and 11860 — minesweepers 1942–45 and files of ships; Captain (D) Halifax, 1940–46.
- RG 24, accession 1983-84/167, box 3929 — drawings and specifications, HMCS *Red Deer.*
- RG 24, vol. 6101 — ship's book, HMCS *Red Deer.*
- RG 24-H (R112-620-X-E) — personnel files for infantry, air force, and navy. At present the archives holds the records of those who died during the war.
- RG 24-D-13 (R112-715-X-E) — Flower Class Corvettes personnel files. Some information applies to minesweepers, etc.
- RG 150, 1992-93/170 — navy pay ledger sheets.

Websites

Awards to the Royal Canadian Navy, *www.rcnvr.com*, the regular navy and merchant marine.

Canadian Naval Memorial Trust, *www.hmcssackville-cnmt.ns.ca*, to honour the HMCS *Sackville*, the Last Corvette.

Canadian Navy, *www.navy.forces.gc.ca.*

Dizzy Lou's Books and Prints, *www.hmcsnavyships.com*. This site offers an excellent general history of the Canadian Navy.

Fleet Air Arm Museum, *www.fleetairarmarchive.net.*

Friends of the HMCS *Haida*, *www.hmcshaida.ca/hhistory.html*. If your ancestor served on a Tribal class Destroyer you'll want to read the story of this ship.

German submarines destroyed by the Canadian Forces 1939–45, *www.familyheritage.ca/Articles/uboat1.html.*

Juno Beach Centre, *www.junobeach.org/e/4/can-tac-per-e.htm*.

Naval Museum of Manitoba, *naval-museum.mb.ca*, provides excellent information about Canadian ships lost at sea.

Naval History, *www.naval-history.net*, archived by British Library and Library of Congress Working with National Maritime Museum & Citizen Science Alliance/University of Oxford.

Newfoundland's Grand Banks, *www.ngb.chebucto.org/NFREG/WWII/ww2-hon-roll-cdnnavy.shtml*. An honour roll of Newfoundlanders killed during the Second World War while serving in the RCN.

The Royal Navy, *www.nationalarchives.gov.uk/documentsonline/royal-navy-service.asp*.

Royal Canadian Navy Regulating Branch and Naval Police, *www.mpmuseum.org/rcnofficers.html*. Pictures of the uniforms worn by the officers of the Royal Canadian Navy, Royal Canadian Naval Volunteer Reserve, and the Royal Canadian Naval Reserve, as well as the Merchant Marine.

Veterans' Affairs, *www.vac-acc.gc.ca*.

The WRENs site, *www.thewrens.com*.

Books

Blatherwick, J. *Royal Canadian Navy: Honours, Decorations, Medals, 1910–1968.* New Westminister, BC: F.J.B. Air Publications, 1992.

Burrow, L. and E. Beaudoin. *Unlucky Lady: The Life & Death of HMCS* Athabaskan. Toronto: McClelland & Stewart, 1989. The story of the sinking of the Canadian Destroyer, *Athabaskan,* sister ship to HMCS *Haida.*

Jenson, L., *Tin Hats, Oilskins & Seaboots: A Naval Journey, 1938–1945.* Toronto: Robin Brass Studio, 2000. An excellent depiction of life in the Royal Navy and on board Canadian ships during the war. Good resource for uniforms and insignia worn by both British and Canadian sailors.

Johnston, M. *Corvettes Canada: Convoy Veterans of WWII Tell Their True Stories*. Toronto: McGraw-Hill Ryerson, 1994.

Lamb, J.B. *The Corvette Navy: True Stories from Canada's Atlantic War*. Toronto: Stoddart Publishing, 2000.

Lamb, J.B. *On The Triangle Run: More True Stories of Canada's Navy*. Toronto: Macmillan of Canada, 1986.

Law, C.A. *White Plumes Astern: The Short, Daring Life of Canada's MTB Flotilla*. Halifax: Nimbus Publishing, 1989.

Macbeth, J., *Ready, Aye, Ready: An Illustrated History of the Royal Canadian Navy*. Toronto: Key Porter, 1989.

MacFarlane, J. M. *Commissioned and Warrant Officers of the Royal Canadian Navy, 1910–1939*. Victoria: Maritime Museum of British Columbia, 1993.

Macpherson, K.R. *Canada's Fighting Ships*. Toronto: Samuel Stevens, Hakkert & Company, 1975. The development of the various ships of the RCN with pictures.

Margison, J.E. *H.M.C.S. Sackville, 1942–1943: Memories of a Gunnery Officer*. Cobalt, ON: Highway Book Shop, 1998.

Milner, M. *North Atlantic Run: The Royal Canadian Navy and the Battle for the Convoys*. Toronto: University of Toronto Press, 1985.

Paquette, C.D. and C.G. Bainbridge. *Honours and Awards: Canadian Naval Forces, World War II*. Victoria: Project Gallantry, 1986.

Reynolds, L.C. *Gunboat 658*. London, U.K.: William Kimber Publishing, 1955. This is the story of a Canadian MTB in the Mediterranean. A hard book to find.

Schull, J. *Far Distant Ships*, Toronto: Stoddart Publishing Ltd., 1987. An overall excellent history of the Royal Canadian Navy during the Second World War.

Watt, F.B. *In All Respects Ready: The Merchant Navy and the Battle of the Atlantic, 1940–1945.* Toronto: Prentice-Hall Canada, 1985.

Weyman, R.C. *In Love and War: A Memoir.* Toronto: Simon & Pierre Pub., 1995. Memoir of a Canadian officer serving with the British Navy.

APPENDIX A

Websites and Other Useful Resources

Note that websites change from time to time. If you cannot link to a particular website, try typing just the first portion up to the .ca or .uk or .org

National/International Websites

Library and Archives Canada,
    www.collectionscanada.gc.ca/militaire.
Canadian War Museum,
    www.warmuseum.ca.
Veterans' Affairs Canada,
    www.vac-acc.gc.ca.
National Archives, U.K.,
    www.nationalarchives.gov.uk.
Imperial War Museum, U.K.,
    www.iwmcollections.org.uk.
United States Archives,
    www.archives.gov.

Provincial Websites

Alberta,
 alberta.ca.
British Columbia,
 www.bcarchives.gov.bc.ca.
Manitoba,
 www.gov.mb.ca/chc/archives.
New Brunswick,
 www.gnb.ca.
Newfoundland,
 www.gnb.ca.
Northwest Territories,
 www.gov.nt.ca.
Nova Scotia,
 www.gov.ns.ca/nsarm.
Nunavut,
 www.gov.nu.ca.
Ontario,
 www.archives.gov.on.ca.
Prince Edward Island,
 www.gov.pe.ca/archives.
Quebec,
 www.banq.qc.ca.
Saskatchewan,
 www.saskarchives.com/web/about-where.html.
Yukon,
 www.gov.yk.ca.

General Information Websites

Canadian Broadcasting Corporation Archives,
archives.cbc.ca.
Early Canadiana Online Project,
www.canadiana.org/ECO.
Family History Research, Mormon Church,
www.familysearch.com.
There are also many Canadian universities that have archives with military-related information.

Gateway Websites

Canadian Military Heritage Project,
www.rootsweb.ancestry.com/~canmil.
Cyndi's List,
www.cyndislist.com/milres.htm.
Mary's Genealogy Treasures,
www3.telus.net/public/mtoll.
Olivetree Genealogy,
www.olivetreegenealogy.com/mil.
Rootsweb,
www.rootsweb.ancestry.com/~canmil.

Pay-per-view Websites

Ancestry, *www.ancestry.com*, a wide variety of military records starting in the seventeenth century. Recently added are British and German deserters, discharges, and prisoners of war who may have remained in Canada and the U.S., 1774–83.

Family Relatives, *www.familyrelatives.com*, claims to have over two million military records available online. Has recently added the Peninsula Wars Medal Recipients, Waterloo Medal Roll, and records back to the seventeenth century.

Find My Past, *www.findmypast.com*, British military records include military marriages, births, and deaths.

Ancestry.com and *findmypast.com* are available free of charge at all Family History Centers and at some local public libraries.

Always check for online digitized historic newspapers. The *Toronto Star* and *Globe and Mail* have pay-per-view websites that may be viewed for free through some public libraries.

Regimental Websites

Algonquin Regiment,
   www.army.forces.gc.ca/33cbg/AR.asp.
Argyll and Sutherland Highlanders (Princess Louise's),
   www.argylls.ca.
Black Watch (Royal Highland Regiment),
   www.blackwatchcanada.com.
Brockville Rifles,
   www.army.ca/inf/brock.php.
Calgary Highlanders,
   www.calgaryhighlanders.com.
Cameron Highlanders of Ottawa,
   www.camerons.ca.
Canadian Airborne/Parachute Regiment,
   www.commando.org.

Canadian Grenadier Guards,
www.grenadiers.ca.
Canadian Scottish Regiment (Princess Mary's),
www.islandnet.com/~csrmuse.
Essex and Kent Scottish Regiment,
www.army.ca/inf/eksr.php.
48th Highlanders of Canada,
www.48highlanders.com.
Fusiliers de Sherbrooke,
www.army.gc.ca/fusiliers_sherbrooke.
Fusiliers du St-Laurent,
www.army.forces.gc.ca/35gbc/unites-units/fusdustl-eng.aspx.
Fusiliers Mont-Royal,
lesfusiliersmont-royal.com.
Governor General's Foot Guards,
www.army.ca/inf/ggfg.php.
Grey and Simcoe Foresters,
www.foresters.0catch.com.
Hastings and Prince Edward Regiment,
www.theregiment.ca/hastypee.html.
Highland Fusiliers of Canada,
www.army.ca/inf/hfc.php.
Irish Regiment of Canada,
www.army.ca/inf/irrc.php.
Lake Superior Scottish,
www.thunderbaymuseum.com/lsr.htm.
Lanark and Renfrew Scottish Regiment,
www.army.ca/inf/lrsr.php.
Lincoln and Welland Regiment,
www.iaw.com/~awoolley/lincweld.html.
Lorne Scots (Peel, Dufferin, and Halton),
www.lornescots.ca.

Loyal Edmonton Regiment,
www.loyaleddies.com.

North Saskatchewan Regiment,
www.army.forces.gc.ca/NORTH_SASKATCHEWAN_REGT.

Nova Scotia Highlanders,
www.parl.ns.ca/highlanders.

Perth Regiment,
www.perthregiment.org.

Princess Louise Fusiliers,
www.army.dnd.ca/Princess_Louise_Fusiliers.

Princess of Wales's Own Regiment,
www.army.ca/inf/pwor.php.

Princess Patricia's Canadian Light Infantry,
www.ppcli.com.

Queen's Own Cameron Highlanders,
www.thequeensowncameronhighlandersofcanada.net.

Queen's Own Rifles of Canada,
www.qor.com.

Regiment de la Chaudière,
www.armee.gc.ca/rdechaud.

Regiment de Maisonneuve,
www.armee.forces.gc.ca/regt_maisonneuve.

Regiment du Saguenay,
www.army.ca/inf/rdusag.php.

Rocky Mountain Rangers,
www.army.forces.gc.ca/rocky_mountain_rangers.

Royal 22nd Regiment,
www.r22er.com.

Royal Canadian Regiment,
www.theroyalcanadianregiment.ca.

Royal Hamilton Light Infantry,
www.rhli.ca.

Royal Montreal Regiment,
   www.royalmontrealregiment.com.
Royal New Brunswick Regiment,
   www.army.ca/inf/rnbr.php.
Royal Newfoundland Regiment,
   www.army.ca/inf/rnfldr.php.
Royal Regiment of Canada,
   www.army.forces.gc.ca/rrc.
Royal Regina Rifles,
   www.reginarifles.ca.
Royal Westminster Regiment,
   www.royal-westies-assn.ca.
Royal Winnipeg Rifles,
   www.mts.net/~rwpgrif.
Seaforth Highlanders of Canada,
   www.seaforth-highlanders.ca.
Stormont, Dundas and Glengary Highlanders,
   www.army.ca/inf/sdgh.php.
Toronto Scottish Regiment,
   www.tsrpd.com.
Voltigeurs de Quebec,
   www.voltigeursdequebec.net.
West Nova Scotia Regiment,
   www.army.ca/wnsr.

Royal Canadian Armoured Corps

British Columbia Dragoons,
   www.army.forces.gc.ca/BCDRAGOONS/content_e.html.
British Columbia Regiment,
   www.bcregiment.com.

Calgary Regiment (King's Own),
www.kingsown.ca.

8th Princess Louise's New Brunswick Hussars,
www.rcaca.org/includes/r-PLNBH.asp.

Elgin Regiment,
www.rcaca.org/includes/r-Elgin.asp.

First Hussars,
www.firsthussars.ca.

Fort Garry Horse,
www.fortgarryhorse.ca.

Governor General's Horse Guard,
www.gghg.org.

Halifax Rifles,
www.army.ca/wiki/index.php/The_Halifax_Rifles_(RCAC).

Lord Strathcona's Horse,
www.strathconas.ca.

New Brunswick Rangers,
www.ordersofbattle.com/UnitData.aspx?UniX=8427&tab.

Ontario Regiment,
www.ontrmuseum.ca.

Prince Edward Island Light Horse,
www.archives.pe.ca/exhibit.php3?number=1018866&lang=E&t hemenum=2&sectionnum=4.

Queens York Rangers,
www.qyrang.ca.

Regiment De Hull,
www.army.forces.gc.ca/regt_hull.

Royal Canadian Dragoons,
www.dragoons.ca.

Royal Canadian Hussars,
www.army.dnd.ca/rch.

Saskatchewan Dragoons,
   www.saskd.ca/saskd.htm.
Sherbrooke Hussars,
   www.armee.gc.ca/sherh.
South Alberta Light Horse,
   www.salh.net.
Three Rivers Regiment,
   www.12rbc.ca.
12th Manitoba Dragoons,
   www.12mbdragoons.com.
Windsor Regiment,
   www.army.ca/wiki/index.php/The_Windsor_Regiment.

Canadian Corps

Canadian Forestry Corps
   — no website at present
Royal Canadian Artillery,
   www.artillery.net.
Royal Canadian Chaplain Service
   — learn more at *canadiansoldiers.com.*
Royal Canadian Corps of Engineers,
   www.reubique.com/rce.htm.
Royal Canadian Corps of Signals,
   www.rcsigs.ca.
Royal Canadian Medical/Dental Corps,
   rcdca.cfdental.ca.
Royal Canadian Ordinance Corps,
   www.rcocassn.com.
Royal Canadian Postal Corps — learn more at
   canadiansoldiers.com.

Royal Canadian Provost Corps,
   www.canadianprovostcorps.ca/history.htm.
Royal Canadian Service Corps,
   www.rcasc.org.
Veteran Guards of Canada,
   www.cmhg.gc.ca.
Many of the cap badges or uniforms you discover are stamped
"William Scully Ltd." This company, located in Montreal, Quebec,
has manufactured military accoutrements for the Canadian government for years: *www.williamscully.ca.*

General Reference

Mitchell, M. *Ducimu: The Regiments of the Canadian Infantry.*
Ottawa: Canadian War Museum, 1992. A history of the various
regiments of the Canadian Army with descriptions of badges,
colours, and current headquarters.

NOTES

Preface: How to Use This Guide

1. *www.collectionscanada.gc.ca/whats-new/013-504-e.html*, accessed 14 December 2010.
2. *www.familysearch.org/eng/library/fhc/frameset_fhc.asp*, accessed 15 December 2010.

Introduction

1. Anna Jameson, *Winter Studies and Summer Rambles* (reprinted by Toronto: McClelland & Stewart, 1990), 49–50.

Chapter One

1. Thomas Jefferson to William Duane, 1812.08.04, found in C. Benn, *Historic Fort York, 1793–1993* (Toronto: Natural Heritage Press, 1993), 45.
2. LAC, RG 8, series I, finding aid 1800.
3. J.M. Hitsman, *The Incredible War of 1812* (Toronto: University of Toronto Press, Toronto, 1965), 22.
4. W.D. Raymond, *Loyalists in Arms, 1775–1783: A Short History of the British American Regiments with Roll of Officers* (Milton: Global Heritage Press, 2001), 26.

5. W.R. Lauber, *Index of Essex and Kent Militia Records 1812–1815* (Chatham, ON: Kent Branch, OGS, 1995), intro.

6. Angela Files and Tess M. Rowe, comp., *Register of Persons Connected with High Treason, War of 1812–14* (Brantford, ON: Brant County Branch OGS, 1985).

7. *Canadian Recipients of the Military General Service, Egypt Medal* and *North West Canada* (London: Spink and Son Ltd., 1975), 1–3.

8. LAC, RG 8-1, vol. 1061 B, pg. 39, microfilm C-3369.

9. LAC, RG 1 L 3L, vol. 40, pages 20030–20037, reel C-2508.

Chapter Two

1. M.A. FitzGibbon, *A Veteran of the War of 1812* (Toronto: William Briggs Publishing, 1894), 220–21.

2. Susanna Moodie, *Roughing It in the Bush* (Ottawa: Carleton University Press, 1995, originally published 1852), 527.

3. C. Benn, *Historic Fort York, 1793–1993* (Toronto: Natural Heritage, 1993), 100.

4. Olive Tree Genealogy, *www.olivetreegenealogy.com/ships/vandsland1839.shtml*, accessed 22 December 2010.

5. *Ibid.*

6. Toronto Historic Plaques, 1981, located at Joseph Sheard Parkette, Toronto.

7. A. Brooke, and D. Brandon, *Bound for Botany Bay, British Convict Voyages to Australia* (London: The National Archives, U.K., 2005), 13.

8. C.P. Stacey, *An Introduction to the Study of Military History for Canadian Students*, 3rd ed. (Ottawa: Directorate of Training Canadian Forces Headquarters, 1973), 12.

Chapter Three

1. G.A Brown, *Canada General Service Medal, 1866–1870* (Langley, BC: Battleline Books, 1983), 1–3.
2. J.MacDonald, J., *Troublous Times in Canada: A History of the Fenian Raids of 1866 and 1870* (Toronto: W.S. Johnston, 1910), appendix.
3. *Ibid.*, 6.
4. C.P. Stacey, *Records of the Nile Voyageurs, 1884–1885* (Toronto: Champlain Society, 1959), 61, 88, 114.
5. *Ibid.*
6. *Ibid.*
7. D. Morton, *The Last War Drum* (Toronto: Hakkert, 1972), 178. Also in D. Graves, *Fighting for Canada* (Toronto: Robin Brass Studio Publishers, 2000), 150.
8. LAC, RG 9 II-B-1 vols 77–79.
9. RG 9, II-A-5, volume 11, page 56, microfilm reel C-1863.
10. P. Berton, *Klondike: The Last Great Gold Rush, 1896–1899* (Toronto: McClelland & Stewart Ltd., 1972), 215.

Chapter Four

1. C. Barnett, *Britain and Her Army, 1509–1970: A Military, Political and Social Survey* (New York: Morrow & Co., 1970), 338–40, 346–47. See also R. Dixon-Smith, "Tracing Anglo-Boer War Ancestors," *Your Family History Magazine*, Issue 2 (June 2010), 30–4.
2. W.S. Evans, *The Canadian Contingents and Canadian Imperialism* (Toronto: Publishers Syndicate, 1901); Chamberlain in telegraph to Lord Minto, Governor General of Canada, 54.
3. *Ibid.*, 77–8.
4. *Ibid.*, 124.
5. *Ibid.*, 127.

6. E.W.B. Morrison, *With the Guns, D. Battery, Royal Canadian Artillery* (Winnipeg: Hignell Printing Limited, 1901), 226.

7. Evans.

8. Stacey, *An Introduction to the Study of Military History for Canadian Students*, 22.

Chapter Five

1. J.C. Hopkins, *Canada at War: A Record of Heroism and Achievement, 1914–1918* (Toronto: Canadian Annual Review Ltd., 1919), 93.

2. D. Morton, *A Military History of Canada* (Toronto: McClelland & Stewart, 2007), 138.

3. Collection of author.

4. E. Wigney, *Serial Numbers of the CEF* (Nepean, ON: E.H. Wigney Publisher, 1996), 13.

5. Tim Cook, *The Madman and the Butcher: The Sensational Wars of Sam Hughes and General Arthur Currie* (Toronto: Penguin Group Pub., 2010), 166.

6. D.W. Love, *A Call to Arms: The Organization and Administration of Canada's Military in World War One* (Winnipeg & Calgary: Bunker to Bunker Books, 1999), 167–75.

7. Statistics are readily available online from a variety of sources. Check *www.warmuseum.ca/cwm/exhibitions/guerre/home-e.aspx*, accessed 18 January 2011.

8. T Barris, *Victory at Vimy, Canada Comes of Age: April 9–12, 1917* (Toronto: Thomas Allen Publishers, 2007), 82.

9. Library and Archives Canada, insert accompanying First World War service records.

10. Overseas Military Forces of Canada, *Report of the Ministry, Overseas Military Forces of Canada* (London, 1918), 58.

11. D. Morton, *Silent Battle, Canadian Prisoners of War in Germany, 1914–1919* (Toronto: Lester Publishing Ltd., 1992), 12–3.

12. LAC, box 30, acc 2004-01505-5, I.D. 15180.
13. LAC box 63, acc 2004-01505-5. I.D. 7672.

Chapter Six

1. J. Bouchery, *From D-Day to VE-Day: The Canadian Soldier* (Paris: Histoire and Collections, 2004), for a complete, detailed, list of Canadian regiments, equipment, etc.
2. C.P. Stacey, *Six Years of War: The Army in Canada, Britain and the Pacific* (Ottawa: Queen's Printer, 1966), 488–91.
3. *Ibid.*, 387–88.
4. G.W.L. Nicholson, *The Canadians in Italy 1943–1945* (Ottawa: R. Duhamel, 1966), 681.
5. C.P. Stacey, *The Victory Campaign: The Operations in North-West Europe, 1944–1945* (Ottawa: Queen's Printer, 1966), 270.
6. LAC, categories used to define fitness of recruits, always found on service records. F.O. K.J. Cox, RCAF, was rated A1B; Stoker Ray Mecoy, RCNVR, A; and Infantryman L. G. Cox, RCA SC, B1.
7. Les Chater, *Behind the Fence: Life as a POW in Japan 1942–1945* (St. Catharines, ON: Vanwell, 2001), 280.

Chapter Seven

1. *www.navalandmilitarymuseum.org/resource_pages/pavingtheway/ cwac.html*, accessed 18 January 2011.
2. M.A. FitzGibbon, *A Veteran of 1812: The Life of James FitzGibbon* (Toronto, William Briggs, 1894), 84.
3. A. Venning, *Following the Drum: The Lives of Army Wives and Daughters Past and Present* (London, U.K.: Headline Book Publishing, 2005), 12.

4. *Ibid.*

5. Lieutenant John Le Couteur, *Merry Hearts Make Light Days*, edited by Donald E. Graves (Ottawa: Carleton University Press, 1994), 234.

Chapter Eight

1. C.W. Hunt, *Dancing in the Sky: The Royal Flying Corps in Canada* (Toronto: Dundurn Press, 2009), 8.

2. *Ibid*, 27.

3. A.G. Lee, *No Parachute: The Exploits of a Fighter Pilot in the First World War* (London, UK: Arrow Books Ltd., 1969), 13–4.

4. Hunt, 109.

5. *Ibid.*

6. R. Collishaw, *The Black Flight: The Story of a Great War Fighter Ace* (Ottawa: CEF Books, Ottawa, 2008), Preface.

7. Medal rolls, Royal Flying Corps, WO 372/15, *nationalarchives. gov.uk/documentsonline*, accessed 23 January 2011.

8. *www.bombercommandmuseum.ca/fatherlardie.html*, accessed 19 January 2011.

9. D.L. Bashow, *No Prouder Place: Canadians and the Bomber Command Experience, 1939–1945* (St. Catharines: Vanwell, 2005), 456.

10. L. Milberry, and H. Halliday, *The Royal Canadian Air Force At War, 1939–1945* (Toronto: CANAV Books, 1990), 161, (Fighter Command), 271 (Bomber Command).

11. *Ibid.*, 28.

12. Bill Olmstead, *Blue Skies* (Toronto: Stoddart, 1987), 4.

13. B. Nolan, *Hero: The Buzz Beurling Story* (Toronto: Lester & Orpen, Denys, 1981), 103.

14. R. Collins, *The Long and the Short and the Tall* (Saskatoon: Western Producer Prairie Books, 1986), 51.

15. Milberry and Halliday, 28.
16. Olmstead, 13.
17. *en.wikipedia.org/wiki/John_Gillespie_Magee,_Jr*, accessed 18 January 2011.
18. Bashow, 455.
19. Olmstead, 249.
20. *London Gazette*, 30 March 1943, No. 36051: 2677, *www.london-gazette.co.uk/issues/all=Sherk/start=1*, accessed 18 January 2011.
21. *Ibid.*
22. London Gazette, 1 January 1945, *www.london-gazette.co.uk/issues/36866/supplements/102*, accessed 23 January 2011.
23. Mary Byrne and Bill Zahn, *Newsletter of the Schurch Family Association of North America*, Vol.22B, November 2004, 21.

Chapter Nine
1. J.M. Hitsman, *The Incredible War of 1812* (Toronto: Robin Brass Studio, 1999), 28.
2. R. Malcomsom, *Warships of the Great Lakes, 1754–1834* (Edison, NJ: Knickerbocker Press, 2004), 71, 85, 88.
3. *Ibid.*; Hitsman, 28–31; and W.A.B. Douglas, *The Naval War of 1812–1814: On the Great Lakes and Lake Champlain* (Ottawa: National Museum of Man, 1977), 4, 6, 8–10.
4. D. Perkins, *Canada's Submariners, 1914–1923* (Erin, ON: Boston Mills Press, 1989), 16–7.
5. J. Schull, *Far Distant Ships* (Toronto: Stoddart, 1987), 425–26.
6. L. Jenson, *Tin Hats, Oilskins & Seaboots* (Toronto: Robin Brass Studios, 2000), 303.
7. J. MacBeth, *Ready, Aye, Ready: An Illustrated History of the Royal Canadian Navy* (Toronto: Key Porter, 1989), 29.

ACKNOWLEDGEMENTS

I have always believed that the best way to learn a subject is to have to teach it or actually roll up your sleeves and do it. This has been the case with this resource guide as I learned about our own Archives and the intricacies of publishing a piece of work. There are many people who need to be thanked for this journey.

Without the support of the Ontario Genealogy Society and Dundurn Press, whose editors Ruth Chernia and Cheryl Hawley patiently directed me through the writing and publishing process, I am sure I would have given up long ago. I would also be amiss if I didn't thank the staff at our own Library and Archives Canada. The resources they provided and the professional way in which they handled my requests and many visits is a credit to their professionalism. Many of the support documents provided in this text are available on their website and they readily gave permission to include material in published sources.

The last thanks have to go to the Institute for Genealogical Studies at the University of Toronto. It was through my involvement and study with the institute that I was motivated to search out the military records associated with my own family, visit the archives, and then prepare this resource guide. It has been an interesting, demanding journey.

INDEX

OF RELATED INTEREST

CONSERVING, PRESERVING, AND RESTORING YOUR HERITAGE
A Professional's Advice
Kim Kennis
978-1-554884629
$19.99

Artifacts, whether found in museums, our community, or our homes, offer glimpses into the past. Be they documents, photographs, books, or clothing, as custodians of our history, we're faced with how to maintain these items. Professional conservator Kennis Kim tells us how. Topics include: creating an accession list; the nature of conservation, restoration, and preservation; deciding on display, storage, or using the artifact; common threats such as light, humidity, insects, and rodents; and when to call a professional. Here is all that's needed to determine what can be done to preserve precious articles for future generations.

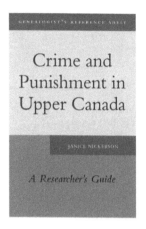

CRIME AND PUNISHMENT IN UPPER CANADA

A Researcher's Guide

Janice Nickerson

978-1-554887705

$19.99

Crime and Punishment in Upper Canada provides genealogists and social historians with context and tools to understand the criminal justice system and locate sources on criminal activity and its consequences for the Upper Canada period (1791–1841) of Ontario's history.

Illustrative examples further aid researchers in this era of the province's past, which is notoriously difficult to investigate due to paucity of records and indexes. An entertaining, educational read, the book features chapters with detailed inventories of available records in federal, provincial, and local repositories; published transcripts and indexes; online transcripts and indices; and suggestions for additional reading.

Also included are engravings (jails and courthouses, public hangings, judges), maps (showing the boundaries of districts), charts (for statistics such as frequencies of different kinds of offences), and document examples (court minutes, jail registers, newspaper reports, et cetera), while case studies demonstrate the use and relevance of various records.

DUNDURN
www.dundurn.com

What did you think of this book?
Visit www.dundurn.com for reviews, videos, updates, and more!